GEORGE WASHINGTON

IN HIS OWN WORDS

GEORGE
WASHINGTON

IN HIS OWN WORDS

Maureen Harrison & Steve Gilbert
Editors

BARNES
&NOBLE
BOOKS
NEW YORK

Published in paperback as *George Washington: Word for Word*

Copyright © 1997 by Excellent Books

This edition published by Barnes & Noble, Inc.,
by arrangement with Excellent Books.

1997 Barnes & Noble Books

Book design by Excellent Books.

ISBN 0-7607-0607-7

Printed and bound in the United States of America

97 98 99 00 01 M 9 8 7 6 5 4 3 2 1

QF

The time is now near at hand which must probably determine whether Americans are to be freemen or slaves; whether they are to have any property they can call their own; whether their houses and farms are to be pillaged and destroyed, and themselves consigned to a state of wretchedness from which no human efforts will deliver them. The fate of unborn millions will now depend, under God, on the courage and conduct of this army. Our cruel and unrelenting enemy leaves us only the choice of brave resistance, or the most abject submission. We have, therefore, to resolve to conquer or die.

—George Washington, 1776

INTRODUCTION

George Washington: In His Own Words is designed to easily acquaint readers, young and old alike, with the essential writings of the first American president. We have carefully selected from a lifetime of Washington's public speeches and private writings those documents which we think will give the reader a real insight into the life and times of "The Father Of Our Country." Some are famous, some are obscure, all are interesting, thought-provoking, and informative.

The anthology is divided into eight sections. Seven of these contain material from specific periods of Washington's life. The eighth, *Washingtoniana*, is a representative selection of short extracts from his writings from the age of twenty-two until the year of his death.

All serious researchers of the writings of George Washington owe, as we do, a great debt of gratitude to those who have preceded us. This book could not have been written without reference to Jared Sparks' *The Writings Of George Washington*, John Fredrick Schroeder's *Maxims Of Washington*, and William Newton's *Last Will And Testament Of George Washington*. We also gratefully acknowledge for their assistance the reference librarians at the Library of Congress, the National Archives, Columbia University, and the New York Public Library.

It is not within the narrow scope of this anthology of George Washington's writings to discuss the details of his life or sort out the myth from the man. The life of Washington has been extensively chronicled in many books of varying quality and accuracy over the years. We have included in our bibliography what we consider to be the best of the works on Washington. Among our favorites are Douglas Southhall Freeman's *George Washington*, Washington Irving's *Life Of George Washington*, and James Thomas Flexner's *George Washington*.

A few words about Washington's English. We have left unchanged George Washington's eighteenth-century spelling and grammar. To have changed the spelling of words such as "courtesie" and "drest" to the modern versions would have somehow changed their flavor. Some words, like "disfurnish," "effectually," and "independency," are no longer in common use but, as they are in keeping with the language as Washington spoke and wrote it, we have also left them unchanged. Any editorial changes or explanations we have added can be found in [brackets].

We hope that the reader finds in *George Washington: In His Own Words* a true and lasting appreciation for the man, as well as for the president.

—M.H. & S.G.

TABLE OF CONTENTS

GENERAL GEORGE WASHINGTON'S
ADVICE TO THE UNITED STATES
63

It appears to me there is an option still left to the United States of America, that it is in their choice, and depends upon their conduct, whether they will be respectable and prosperous, or contemptable and miserable as a nation.

PRESIDENTIAL PAPERS
79

The great rule of conduct for us, in regard to foreign nations, is, in extending our commercial relations, to have with them as little political connection as possible. So far as we have already formed engagements, let them be fulfilled with perfect good faith. Here let us stop.

WASHINGTONIANA:
EXTRACTS FROM WASHINGTON'S WRITINGS
173

The honor and safety of our bleeding country, and every other motive that can influence the brave and heroic patriot, call loudly upon us, to acquit ourselves with resolution. In short, we must now determine, to be enslaved or free. If we make freedom our choice, we must obtain it, by the blessing of Heaven on our united and vigorous efforts.

THE LAST WILL AND TESTAMENT OF
GEORGE WASHINGTON
337

I, George Washington of Mount Vernon, a citizen of the United States and lately President of the same, do make, ordain and declare this instrument, which is written with my own hand and every page thereof subscribed with my name, to be my last Will and Testament.

BIBLIOGRAPHY
357

First in war, first in peace, first in the hearts of his countrymen.
—From Washington's Eulogy by General Henry Lee

INDEX
365

"George," said his father, "do you know who killed that beautiful little cherry tree yonder in the garden?" Looking at his father with the sweet face of youth brightened with the inexpressible charm of all-conquering truth, young George Washington bravely cried out, "I cannot tell a lie, Pa. I did it with my little hatchet."
—From Parson Weems' *Life Of George Washington The Great: With Curious Anecdotes, Equally Honorable To Himself And Exemplary To His Young Countrymen* (5th Edition, 1806)

MASTER GEORGE WASHINGTON'S RULES OF CIVILITY AND DECENT BEHAVIOR IN COMPANY AND CONVERSATION

Washington's *Rules Of Civility* were written in the 1740's between his eleventh and sixteenth years. *The Rules* are a collection of one hundred and ten maxims on respect for, deference to, and consideration of others. Some now seem trivial and antiquated, while others are still very relevant and timely. All form a strict code of personal behavior, conscientiousness, and self-control which Washington adopted in his youth and maintained throughout his life as his own.

MASTER GEORGE WASHINGTON'S RULES OF CIVILITY AND DECENT BEHAVIOR IN COMPANY AND CONVERSATION

Rule 1. Every action done in company ought to be with some sign of respect, to those that are present.

Rule 2. When in company, put not your hands to any part of the body, not usually discovered.

Rule 3. Shew nothing to your friend that may affright him.

Rule 4. In the presence of others, sing not to yourself with a humming noise, nor drum with your fingers or feet.

Rule 5. If you cough, sneeze, sigh, or yawn, do it not loud but privately; and speak not in your yawning, but put your handkerchief or hand before your face and turn aside.

Rule 6. Sleep not when others speak, sit not when others stand, speak not when you should hold your peace, walk not on when others stop.

Rule 7. Put not off your clothes in the presence of others, nor go out your chamber half drest.

Rule 8. At play and at fire its good manners to give place to the last commer, and affect not to speak louder than ordinary.

Rule 9. Spit not in the fire, nor stoop low before it; neither put your hands into the flames to warm them, nor set your feet upon the fire especially if there be meat before it.

Rule 10. When you sit down, keep your feet firm and even, without putting one on the other or crossing them.

Rule 11. Shift not yourself in the sight of others nor gnaw your nails.

Rule 12. Shake not the head, feet, or legs; rowl not the eyes; lift not one eyebrow higher than the other; wry not the mouth; and bedew no man's face with your spittle, by approaching too near him when you speak.

Rule 13. Kill no vermin as fleas, lice, ticks, etc. in the sight of others; if you see any filth or thick spittle, put your foot dexteriously upon it; if it be upon the clothes of your companions, put if off privately, and if it be upon your own clothes, return thanks to him who puts it off.

Rule 14. Turn not your back to others, especially in speaking; jog not the table or desk on which another reads or writes; lean not upon any one.

Rule 15. Keep your nails clean and short, also your hands and teeth clean, yet without shewing any great concern for them.

Rule 16. Do not puff up the cheeks, loll not out the tongue, rub the hands, or beard, thrust out the lips, or bite them or keep the lips too open or too close.

Rule 17. Be no flatterer, neither play with any that delights not to be play'd withal.

Rule 18. Read no letters, books, or papers in company, but when there is a necessity for the doing of it, you must ask leave: come not near the books or writings of another so as to read them unless desired, or give your opinion of them unask'd; also look not nigh when another is writing a letter.

Rule 19. Let your countenance be pleasant but in serious matters somewhat grave.

Rule 20. The gestures of the body must be suited to the discourse you are upon.

Rule 21. Reproach none for the infirmaties of nature, nor delight to put them that have in mind thereof.

Rule 22. Shew not yourself glad at the misfortune of another though he were your enemy.

Rule 23. When you see a crime punished, you may be inwardly pleased; but always shew pity to the suffering offender.

Rule 24. Do not laugh too loud or too much at any publick spectacle.

Rule 25. Superfluous complements and all affectation of ceremony are to be avoided, yet where due they are not to be neglected.

Rule 26. In pulling off your hat to persons of distinction, as noblemen, justices, churchmen, etc., make a reverence, bowing more or less according to the custom of the better bred, and quality of the person. Amongst your equals expect not always that they should begin with you first, but to pull off the hat when there is no need is affectation; in the manner of saluting and resaluting in words, keep to the most usual custom.

Rule 27. 'Tis ill manners to bid one more eminent than yourself be covered as well as not to do it to whom it's due, likewise he that makes too much haste to put on his hat does not well, yet he ought to put it on at the first, or at most the second time of being ask'd; now what is herein spoken, of qualification in behaviour in saluting, ought also to be observed in taking of place, and sitting down for ceremonies without bounds is troublesome.

Rule 28. If any one come to speak to you while you are sitting, stand up tho he be your inferiour, and when you present seats let it be to every one according to his degree.

Rule 29. When you meet with one of greater quality than yourself, stop, and retire, especially if it be at a door or any straight place to give way for him to pass.

Rule 30. In walking the highest place in most countrys seems to be on the right hand; therefore place yourself on the left of him whom you desire to honour: but if three walk together the middest place is the most honorable; the wall is usually given to the most worthy if two walk together.

Rule 31. If any one far surpasses others, either in age, estate, or merit, yet would give place to a meaner than himself in his own lodging or elsewhere, the one ought not to except it, so he on the other part should not use much earnestness nor offer it above once or twice.

Rule 32. To one that is your equal, or not much inferior you are to give the chief place in your lodging and he to who 'tis offered ought at the first to refuse it but at the second to accept though not without acknowledging his own unworthiness.

Rule 33. They that in dignity or in office have in all places preceedency, but whilst they are young they ought to respect those that are their equals in birth or other qualitys, though they have no publick charge.

Rule 34. It is good manners to prefer them to whom we speak before ourselves especially if they be above us with whom in no sort we ought to begin.

Rule 35. Let your discourse with men of business be short and comprehensive.

Rule 36. Artificers and persons of low degree ought not to use many ceremonies to lords, or others of high degree but respect and highly honour them, and those of high degree ought to treat them with affibility and courtesie, without arrogancy.

Rule 37. In speaking to men of quality do not lean nor look them full in the face, nor approach too near them; at least keep a full pace from them.

Rule 38. In visiting the sick, do not presently play the physician if you be not knowing therein.

Rule 39. In writing or speaking, give to every person his due title according to his degree and the custom of the place.

Rule 40. Strive not with your superiors in argument, but always submit your judgment to others with modesty.

Rule 41. Undertake not to teach your equal in the art himself professes; it savours of arrogancy.

Rule 42. Let thy ceremonies in courtesie be proper to the dignity of his place with whom thou conversest, for it is absurd to act ye the same with a clown and a prince.

Rule 43. Do not express joy before one sick or in pain for that contrary passion will aggravate his misery.

Rule 44. When a man does all he can though it succeeds not well, blame not him that did it.

Rule 45. Being to advise or reprehend any one, consider whether it ought to be in publick or in private; presently, or at some other time, in what terms to do it, and in reproving shew no sign of cholar but do it with all sweetness and mildness.

Rule 46. Take all admonitions thankfully in what time or place soever given but afterwards not being culpable take a time and place convenient to let him know it that gave them.

Rule 47. Mock not nor jest at any thing of importance; break no jest that are sharp biting and if you deliver any thing witty and pleasant abstain from laughing thereat yourself.

Rule 48. Wherein you reprove another be unblameable yourself; for example is more prevalent than precepts.

Rule 49. Use no reproachfull language against any one; neither curse nor revile.

Rule 50. Be not hasty to believe flying reports to the disparagement of any.

Rule 51. Wear not your clothes, foul, unript or dusty but see they be brushed once every day at least and take heed that you approach not to any uncleanness.

Rule 52. In your apparel be modest and endeavour to accommodate nature, rather than to procure admiration; keep to the fashion of your equals such as are civil and orderly with respect to times and places.

Rule 53. Run not in the streets, neither go too slowly nor with mouth open, go not shaking your arms, kick not the earth with your feet, go not upon the toes, nor in a dancing fashion.

Rule 54. Play not the peacock, looking every where about you, to see if you be well deck't, if your shoes fit well, if your stockings sit neatly, and clothes handsomely.

Rule 55. Eat not in the streets, nor in your house, out of season.

Rule 56. Associate yourself with men of good quality if you esteem your own reputation; for 'tis better to be alone than in bad company.

Rule 57. In walking up and down in a house, only with one in company, if he be greater than yourself, at the first give him the right hand and stop not till he does, and be not the first that turns, and when you do turn let it be with your face towards him; if he be a man of great quality, walk not with him cheek by joul but somewhat behind him; but yet in such a manner that he may easily speak to you.

Rule 58. Let your conversation be without malice or envy, for 'tis a sign of a tractable and commendable nature: and in all causes of passion admit reason to govern.

Rule 59. Never express anything unbecoming, nor act against your rules moral before your inferiours.

Rule 60. Be not immodest in urging your friends to discover a secret.

Rule 61. Utter not base and frivolous things amongst grave and learn'd men, nor very difficult questions or subjects, among the ignorant, or things hard to be believed; stuff not your discourse with sentences amongst your betters nor equals.

Rule 62. Speak not of doleful things in a time of mirth or at the table; speak not of melancholy things as death and wounds, and if others mention them change if you can the discourse; tell not your dreams, but to your intimate friend.

Rule 63. A man ought not to value himself of his achievements, or rare qualities of wit; much less of his riches, virtue, or kindred.

Rule 64. Break not a jest where none take pleasure in mirth; laugh not aloud, nor at all without occasion; deride no man's misfortune, tho' there seem to be some cause.

Rule 65. Speak not injurious words neither in jest nor earnest; scoff at none although they give occasion.

Rule 66. Be not froward but friendly and courteous; the first to salute, hear and answer, and be not pensive when it's a time to converse.

Rule 67. Detract not from others; neither be excessive in commanding.

Rule 68. Go not thither, where you know not, whether you shall be welcome or not. Give not advice without being ask'd and when desired do it briefly.

Rule 69. If two contend together, take not the part of either unconstrained; and be not obstinate in your own opinion; in things indifferent be of the major side.

Rule 70. Reprehend not the imperfections of others for that belongs to parents, masters, and superiours.

Rule 71. Gaze not on the marks or blemishes of others and ask not how they came. What you may speak in secret to your friend deliver not before others.

Rule 72. Speak not in an unknown tongue in company but in your own language and that as those of quality do and not as the vulgar; sublime matters treat seriously.

Rule 73. Think before you speak; pronounce not imperfectly nor bring out your words too hastily but orderly and distinctly.

Rule 74. When another speaks be attentive your self and disturb not the audience; if any hesitate in his words, help him, nor prompt him without desired, interrupt him not, nor answer him till his speech be ended.

Rule 75. In the midst of discourse ask not of what one treateth but if you perceive any stop because of your coming you may well intreat him gently to proceed: if a person of quality comes in while your conversing it's handsome to repeat what was said before.

Rule 76. While you are talking, point not with your finger at him of whom you discourse, nor approach too near him to whom you talk, especially to his face.

Rule 77. Treat with men at fit times about business and whisper not in the company of others.

Rule 78. Make no comparisons and if any of the company be commended for any brave act of virtue, commend not another for the same.

Rule 79. Be not apt to relate news if you know not the truth thereof. In discoursing of things you have heard, name not your author; always a secret discover not.

Rule 80. Be not tedious in discourse or in reading unless you find the company pleased therewith.

Rule 81. Be not curious to know the affairs of others, neither approach those that speak in private.

Rule 82. Undertake not what you cannot perform, but be careful to keep your promise.

Rule 83. When you deliver a matter do it without passion and with discretion, however mean the person be you do it to.

Rule 84. When your superiours talk to any body hearken not, neither speak nor laugh.

Rule 85. In company of those of higher quality than yourself, speak not till you are ask'd a question, then stand upright, put off your hat, and answer in few words.

Rule 86. In disputes, be not so desirous to overcome as not to give liberty to each one to deliver his opinion, and submit to the judgment of the major part, especially if they are judges of the dispute.

Rule 87. Let thy carriage be such as becomes a man grave, settled, and attentive to that which is spoken. Contradict not at every turn what others say.

Rule 88. Be not tedious in discourse, make not many digressions, nor repeat often the same manner of discourse.

Rule 89. Speak not evil of the absent for it is unjust.

Rule 90. Being set at meat, scratch not, neither spit, cough, or blow your nose, except there's a necessity for it.

Rule 91. Make no shew of taking great delight in your victuals, feed not with greediness; cut your bread with a knife, lean not on the table, neither find fault with what you eat.

Rule 92. Take no salt or cut bread with your knife greasy.

Rule 93. Entertaining any one at table, it is decent to present him with meat; undertake not to help others undesired by the master.

Rule 94. If you soak bread in the sauce, let it be no more than what you put in your mouth at a time, and blow not your broth at table, but stay till cools of it self.

Rule 95. Put not your meat to your mouth with your knife in your hand, neither spit forth the stones of any fruit pye upon a dish, nor cast anything under the table.

Rule 96. It's unbecoming to stoop much to one's meat; keep your fingers clean and when foul, wipe them on a corner of your table napkin.

Rule 97. Put not another bit into your mouth till the former be swallowed; let not your morsels be too big for the gowls.

Rule 98. Drink not nor talk with your mouth full; neither gaze about you while you are a drinking.

Rule 99. Drink not too leisurely nor yet too hastily. Before and after drinking, wipe your lips; breathe not then or ever with too great a noise, for it's uncivil.

Rule 100. Cleanse not your teeth with the table cloth, napkin, fork, or knife, but if others do it let it be done with a pick tooth.

Rule 101. Rinse not your mouth in the presence of others.

Rule 102. It is out of use to call upon the company often to eat, nor need you drink to others every time you drink.

Rule 103. In company of your betters, be not longer in eating than they are; lay not your arm but only your hand upon the table.

Rule 104. It belongs to the chiefest in company to unfold his napkin and fall to meat first, but he ought then to begin in time and to dispatch with dexterity that the slowest may have time allowed him.

Rule 105. Be not angry at table, whatever happens and if you have reason to be so, shew it not, put on a cheerfull countenance, especially if there be strangers, for good humour makes one dish of meat a feast.

Rule 106. Set not yourself at the upper of the table but, if it be your due or that the master of the house will have it so, contend not, least you should trouble the company.

Rule 107. If others talk at table be attentive but talk not with meat in your mouth.

Rule 108. When you speak of God or his attributes, let it be seriously and with reverence; honor and obey your natural parents altho they be poor.

Rule 109. Let your recreations be manfull, not sinfull.

Rule 110. Labour to keep alive in your breast that little spark of celestial fire called conscience.

MAJOR GEORGE WASHINGTON'S JOURNAL OF HIS MISSION TO THE FRENCH FORCES IN THE OHIO VALLEY

Washington's *Journal* was written in 1754 when he was twenty-one. On the eve of the French and Indian War, Virginia's Colonial Governor sent young Major Washington on a mission to deliver a warning to the French forces to leave English territory. Washington's *Journal*, written over the course of his three-month mission, records his arduous midwinter journey of nearly nine hundred miles through the forests, across the rivers, and over the mountains of Virginia, Maryland, and Pennsylvania.

MAJOR GEORGE WASHINGTON'S JOURNAL OF HIS MISSION TO THE FRENCH FORCES IN THE OHIO VALLEY NOVEMBER 1753–JANUARY 1754

I was commissioned and appointed by the Honorable Robert Dinwiddie, Esquire, Governor of Virginia, to visit and deliver a letter to the commandant of the French forces on the Ohio, and set out on the intended journey on the same day; the next, I arrived at Fredericksburg, and engaged Mr. Jacob Vanbraam to be my French interpreter, and proceeded with him to Alexandria, where we provided necessaries. From thence we went to Winchester, and got baggage, horses, etc., and from thence we pursued the new road to Will's Creek, where we arrived on the 14th of November.

Here I engaged Mr. Gist to pilot us out, and also hired four others as servitors, Barnaby Currin and John McQuire, Indian traders, Henry Steward, and William Jenkins; and in company with those persons left the inhabitants the next day.

The excessive rains and vast quantity of snow, which had fallen, prevented our reaching Mr. Frazier's, an Indian trader, at the mouth of Turtle Creek, on Monongahela River, until Thursday the 22d. We were informed here, that expresses had been sent a few days before to the traders down the river, to acquaint them with the French general's death, and the return of the major part of the French army into winter-quarters.

The waters were quite impassable without swimming our horses, which obliged us to get the loan of a canoe from Frazier, and to send Barnaby Currin and Henry Steward down the Monongahela, with our baggage, to meet us at the Fork of the Ohio, about ten miles; there to cross the Allegany.

As I got down before the canoe, I spent some time in viewing the rivers, and the land in the Fork, which I think extremely well situated for a fort, as it has the absolute command of both rivers. The land at the point is twenty, or twenty-five feet above the common surface of the water; and a considerable bottom of flat, well-timbered land all around it, very convenient for building. The rivers are each a quarter of a mile or more across, and run here very nearly at right angles; Allegany bearing northeast; and Monongahela southeast. The former of these two is a very rapid and swift running water, the other deep and still, without any perceptible fall.

About two miles from this on the southeast side of the river, at the place where the Ohio Company intended to erect a fort, lives Shingiss, King of the Delawares. We called upon him, to invite him to council at the Logstown.

As I had taken a good deal of notice yesterday of the situation at the Fork, my curiosity led me to examine this more particularly, and I think it greatly inferior, either for defence or advantages; especially the latter. For a fort at the Fork would be equally well situated on the Ohio, and have the entire command of the Monongahela, which runs up our settlement, and is extremely well designed for water-carriage, as it is of a deep, still nature. Besides, a fort at the Fork might be built at much less expense than at the other places.

Nature has well contrived this lower place for water defence; but the hill whereon it must stand being about a quarter of a mile in length, and then descending gradually on the land side, will render it difficult and very expensive to make a sufficient fortification there. The whole flat upon the hill must be taken in, the side next the descent made extremely high, or else the hill itself cut away; otherwise the enemy may raise batteries within that distance without being exposed to a single shot from the fort.

Shingiss attended us to the Logstown, where we arrived between sun-setting and dark, the twenty-fifth day after I left Williamsburg. We travelled over some extremely good and bad land to get to this place.

As soon as I came into town, I went to Monacatoocha (as the Half-King was out at his hunting cabin on Little Beaver Creek, about fifteen miles off), and informed him by John Davidson, my Indian interpreter, that I was sent a messenger to the French general; and was ordered to call upon the Sachems of the Six Nations to acquaint them with it. I gave him a string of wampum and a twist of tobacco, and desired him to send for the Half-King, which he promised to do by a runner in the morning, and for other sachems. I invited him and the other great men present to my tent, where they stayed about an hour and returned.

According to the best observations I could make, Mr. Gist's new settlement (which we passed by) bears about west northwest seventy miles from Will's Creek; Shannopins, or the Fork, north by west, or north northwest, about fifty miles from that; and from thence to the Logstown, the course is nearly west about eighteen or twenty miles; so that the whole distance, as we went and computed it, is at least one hundred and thirty-five or one hundred and forty miles from our back inhabitants.

25th—Came to town four of ten Frenchmen, who had deserted from a company at the Kuskuskas, which lies at the mouth of this river. I got the following account from them.

They were sent from New Orleans with a hundred men and eight canoe-loads of provisions to this place, where they expected to have met the same number of men, from the forts on this side of Lake Erie, to convoy them and the stores up, who were not arrived when they ran off.

I inquired into the situation of the French on the Mississippi, their numbers, and what forts they had built. They informed me, that there were four small forts between New Orleans and the Black Islands, garrisoned with about thirty or forty men, and a few small pieces in each. That at New Orleans, which is near the mouth of the Mississippi, there are thirty-five companies of forty men each, with a pretty strong fort mounting eight carriage-guns; and at the Black Islands there are several companies and a fort with six guns. The Black Islands are about a hundred and thirty leagues above the mouth of the Ohio, which is about three hundred and fifty above New Orleans. They also acquainted me, that there was a small palisadoed fort on the Ohio, at the mouth of the Obaish, about sixty leagues from the Mississippi. The Obaish heads near the west end of Lake Erie, and affords the communication between the French on the Mississippi and those on the lakes. These deserters came up from the lower Shannoah town with one Brown, an Indian trader, and were going to Philadelphia.

About three o'clock this evening the Half-King came to town. I went up and invited him with Davidson, privately, to my tent, and desired him to relate some of the particulars of his journey to the French commandant, and of his reception there; also, to give me an account of the ways and distance. He told me, that the nearest and levelest way was now impassable, by reason of many large, miry savannas; that we must be obliged to go by Venango, and should not get to the near fort in less than five or six nights' sleep, good travelling. When he went to the fort, he said he was received in a very stern manner by the late commander, who asked him very abruptly what he had come about, and to declare his business, which he said he did in the following speech.

"Fathers, I am come to tell you your own speeches, what your own mouths have declared. Fathers, you, in former days, set a silver basin before us, wherein there was the leg of a beaver, and desired all the nations to come and eat of it, to eat in peace and plenty, and not to be churlish to one another; and that if any such person should be found to be a disturber, I here lay down by the edge of the dish a rod, which you must scourge them with; and if your father should get foolish, in my old days, I desire you may use it upon me as well as others.

"Now, fathers, it is you who are the disturbers in this land, by coming and building your towns, and taking it away unknown to us, and by force.

"Fathers, we kindled a fire a long time ago, at a place called Montreal, where we desired you to stay, and not to come and intrude upon our land. I now desire you may despatch to that place; for be it known to you, fathers, that this is our land and not yours.

"Fathers, I desire you may hear me in civilness; if not, we must handle that rod which was laid down for the use of the obstreperous. If you had come in a peaceable manner, like our brothers the English, we would not have been against your trading with us as they do; but to come, fathers, and build houses upon our land, and to take it by force, is what we cannot submit to.

"Fathers, both you and the English are white, we live in a country between; therefore, the land belongs to neither one nor the other. But the Great Being above allowed it to be a place of residence for us; so, fathers, I desire you to withdraw, as I have done our brothers the English; for I will keep you at arm's length. I lay this down as a trial for both, to see which will have the greatest regard to it, and that side we will stand by, and make equal sharers with us. Our brothers, the English, have heard this, and I come now to tell it to you; for I am not afraid to discharge you off this land."

This he said was the substance of what he spoke to the general, who made this reply.

"Now, my child, I have heard your speech; you spoke first, but it is my time to speak now. Where is my wampum that you took away, with the marks of towns on it? This wampum I do not know, which you have discharged me off the land with; but you need not put yourself to the trouble of speaking, for I will not hear you. I am not afraid of flies or musquitoes, for Indians are such as those; I tell you down that river I will go, and build upon it, according to my command. If the river was blocked up, I have forces sufficient to burst it open, and tread under my feet all that stand in opposition, together with their alliances; for my force is as the sand upon the sea-shore; therefore here is your wampum; I sling it at you. Child, you talk foolish; you say this land belongs to you, but there is not the black of [the dirt under] my nail [which is] yours. I saw that land sooner than you did, before the Shannoahs and you were at war; Lead was the man who went down and took possession of that river. It is my land, and I will have it, let who will stand up for, or say against it. I will buy and sell with the English (mockingly). If people will be ruled by me, they may expect kindness, but not else."

The Half-King told me he had inquired of the general after two Englishmen, who were made prisoners, and received this answer.

"Child, you think it a very great hardship that I made prisoners of those two people at Venango. Don't you concern yourself with it; we took and carried them to Canada, to get intelligence of what the English were doing in Virginia."

He informed me, that they had built two forts, one on Lake Erie, and another on French Creek, near a small lake, about fifteen miles asunder, and a large wagon-road between. They are both built after the same model, but different in size; that on the lake the largest. He gave me a plan of them of his own drawing.

The Indians inquired very particularly after their brothers in Carolina gaol.

They also asked what sort of a boy it was, who was taken from the South Branch; for they were told by some Indians, that a party of French Indians had carried a white boy by Kuskuska Town, towards the lakes.

26th—We met in council at the long-house about nine o'clock, where I spoke to them as follows.

"Brothers, I have called you together in council, by order of your brother, the Governor of Virginia, to acquaint you, that I am sent with all possible despatch, to visit and deliver a letter to the French commandant, of very great importance to your brothers, the English; and I dare say to you, their friends and allies.

"I was desired, brothers, by your brother, the Governor, to call upon you, the sachems of the nations, to inform you of it, and to ask your advice and assistance to proceed the nearest and best road to the French. You see, brothers, I have gotten thus far on my journey.

"His Honor likewise desired me to apply to you for some of your young men to conduct and provide provisions for us on our way, and be a safeguard against those French Indians, who have taken up the hatchet against us. I have spoken thus particularly to you, brothers, because his Honor our Governor treats you as good friends and allies, and holds you in great esteem. To confirm what I have said, I give you this string of wampum."

After they had considered for some time on the above discourse, the Half-King got up and spoke.

"Now, my brother, in regard to what my brother, the Governor, had desired of me I return you this answer.

"I rely upon you as a brother ought to do, as you say we are brothers, and one people. We shall put heart in hand and speak to our fathers, the French, concerning the speech they made to me; and you may depend that we will endeavour to be your guard.

"Brother, as you have asked my advice, I hope you will be ruled by it, and stay until I can provide a company to go with you. The French speech-belt is not here; I have to go for it to my hunting-cabin. Likewise, the people whom I have ordered in are not yet come, and cannot until the third night from this; until which time, brother, I must beg you to stay.

"I intend to send the guard of Mingoes, Shannoahs, and Delawares, that our brothers may see the love and loyalty we bear them."

As I had orders to make all possible despatch, and waiting here was very contrary to my inclination, I thanked him in the most suitable manner I could, and told him that my business required the greatest expedition, and would not admit of that delay. He was not well pleased that I should offer to go before the time he had appointed, and told me, that he could not consent to our going without a guard, for fear some accident should befall us, and draw a reflection upon him. Besides, said he, this is a matter of no small moment, and must not be entered into without due consideration; for I intend to deliver up the French speech-belt, and make the Shannoahs and Delawares do the same. And accordingly he gave orders to King Shingiss, who was present, to attend on Wednesday night with the wampum; and two men of their nation to be in readiness to set out with us the next morning. As I found it was impossible to get off without affronting them in the most egregious manner, I consented to stay.

I gave them back a string of wampum, which I met with at Mr. Frazier's, and which they sent with a speech to his Honor the Governor, to inform him, that three nations of French Indians, namely, Chippewas, Ottowas, and Orundaks, had taken up the hatchet against the English; and desired them to repeat it over again. But this they postponed doing until they met in full council with the Shannoah and Delaware chiefs.

27th—Runners were despatched very early for the Shannoah chiefs. The Half-King set out himself to fetch the French speech-belt from his hunting-cabin.

28th—He returned this evening, and came with Monacatoocha, and two other sachems to my tent; and begged (as they had complied with his Honor the Governor's request, in pro-

viding men, etc.) to know on what business we were going
to the French. This was a question I had all along expected,
and had provided as satisfactory answers as I could; which
allayed their curiosity a little.

Monacatoocha informed me, that an Indian from Venango
brought news, a few days ago, that the French had called all
the Mingoes, Delawares, etc. together at that place; and told
them, that they intended to have been down the river this
fall, but the waters were growing cold, and the winter advancing, which obliged them to go into quarters; but that
they might assuredly expect them in the spring, with a far
greater number; and desired that they might be quite pas-
sive, and not intermeddle unless they had a mind to draw all
their force upon them; for that they expected to fight the
English three years (as they supposed there would be some
attempts made to stop them), in which time they should
conquer. But that if they should prove equally strong, they
and the English would join to cut them all off, and divide
the land between them; that though they had lost their general, and some few of their soldiers, yet there were men
enough to reinforce them, and make them masters of the
Ohio.

This speech, he said, was delivered to them by one Captain
Joncaire, their interpreter in chief, living at Venango, and a
man of note in the army.

29th—The Half-King and Monacatoocha came very early,
and begged me to stay one day more; for notwithstanding
they had used all the diligence in their power, the Shannoah
chiefs had not brought the wampum they ordered, but would
certainly be in to-night; if not, they would delay me no
longer, but would send it after us as soon as they arrived.
When I found them so pressing in their request, and knew
that the returning of wampum was the abolishing of

agreements, and giving this up was shaking off all dependence upon the French, I consented to stay, as I believed an offence offered at this crisis might be attended with greater ill consequence, than another day's delay. They also informed me, that Shingiss could not get in his men, and was prevented from coming himself by his wife's sickness (I believe by fear of the French), but that the wampum of that nation was lodged with Kustalogo, one of their chiefs, at Venango.

In the evening, late, they came again, and acquainted me that the Shannoahs were not yet arrived, but that it should not retard the prosecution of our journey. He delivered in my hearing the speech that was to be made to the French by Jeskakake, one of their old chiefs, which was giving up the belt the late commandant had asked for, and repeating nearly the same speech he himself had done before.

He also delivered a string of wampum to this chief, which was sent by King Shingiss, to be given to Kustalogo, with orders to repair to the French, and deliver up the wampum.

He likewise gave a very large string of black and white wampum, which was to be sent up immediately to the Six Nations, if the French refused to quit the land at this warning; which was the third and last time, and was the right of this Jeskakake to deliver.

30th—Last night, the great men assembled at their council house, to consult further about this journey, and who were to go; the result of which was, that only three of their chiefs, with one of their best hunters, should be our convoy. The reason they gave for not sending more, after what had been proposed at council the 26th, was, that a greater number might give the French suspicions of some bad design, and cause them to be treated rudely; but I rather think they could not get their hunters in.

We set out about nine o'clock with the Half-King, Jeskakake, White Thunder, and the Hunter; and travelled on the
road to Venango, where we arrived the 4th of December,
without any thing remarkable happening but a continued
series of bad weather.

This is an old Indian town, situated at the mouth of French
Creek, on the Ohio; and lies near north about sixty miles
from the Logstown, but more than seventy the way we were
obliged to go.

We found the French colors hoisted at a house from which
they had driven Mr. John Frazier, an English subject. I immediately repaired to it, to know where the commander re-
sided. There were three officers, one of whom, Captain
Joncaire, informed me that he had the command of the Ohio;
but that there was a general officer at the near fort, where he
advised me to apply for an answer. He invited us to sup with
them, and treated us with the greatest complaisance.

The wine, as they dosed themselves pretty plentifully with
it, soon banished the restraint which at first appeared in their
conversation, and gave a license to their tongues to reveal
their sentiments more freely.

They told me, that it was their absolute design to take possession of the Ohio, and by G— they would do it; for that,
although they were sensible the English could raise two men
for their one, yet they knew their motions were too slow and
dilatory to prevent any undertaking of theirs. They pretend
to have an undoubted right to the river from a discovery
made by one La Salle, sixty years ago; and the rise of this
expedition is, to prevent our settling on the river or waters
of it, as they heard of some families moving out in order
thereto. From the best intelligence I could get, there have

been fifteen hundred men on this side Ontario Lake. But upon the death of the general, all were recalled to about six or seven hundred, who were left to garrison four forts, one hundred and fifty or thereabout in each. The first of them is on French Creek, near a small lake, about sixty miles from Venango, near north northwest; the next lies on Lake Erie, where the greater part of their stores are kept, about fifteen miles from the other; from this it is one hundred and twenty miles to the carrying-place, at the Falls of Lake Erie, where there is a small fort, at which they lodge their goods in bringing them from Montreal, the place from whence all their stores are brought. The next fort lies about twenty miles from this, on Ontario Lake. Between this fort and Montreal, there are three others, the first of which is nearly opposite to the English fort Oswego. From the fort on Lake Erie to Montreal is about six hundred miles, which, they say, requires no more (if good weather) than four weeks' voyage, if they go in barks or large vessels, so that they may cross the lake; but if they come in canoes, it will require five or six weeks, for they are obliged to keep under the shore.

December 5th—Rained excessively all day, which prevented our travelling. Captain Joncaire sent for the Half-King, as he had but just heard that he came with me. He affected to be much concerned that I did not make free to bring them in before. I excused it in the best manner of which I was capable, and told him, I did not think their company agreeable, as I had heard him say a good deal in dispraise of Indians in general; but another motive prevented me from bringing them into his company; I knew that he was an interpreter, and a person of very great influence among the Indians, and had lately used all possible means to draw them over to his interest; therefore I was desirous of giving him no opportunity that could be avoided.

When they came in, there was great pleasure expressed at seeing them. He wondered how they could be so near without coming to visit him, made several trifling presents, and applied liquor so fast, that they were soon rendered incapable of the business they came about, notwithstanding the caution which was given.

6th—The Half-King came to my tent, quite sober, and insisted very much that I should stay and hear what he had to say to the French. I fain would have prevented him from speaking any thing until he came to the commandant, but could not prevail. He told me, that at this place a council-fire was kindled, where all their business with these people was to be transacted, and that the management of the Indian affairs was left solely to Monsieur Joncaire. As I was desirous of knowing the issue of this, I agreed to stay; but sent our horses a little way up French Creek, to raft over and encamp; which I knew would make it near night.

About ten o'clock they met in council. The King spoke much the same as he had before done to the general; and offered the French speech-belt which had before been demanded, with the marks of four towns on it, which Monsieur Joncaire refused to receive, but desired him to carry it to the fort to the commander.

7th—Monsieur La Force, commissary of the French stores, and three other soldiers, came over to accompany us up. We found it extremely difficult to get the Indians off to-day, as every stratagem had been used to prevent their going up with me. I had last night left John Davidson (the Indian interpreter), whom I brought with me from town, and strictly charged him not to be out of their company, as I could not get them over to my tent; for they had some business with Kustalogo, chiefly to know why he did not deliver up the French speech-belt which he had in keeping; but I was obliged to send Mr. Gist over to-day to fetch them, which he did with great persuasion.

At twelve o'clock, we set out for the fort, and were prevented arriving there until the 11th by excessive rains, snows, and bad travelling through many mires and swamps; these we were obliged to pass to avoid crossing the creek, which was impassable, either by fording or rafting, the water was so high and rapid.

We passed over much good land since we left Venango, and through several extensive and very rich meadows, one of which, I believe, was nearly four miles in length, and considerably wide in some places.

12th—I prepared early to wait upon the commander, and was received and conducted to him by the second officer in command. I acquainted him with my business, and offered my commission and letter; both of which he desired me to keep until the arrival of Monsieur Reparti, captain at the next fort, who was sent for and expected every hour.

This commander is a knight of the military order of St. Louis, and named Legardeur de St. Pierre. He is an elderly gentleman, and has much the air of a soldier. He was sent over to take the command immediately upon the death of the late general, and arrived here about seven days before me.

At two o'clock, the gentleman who was sent for arrived, when I offered the letter, etc. again, which they received, and adjourned into a private apartment for the captain to translate, who understood a little English. After he had done it, the commander desired I would walk in and bring my interpreter to peruse and correct it: which I did.

13th—The chief officers retired to hold a council of war, which gave me an opportunity of taking the dimensions of the fort, and making what observations I could.

It is situated on the south or west fork of French Creek, near the water; and is almost surrounded by the creek, and a small branch of it, which form a kind of island. Four houses compose the sides. The bastions are made of piles driven into the ground, standing more than twelve feet above it, and sharp at top, with port-holes cut for cannon, and loop-holes for the small arms to fire through. There are eight six-pounds pieces mounted in each bastion, and one piece of four pounds before the gate. In the bastions are a guard-house, chapel, doctor's lodging, and the commander's private store; round which are laid platforms for the cannon and men to stand on. There are several barracks without the fort, for the soldiers' dwellings, covered, some with bark, and some with boards, made chiefly of logs. There are also several other houses, such as stables, smith's shop, etc.

I could get no certain account of the number of men here; but, according to the best judgment I could form, there are a hundred, exclusive of officers, of whom there are many. I also gave orders to the people who were with me, to take an exact account of the canoes, which were hauled up to convey their forces down in the spring. This they did, and told fifty of birch bark, and a hundred and seventy of pine; besides many others, which were blocked out, in readiness for being made.

14th—As the snow increased very fast, and our horses daily became weaker, I sent them off unloaded, under the care of Barnaby Currin and two others, to make all convenient despatch to Venango, and there to wait our arrival, if there was a prospect of the river's freezing; if not, then to continue down to Shannopin's Town, at the Fork of the Ohio, and there to wait until we came to cross the Allegany; intending myself to go down by water, as I had the offer of a canoe or two.

As I found many plots concerted to retard the Indians' business, and prevent their returning with me, I endeavoured all that lay in my power to frustrate their schemes, and hurried them on to execute their intended design. They accordingly pressed for admittance this evening, which at length was granted them, privately, to the commander and one or two other officers. The Half-King told me, that he offered the wampum to the commander, who evaded taking it, and made many fair promises of love and friendship; said he wanted to live in peace and trade amicably with them, as a proof of which, he would send some goods immediately down to the Logstown for them. But I rather think the design of that is to bring away all our straggling traders they meet with, as I privately understood they intended to carry an officer, with them. And what rather confirms this opinion, I was inquiring of the commander by what authority he had made prisoners of several of our English subjects. He told me that the country belonged to them; that no Englishman had a right to trade upon those waters; and that he had orders to make every person prisoner, who attempted it on the Ohio, or the waters of it.

I inquired of Captain Reparti about the boy, that was carried by this place, as it was done while the command devolved on him, between the death of the late general, and the arrival of the present. He acknowledged, that a boy had been carried past; and that the Indians had two or three white men's scalps (I was told by some of the Indians at Venango, eight), but pretended to have forgotten the name of the place where the boy came from, and all the particular facts, though he had questioned him for some hours, as they were carrying him past. I likewise inquired what they had done with John

Trotter and James McClocklan, two Pennsylvania traders, whom they had taken with all their goods. They told me, that they had been sent to Canada, but were now returned home.

This evening I received an answer to his Honor the Governor's letter from the commandant.

15th—The commandant ordered a plentiful store of liquor, and provision to be put on board our canoes, and appeared to be extremely complaisant, though he was exerting every artifice, which he could invent, to set our Indians at variance with us, to prevent their going until after our departure; presents, rewards, and every thing, which could be suggested by him or his officers. I cannot say that ever in my life I suffered so much anxiety, as I did in this affair. I saw that every stratagem, which the most fruitful brain could invent, was practised to win the Half-King to their interest; and that leaving him there was giving them the opportunity they aimed at. I went to the Half-King and pressed him in the strongest terms to go; he told me that the commandant would not discharge him until the morning. I then went to the commandant, and desired him to do their business, and complained of ill treatment; for keeping them, as they were part of my company, was detaining me. This he promised not to do, but to forward my journey as much as he could. He protested he did not keep them, but was ignorant of the cause of their stay; though I soon found it out. He had promised them a present of guns, if they would wait until the morning. As I was very much pressed by the Indians to wait this day for them, I consented, on a promise that nothing should hinder them in the morning.

16th—The French were not slack in their inventions to keep the Indians this day also. But as they were obliged, according to promise, to give the present, they then endeavoured to try the power of liquor, which I doubt not would have prevailed at any other time than this; but I urged and insisted with the King so closely upon his word, that he refrained, and set off with us as he had engaged.

We had a tedious and very fatiguing passage down the creek. Several times we had like to have been staved against rocks; and many times were obliged all hands to get out and remain in the water half an hour or more, getting over the shoals. At one place, the ice had lodged, and made it impassable by water; we were, therefore, obliged to carry our canoe across the neck of land, a quarter of a mile over. We did not reach Venango until the 22d, where we met with our horses.

This creek is extremely crooked. I dare say the distance between the fort and Venango cannot be less than one hundred and thirty miles, to follow the meanders.

23d—When I got things ready to set off, I sent for the Half-King, to know whether he intended to go with us or by water. He told me that White Thunder had hurt himself much, and was sick, and unable to walk; therefore he was obliged to carry him down in a canoe. As I found he intended to stay here a day or two, and knew that Monsieur Joncaire would employ every scheme to set him against the English, as he had before done, I told him, I hoped he would guard against his flattery, and let no fine speeches influence him in their favor. He desired I might not be concerned, for he knew the French too well, for any thing to engage him in their favor; and that though he could not go down with us, he yet would endeavour to meet at the Fork with Joseph Campbell, to deliver a speech for me to carry to his Honor the Governor. He told me he would order the Young Hunter to attend us, and get provisions, etc. if wanted.

Our horses were now so weak and feeble, and the baggage so heavy (as we were obliged to provide all the necessaries which the journey would require), that we doubted much their performing it. Therefore, myself and others, except the drivers, who were obliged to ride, gave up our horses for packs, to assist along with the baggage. I put myself in an Indian walking-dress, and continued with them three days, until I found there was no probability of their getting home in any reasonable time. The horses became less able to travel every day; the cold increased very fast; and the roads were becoming much worse by a deep snow, continually freezing; therefore, as I was uneasy to get back, to make report of my proceedings to his Honor the Governor, I determined to prosecute my journey, the nearest way through the woods, on foot.

Accordingly, I left Mr. Vanbraam in charge of our baggage, with money and directions to provide necessaries from place to place for themselves and horses, and to make the most convenient despatch in travelling.

I took my necessary papers, pulled off my clothes, and tied myself up in a watch-coat. Then, with gun in hand, and pack on my back, in which were my papers and provisions, I set out with Mr. Gist, fitted in the same manner, on Wednesday the 26th. The day following, just after we had passed a place called Murdering Town (where we intended to quit the path and steer across the country for Shannopin's Town), we fell in with a party of French Indians, who had lain in wait for us. One of them fired at Mr. Gist or me, not fifteen steps off, but fortunately missed. We took this fellow into custody, and kept him until about nine o'clock at night, then let him go, and walked all the remaining part of the night without making any stop, that we might get the start so far, as to be out of the reach of their pursuit the next day, since we were well assured they would follow our track as soon as it was light. The next day we continued travelling until quite dark, and got to the river about two miles above Shannopin's. We expected to have found the river frozen, but it was not, only about fifty yards from each shore. The ice, I suppose, had broken up above, for it was driving in vast quantities.

There was no way for getting over but on a raft, which we set about, with but one poor hatchet, and finished just after sun-setting. This was a whole day's work; we next got it launched, then went on board of it, and set off; but before we were half way over, we were jammed in the ice in such a manner, that we expected every moment our raft to sink, and ourselves to perish. I put out my setting-pole to try to stop the raft, that the ice might pass by, when the rapidity of the stream threw it with so much violence against the pole, that it jerked me out into ten feet water; but I fortunately saved myself by catching hold of one of the raft-logs. Notwithstanding all our efforts, we could not get to either shore, but were obliged, as we were near an island, to quit our raft and make to it.

The cold was so extremely severe, that Mr. Gist had all his fingers and some of his toes frozen, and the water was shut up so hard, that we found no difficulty in getting off the island on the ice in the morning, and went to Mr. Frazier's. We met here with twenty warriors, who were going to the southward to war; but coming to a place on the head of the Great Kenhawa, where they found seven people killed and scalped (all but one woman with very light hair), they turned about and ran back, for fear the inhabitants should rise and take them as the authors of the murder. They report that the bodies were lying about the house, and some of them much torn and eaten by the hogs. By the marks which were left, they say they were French Indians of the Ottoway nation, who did it.

As we intended to take horses here, and it required some time to find them, I went up about three miles to the mouth of Youghiogany, to visit Queen Aliquippa, who had expressed great concern that we passed her in going to the fort. I made her a present of a watch-coat and a bottle of rum, which latter was thought much the better present of the two.

Tuesday, the 1st of January, we left Mr. Frazier's house, and arrived at Mr. Gist's, at Monongahela, the 2d, where I bought a horse and saddle. The 6th, we met seventeen horses loaded with materials and stores for a fort at the Fork of the Ohio, and the day after, some families going out to settle. This day, we arrived at Will's Creek, after as fatiguing a journey as it is possible to conceive, rendered so by excessive bad weather. From the 1st day of December to the 15th, there was but one day on which it did not rain or snow incessantly; and throughout the whole journey, we met with nothing but one continued series of cold, wet weather, which occasioned very uncomfortable lodgings, especially after we had quitted our tent, which was some screen from the inclemency of it.

On the 11th, I got to Belvoir, where I stopped one day to take necessary rest; and then set out and arrived in Williamsburg the 16th, when I waited upon his Honor the Governor, with the letter I had brought from the French commandant, and to give an account of the success of my proceedings. This I beg leave to do by offering the foregoing narrative, as it contains the most remarkable occurrences, which happened in my journey.

I hope what has been said will be sufficient to make your Honor satisfied with my conduct; for that was my aim in undertaking the journey, and chief study throughout the prosecution of it.

THE FAIRFAX COUNTY RESOLVES
GEORGE WASHINGTON, CHAIRMAN

The Resolves were written by a Committee chaired by George Washington in 1774 when he was forty-two. On the eve of the Revolutionary War, the leading men of Fairfax County, Virginia, appointed a Committee to draw up a document expressing their mutual opinions, their resolves, on what should be done about Britain's mistreatment of her American colonies. When his committee's work was completed and approved, Washington was selected to present the *Fairfax County Resolves* to the Virginia General Assembly.

THE FAIRFAX COUNTY RESOLVES
GEORGE WASHINGTON, CHAIRMAN
JULY 18, 1774

At a general meeting of the freeholders and inhabitants of the County of Fairfax on Monday, the 18th day of July, 1774, at the Court-House; George Washington, Chairman, and Robert Harrison, Clerk of the said meeting;

1. Resolved, That this colony and dominion of Virginia cannot be considered as a conquered country; and if it was, that the present inhabitants are the descendants not of the conquered, but of the conquerors. That the same was not settled at the national expense of England, but at the private expense of the adventurers, our ancestors, by solemn compact with, and under the auspices and protection of, the British crown; upon which we are in every respect as dependent, as the people of Great Britain, and in the same manner subject to all his Majesty's just, legal, and constitutional prerogatives. That our ancestors, when they left their native land and settled in America, brought with them (even if the same had not been confirmed by charters) the civil constitution and form of government of the country they came from; and were, by the laws of nature and nations, entitled to all its privileges, immunities, and advantages; which have descended to us their posterity, and ought of right to be as fully enjoyed, as if we had still continued within the realm of England.

2. Resolved, That the most important and valuable part of the British constitution, upon which its very existence depends, is the fundamental principle of the people's being governed by no laws, to which they have not given their consent by representatives freely chosen by themselves; who

are affected by the laws they enact equally with their constituents; to whom they are accountable, and whose burthens they share; in which consists the safety and happiness of the community; for if this part of the constitution was taken away, or materially altered, the government must degenerate either into an absolute and despotic monarchy; or a tyrannical aristocracy, and the freedom of the people be annihilated.

3. Resolved, Therefore, as the inhabitants of the American colonies are not, and, from their situation, cannot be represented in the British Parliament, that the legislative power here can of right be exercised only by our own provincial Assemblies or Parliaments, subject to the assent or negative of the British crown, to be declared within some proper limited time. But as it was thought just and reasonable, that the people of Great Britain should reap advantages from these colonies adequate to the protection they afforded them, the British Parliament have claimed and exercised the power of regulating our trade and commerce, so as to restrain our importing from foreign countries such articles as they could furnish us with, of their own growth or manufacture, or exporting to foreign countries such articles and portions of our produce, as Great Britain stood in need of, for her own consumption or manufactures. Such a power directed with wisdom and moderation, seems necessary for the general good of that great body politic, of which we are a part; although in some degree repugnant to the principles of the constitution. Under this idea our ancestors submitted to it; the experience of more than a century, during the government of his Majesty's royal predecessors, has proved its utility, and the reciprocal benefits flowing from it produced mutual uninterrupted harmony and good will, between the inhabitants of Great Britain and her colonies, who, during that long period, always considered themselves as one and the same people; and though such a power is capable of

abuse, and in some instances has been stretched beyond the original design and institution, yet to avoid strife and contention with our fellow-subjects, and strongly impressed with the experience of mutual benefits, we always cheerfully acquiesced in it, while the entire regulation of our internal policy, and giving and granting our own money, were preserved to our own provincial legislatures.

4. Resolved, That it is the duty of these colonies, on all emergencies, to contribute, in proportion to their abilities, situation, and circumstances, to the necessary charge of supporting and defending the British empire, of which they are part; that while we are treated upon an equal footing with our fellow-subjects, the motives of self-interest and preservation will be a sufficient obligation, as was evident through the course of the last war; and that no argument can be fairly applied to the British Parliament's taxing us, upon a presumption that we should refuse a just and reasonable contribution, but will equally operate in justification of the executive power taxing the people of England, upon a supposition of their representatives refusing to grant the necessary supplies.

5. Resolved, That the claim, lately assumed and exercised by the British Parliament, of making all such laws as they think fit, to govern the people of these colonies, and to extort from us our money without our consent, is not only diametrically contrary to the first principles of the constitution, and the original compacts by which we are dependent upon the British crown and government; but is totally incompatible with the privileges of a free people and the natural rights of mankind, will render our own legislatures merely nominal and nugatory, and is calculated to reduce us from a state of freedom and happiness to slavery and misery.

6. Resolved, That taxation and representation are in their nature inseparable; that the right of withholding or of giving and granting their own money, is the only effectual security to a free people, against the encroachments of despotism and tyranny; and that whenever they yield the one, they must quickly fall a prey to the other.

7. Resolved, That the powers over the people of America now claimed by the British House of Commons, in whose election we have no share, on whose determinations we can have no influence, whose information must be always defective and often false, who in many instances may have a separate, and in some an opposite interest to ours, and who are removed from those impressions of tenderness and compassion arising from personal intercourse and connexions, which soften the rigors of the most despotic governments, must, if continued, establish the most grievous and intolerable species of tyranny and oppression, that ever was inflicted upon mankind.

8. Resolved, That it is our greatest wish and inclination, as well as interest, to continue our connexion with, and dependence upon the British government; but though we are its subjects, we will use every means, which Heaven hath given us to prevent our becoming its slaves.

9. Resolved, That there is a premeditated design and system, formed and pursued by the British ministry, to introduce an arbitrary government into His Majesty's American dominions; to which end they are artfully prejudicing our sovereign, and inflaming the minds of our fellow-subjects in Great Britain, by propagating the most malevolent falsehoods, particularly that there is an intention in the American colonies to set up for independent states; endeavouring at the same time, by various acts of violence and oppression, by sudden and repeated dissolutions of our Assemblies, whenever they

presume to examine the illegality of ministerial mandates, or deliberate on the violated rights of their constituents, and by breaking in upon the American charters, to reduce us to a state of desperation, and dissolve the original compacts by which our ancestors bound themselves and their posterity to remain dependent upon the British crown; which measures, unless effectually counteracted, will end in the ruin both of Great Britain and her colonies.

10. Resolved, That the several acts of Parliament for raising a revenue upon the people of America without their consent, the creating new and dangerous jurisdictions here, the taking away our trials by jury, the ordering persons, upon criminal accusations, to be tried in another country than that in which the fact is charged to have been committed, the act inflicting ministerial vengeance upon the town of Boston, and the two bills lately brought into Parliament for abrogating the charter of the province of Massachusetts Bay, and for the protection and encouragement of murderers in the said province, are part of the abovementioned iniquitous system. That the inhabitants of the town of Boston are now suffering in the common cause of all British America, and are justly entitled to its support and assistance; and therefore that a subscription ought immediately to be opened, and proper persons appointed in every county of this colony to purchase provisions, and consign them to some gentlemen of character in Boston, to be distributed among the poorer sort of people there.

11. Resolved, That we will cordially join with our friends and brethren of this and the other colonies, in such measures as shall be judged most effectual for procuring redress of our grievances, and that upon obtaining such redress, if the destruction of the tea at Boston be regarded as an invasion of private property, we shall be willing to contribute towards

paying the East India Company the value; but as we consider the said Company as the tools and instruments of oppression in the hands of government, and the cause of our present distress, it is the opinion of this meeting, that the people of these colonies should forbear all further dealings with them, by refusing to purchase their merchandise, until that peace, safety, and good order, which they have disturbed, be perfectly restored. And that all tea now in this colony, or which shall be imported into it shipped before the 1st day of September next, should be deposited in some storehouse to be appointed by the respective committees of each county, until a sufficient sum of money be raised by subscription to reimburse the owners the value, and then to be publicly burned and destroyed; and if the same is not paid for and destroyed as aforesaid, that it remain in the custody of the said committees, at the risk of the owners, until the act of Parliament imposing a duty upon tea, for raising a revenue in America, be repealed; and immediately afterwards be delivered unto the several proprietors thereof, their agents, or attorneys.

12. Resolved, That nothing will so much contribute to defeat the pernicious designs of the common enemies of Great Britain and her colonies, as a firm union of the latter, who ought to regard every act of violence or oppression inflicted upon any one of them, as aimed at all; and to effect this desirable purpose, that a Congress should be appointed, to consist of deputies from all the colonies, to concert a general and uniform plan for the defence and preservation of our common rights, and continuing the connexion and dependence of the said colonies upon Great Britain, under a just, lenient, permanent, and constitutional form of government.

13. Resolved, That our most sincere and cordial thanks be given to the patrons and friends of liberty in Great Britain, for their spirited and patriotic conduct, in support of our

constitutional rights and privileges, and their generous efforts to prevent the present distress and calamity of America.

14. Resolved, That every little jarring interest and dispute, which has ever happened between these colonies, should be buried in eternal oblivion; that all manner of luxury and extravagance ought immediately to be laid aside, as totally inconsistent with the threatening and gloomy propsect before us; that it is the indispensable duty of all gentlemen and men of fortune to set examples of temperance, fortitude, frugality, and industry, and give every encouragement in their power, particularly by subscriptions and premiums, to the improvement of arts and manufactures in America; that great care and attention should be had to the cultivation of flax, cotton, and other materials for manufactures; and we recommend it to such of the inhabitants, as have large stocks of sheep, to sell to their neighbours at a moderate price, as the most certain means of speedily increasing our breed of sheep, and quantity of wool.

15. Resolved, That until American grievances be redressed, by restoration of our just rights and privileges, no goods or merchandise whatsoever ought to be imported into this colony, which shall be shipped from Great Britain or Ireland after the 1st day of September next, except linens not exceeding fifteen pence per yard, coarse woolen cloth, not exceeding two shillings sterling per yard, nails, wire and wire cards, needles and pins, paper, saltpetre, and medicines, which may be imported until the 1st day of September, 1776; and if any goods or merchandise, other than those hereby excepted, should be shipped from Great Britain, after the time aforesaid, to this colony, that the same, immediately upon their arrival, should either be sent back again, by the owners, their agent, or attorneys, or stored and deposited in some warehouse, to be appointed by the committee for each

respective county, and there kept, at the risk and charge of the owners, to be delivered to them, when a free importation of goods hither shall again take place. And that the merchants and venders of goods and merchandise within this colony ought not to take advantage of our present distress, but continue to sell the goods and merchandise which they now have, or which may be shipped to them before the 1st day of September next, at the same rates and prices they have been accustomed to do, within one year last past; and if any person shall sell such goods on any other terms than above expressed, that no inhabitant of this colony should at any time, for ever thereafter, deal with him, his agent, factor, or storekeepers for any commodity whatsoever.

16. Resolved, That it is the opinion of this meeting, that the merchants and venders of goods and merchandise within this colony should take an oath, not to sell or dispose of any goods or merchandise whatsoever, which may be shipped from Great Britain after the 1st day of September next as aforesaid, except the articles before excepted, and that they will, upon receipt of such prohibited goods, either send the same back again by the first opportunity, or deliver them to the committees in the respective counties, to be deposited in some warehouse, at the risk and charge of the owners, until they, their agents, or factors be permitted to take them away by the said committees; the names of those who refuse to take such oath to be advertised by the respective committees in the counties wherein they reside. And to the end that the inhabitants of this colony may know what merchants and venders of goods and merchandise have taken such oath, that the respective committees should grant a certificate thereof to every such person who shall take the same.

17. Resolved, That it is the opinion of this meeting, that during our present difficulties and distress, no slaves ought

to be imported into any of the British colonies on this continent; and we take this opportunity of declaring our most earnest wishes to see an entire stop forever put to such a wicked, cruel, and unnatural trade.

18. Resolved, That no kind of lumber should be exported from this colony to the West Indies, until America be restored to her constitutional rights and liberties, if the other colonies will accede to a like resolution; and that it be recommended to the general Congress to appoint as early a day as possible for stopping such export.

19. Resolved, That it is the opinion of this meeting, if American grievances be not redressed before the 1st day of November, 1775, that all exports of produce from the several colonies to Great Britain should cease; and to carry the said resolution more effectually into execution, that we will not plant or cultivate any tobacco, after the crop now growing; provided the same measure shall be adopted by the other colonies on this continent, as well those who have heretofore made tobacco, as those who have not. And it is our opinion also, if the Congress of deputies from the several colonies shall adopt the measure of non-exportation to Great Britain, as the people will be thereby disabled from paying their debts, that no judgments should be rendered by the courts in the said colonies for any debt, after information of the said measure's being determined upon.

20. Resolved, That it is the opinion of this meeting that a solemn covenant and association should be entered into by the inhabitants of all the colonies upon oath, that they will not, after the times which shall be respectively agreed on at the general Congress, export any manner of lumber to the West Indies, nor any of their produce to Great Britain, or sell or dispose of the same to any person who shall not have

entered into the said covenant and association; and also that
they will not import or receive any goods or merchandise
which shall be shipped from Great Britain after the 1st day
of September next, other than the before enumerated articles,
nor buy or purchase any goods, except as before excepted, of
any person whatsoever, who shall not have taken the oath
herein before recommended to be taken by the merchants
and venders of goods, nor buy or purchase any slaves hereafter imported into any part of this continent until a free ex-
portation and importation be again resolved on by a majority
of the representatives or deputies of the colonies. And that
the respective committees of the counties in each colony, so
soon as the covenant and association becomes general, publish by advertisements in their several counties, a list of the
names of those (if any such there be) who will not accede
thereto; that such traitors to their country may be publicly
known and detested.

21. Resolved, That it is the opinion of this meeting, that
this and the other associating colonies should break off all
trade, intercourse, and dealings, with that colony, province,
or town, which shall decline or refuse to agree to the plan,
which shall be adopted by the general Congress.

22. Resolved, That should the town of Boston be forced to
submit to the late cruel and oppressive measures of government, that we shall not hold the same to be binding upon
us, but will, notwithstanding, religiously maintain and invi-
olably adhere to such measures as shall be concerted by the
general Congress, for the preservation of our lives, liberties,
and fortunes.

23. Resolved, That it be recommended to the deputies of the
general Congress to draw up and transmit an humble and
dutiful petition and remonstrance to his Majesty, asserting

with decent firmness our just and constitutional rights and privileges; lamenting the fatal necessity of being compelled to enter into measures disgusting to his Majesty and his Parliament, or injurious to our fellow-subjects in Great Britain; declaring, in the strongest terms, our duty and affection to his Majesty's person, family, and government, and our desire to continue our dependence upon Great Britain; and most humbly conjuring and beseeching his Majesty not to reduce his faithful subjects of America to a state of desperation, and to reflect, that from our sovereign there can be but one appeal. And it is the opinion of this meeting, that after such petition, and remonstrance shall have been presented to his Majesty, the same should be printed in the public papers, in all the principal towns in Great Britain.

24. Resolved, That George Washington and Charles Broadwater, lately elected our representatives to serve in the General Assembly, be appointed to attend the convention at Williamsburg on the 1st day of August next, and present these resolves, as the sense of the people of this county, upon the measures proper to be taken in the present alarming and dangerous situation of America.

THE NEWBURGH MUTINY ADDRESS

At Army Headquarters in Newburgh, New York, a cabal of officers, owed years of back pay by Congress, was called upon, by an anonymously authored letter, to meet on the night of March 15, 1783, to discuss mutiny. Washington, warned about the treasonous meeting, rushed to Newburgh and, in the stirring *Newburgh Mutiny Address*, ended the threat.

THE NEWBURGH MUTINY ADDRESS
MARCH 15, 1783

Gentlemen:

By an anonymous summons an attempt has been made to convene you together. How inconsistent with the rules of propriety, how unmilitary, and how subversive of all good order and discipline, let the good sense of the army decide.

In the moment of this summons, another anonymous production was sent into circulation; addressed more to the feelings and passions, than to the reason and judgment of the army. The author of the piece is entitled to much credit for the goodness of his pen, and I could wish he had as much credit for the rectitude of his heart; for, as men see through different optics, and are induced by the reflecting faculties of the mind to use different means to obtain the same end, the author of the address should have had more charity, than to mark for suspicion the man, who should recommend moderation and longer forbearance, or in other words, who should not think as he thinks, and act as he advises. But he had another plan in view, in which candor and liberality of sentiment, regard to justice, and love of country, have no part; and he was right to insinuate the darkest suspicion, to effect the blackest designs.

That the address is drawn with great art, and is designed to answer the most insidious purposes, that it is calculated to impress the mind with an idea of premeditated injustice in the sovereign power of the United States, and rouse all those resentments, which must unavoidably flow from such a belief; that the secret mover of this scheme, whoever he may be, intended to take advantage of the passions, while they were warmed by the recollection of past distresses, without giving time for cool, deliberate thinking, and that composure of mind, which is so necessary to give dignity and stability to measures, is rendered too obvious, by the mode of conducting the business, to need other proof than a reference to the proceeding.

Thus much, gentlemen, I have thought it incumbent on me to observe to you, to show upon what principles I opposed the irregular and hasty meeting, which was proposed to be held on Tuesday last, and not because I wanted a disposition to give you every opportunity, consistent with your own honor and the dignity of the army, to make known your grievances. If my conduct heretofore has not evinced to you, that I have been a faithful friend to the army, my declaration of it at this time would be equally unavailing and improper. But, as I was among the first, who embarked in the cause of our common country; as I have never left your side one moment, but when called from you on public duty; as I have been the constant companion and witness of your distresses, and not among the last to feel and acknowledge your merits; as I have ever considered my own military reputation as inseparably connected with that of the army; as my heart has ever expanded with joy, when I have heard its praises, and my indignation has arisen, when the mouth of detraction has been opened against it; it can scarcely be supposed, at this late stage of the war, that I am indifferent to its interests. But how are they to be promoted? The way is plain, says the anonymous addresser; if war continues, remove into the unsettled country; there establish yourselves, and leave an ungrateful country to defend itself. But whom are they to defend? Our wives, our children, our farms and other property, which we leave behind us? Or, in the state of hostile separation, are we to take the two first (the latter cannot be removed) to perish in a wilderness with hunger, cold, and nakedness? If peace takes place, never sheathe your swords, says he, until you have obtained full and ample justice. This dreadful alternative, of either deserting our country in the extremest hour of distress, or turning our arms against it, which is the apparent object, unless Congress can be compelled into instant compliance, has something so shocking in it, that humanity revolts at the idea. My God! What can this writer have in view by recommending such measures? Can he be a friend to the army? Can he be a friend to this country? Rather is he not an insidious foe? Some emissary, perhaps from New York, plotting the ruin of both by sowing the seeds of discord and separation between the civil and military powers of the continent? And what a compliment does he pay to our understandings, when he recommends measures, in either alternative, impracticable in their nature?

But here, gentlemen, I will drop the curtain, because it would be as imprudent in me to assign my reasons for this opinion, as it would be insulting to your conception to suppose you stood in need of them. A moment's reflection will convince every dispassionate mind of the physical impossibility of carrying either proposal into execution.

There might, gentlemen, be an impropriety in my taking notice, in this address to you, of an anonymous production; but the manner in which that performance has been introduced to the army, the effect it was intended to have, together with some other circumstances, will amply justify my observations on the tendency of that writing. With respect to the advice given by the author to suspect the man, who shall recommend moderate measures and longer forbearance, I spurn it, as every man who regards that liberty, and reveres that justice, for which we contend, undoubtedly must. For, if men are to be precluded from offering their sentiments on a matter, which may involve the most serious and alarming consequences, that can invite the consideration of mankind, reason is of no use to us; the freedom of speech may be taken away, and, dumb and silent, we may be led away like sheep to the slaughter.

I cannot, in justice to my own belief and what I have great reason to conceive is the intention of Congress, conclude this address, without giving it as my decided opinion, that that honorable body entertain exalted sentiments of the services of the army, and, from a full conviction of its merits and sufferings, will do it complete justice. That their endeavours to discover and establish funds for this purpose have been unwearied, and will not cease, till they have succeeded, I have no doubt; but, like all other large bodies, where there is a variety of different interests to reconcile, their deliberations are slow. Why then should we distrust them; and, in consequence of that distrust, adopt measures, which may cast a shade over that glory, which has been so justly acquired, and tarnish the reputation of an army, which is celebrated through all Europe for its fortitude and patriotism? And for what is this done? To bring the object we seek nearer? No! Most certainly, in my opinion, it will cast it at a greater distance.

For myself (and I take no merit in giving the assurance, being induced to it from principles of gratitude, veracity, and justice), a grateful sense of the confidence you have ever placed in me, a recollection of the cheerful assistance and prompt obedience I have experienced from you, under every vicissitude of fortune, and the sincere affection I feel for an army I have so long had the honor to command, oblige me to declare in this public and solemn manner, that, in the attainment of complete justice for all your toils and dangers, and in the gratification of every wish, so far as may be done consistently with the great duty I owe to my country, and those powers we are bound to respect, you may freely command my services to the utmost extent of my abilities.

While I give you these assurances, and pledge myself in the most unequivocal manner to exert whatever ability I am possessed of in your favor, let me entreat you, gentlemen, on your part, not to take any measures, which, in the calm light of reason, will lessen the dignity and sully the glory you have hitherto maintained. Let me request you to rely on the plighted faith of your country, and place a full confidence in the purity of the intentions of Congress, that, previous to your dissolution as an army, they will cause all your accounts to be fairly liquidated, as directed in their resolutions, which were published to you two days ago, and that they will adopt the most effectual measures in their power to render ample justice to you for your faithful and meritorious services. And let me conjure you in the name of our common country, as you value your own sacred honor, as you respect the rights of humanity, and as you regard the military and national character of America, to express your utmost horror and detestation of the man, who wishes, under any specious pretences, to overturn the liberties of our country, and who wickedly attempts to open the flood-gates of civil discord, and deluge our rising empire in blood.

By thus determining and thus acting, you will pursue the plain and direct road to the attainment of your wishes; you will defeat the insidious designs of our enemies, who are compelled to resort from open force to secret artifice; you will give one more distinguished proof of unexampled patriotism and patient virtue, rising superior to the pressure of the most complicated sufferings; and you will, by the dignity of your conduct, afford occasion for posterity to say, when speaking of the glorious example you have exhibited to mankind, "Had this day been wanting, the world had never seen the last stage of perfection, to which human nature is capable of attaining."

GENERAL GEORGE WASHINGTON'S
ADVICE TO THE UNITED STATES

Advice To The United States was written in 1783 when George Washington was fifty-one. The eight-year-long Revolutionary War was over. General Washington, preparing to return home to Mount Vernon, believing that he would never return to public life, wrote down his thoughts on how the newly independent United States should act, and so keep, its newly found freedom.

GENERAL GEORGE WASHINGTON'S
ADVICE TO THE UNITED STATES
JUNE 8, 1783

The great object for which I had the honor to hold an appointment in the service of my country, being accomplished, I am now preparing to resign it into the hands of Congress, and to return to that domestic retirement, which, it is well known, I left with the greatest reluctance, a retirement, for which I have never ceased to sigh through a long and painful absence, and in which (remote from the noise and trouble of the world) I meditate to pass the remainder of life in a state of undisturbed repose; but before I carry this resolution into effect, I think it a duty incumbent on me, to make this my last official communication, to congratulate you on the glorious events which Heaven has been pleased to produce in our favor, to offer my sentiments respecting some important subjects, which appear to me, to be intimately connected with the tranquillity of the United States, to take my leave of your Excellency as a public character, and to give my final blessing to that country, in whose service I have spent the prime of my life, for whose sake I have consumed so many anxious days and watchfull nights, and whose happiness being extremely dear to me, will always constitute no inconsiderable part of my own.

Impressed with the liveliest sensibility on this pleasing occasion, I will claim the indulgence of dilating the more copiously on the subjects of our mutual felicitation. When we consider the magnitude of the prize we contended for, the doubtful nature of the contest, and the favorable manner in which it has terminated, we shall find the greatest possible reason for gratitude and rejoicing; this is a theme that will afford infinite delight to every benevolent and liberal mind, whether the event in contemplation, be considered as the source of present enjoyment or the parent of future happiness; and we shall have equal occasion to felicitate ourselves on the lot which Providence has assigned us, whether we view it in a natural, a political or moral point of light.

The citizens of America, placed in the most enviable condition, as the sole lords and proprietors of a vast tract of continent, comprehending all the various soils and climates of the world, and abounding with all the necessaries and conveniencies of life, are now by the late satisfactory pacification, acknowledged to be possessed of absolute freedom and independency; they are, from this period, to be considered as the actors on a most conspicuous theatre, which seems to be peculiarly designated by Providence for the display of human greatness and felicity; here, they are not only surrounded with every thing which can contribute to the completion of private and domestic enjoyment, but Heaven has crowned all its other blessings, by giving a fairer opportunity for political happiness, than any other nation has ever been favored with. Nothing can illustrate these observations more forcibly, than a recollection of the happy conjuncture of times and circumstances, under which our Republic assumed its rank among the nations; the foundation of our empire was not laid in the gloomy age of ignorance and superstition, but at an epocha when the rights of mankind were better understood and more clearly defined, than at any former period, the researches of the human mind, after social happiness, have been carried to a great extent, the treasures of knowledge, acquired by the labours of philosophers, sages and legislatures, through a long succession of years, are laid open for our use, and their collected wisdom may be happily applied in the establishment of our forms of government; the free cultivation of letters, the unbounded extension of commerce, the progressive refinement of manners, the growing liberality of sentiment, and above all, the pure and benign light of revelation, have had a meliorating influence on mankind and increased the blessings of society. At this auspicious period, the United States came into existence as a nation, and if their citizens should not be completely free and happy, the fault will be intirely their own.

Such is our situation, and such are our prospects: but notwithstanding the cup of blessing is thus reached out to us, notwithstanding happiness is ours, if we have a disposition to seize the occasion and make it our own; yet, it appears to me there is an option still left to the United States of America, that it is in their choice, and depends upon their conduct, whether they will be respectable and prosperous, or contemptable and miserable as a nation; this is the time of their political probation, this is the moment when the eyes of the whole world are turned upon them, this is the moment to establish or ruin their national character forever, this is the favorable moment to give such a tone to our Federal Government, as will enable it to answer the ends of its institution, or this may be the ill-fated moment for relaxing the powers of the Union, annihilating the cement of the Confederation, and exposing us to become the sport of European politics, which may play one State against another to prevent their growing importance, and to serve their own interested purposes. For, according to the system of policy the States shall adopt at this moment, they will stand or fall, and by their confirmation or lapse, it is yet to be decided, whether the Revolution must ultimately be considered as a blessing or a curse: a blessing or a curse, not to the present age alone, for with our fate will the destiny of unborn millions be involved.

With this conviction of the importance of the present crisis, silence in me would be a crime; I will therefore speak to your Excellency, the language of freedom and of sincerity, without disguise; I am aware, however, that those who differ from me in political sentiment, may perhaps remark, I am stepping out of the proper line of my duty, and they may possibly ascribe to arrogance or ostentation, what I know is alone the result of the purest intention, but the rectitude of my own heart, which disdains such unworthy motives, the part I have hitherto acted in life, the determination I have formed, of not taking any share in public business hereafter, the ardent desire I feel, and shall continue to manifest, of quietly enjoying in private life, after all the toils of war, the benefits of a wise and liberal government, will, I flatter myself, sooner or later convince my countrymen, that I could have no sinister views in delivering with so little reserve, the opinions contained in this address.

There are four things, which I humbly conceive, are essential to the well being, I may even venture to say, to the existence of the United States as an independent power:

First. An indissoluble Union of the States under one federal head.

Secondly. A sacred regard to public justice.

Thirdy. The adoption of a proper peace establishment, and

Fourthly. The prevalence of that pacific and friendly disposition, among the people of the United States, which will induce them to forget their local prejudices and policies, to make those mutual concessions which are requisite to the general prosperity, and in some instances, to sacrifice their individual advantages to the interest of the community.

These are the pillars on which the glorious fabrick of our independency and national character must be supported; liberty is the basis, and whoever would dare to sap the foundation, or overturn the structure, under whatever specious pretexts he may attempt it, will merit the bitterest execration, and the severest punishment which can be inflicted by his injured country.

On the three first Articles I will make a few observations, leaving the last to the good sense and serious consideration of those immediately concerned.

Under the first head, altho' it may not be necessary or proper for me in this place to enter into a particular disquisition of the principles of the Union, and to take up the great question which has been frequently agitated, whether it be expedient and requisite for the States to delegate a larger proportion of power to Congress, or not, yet it will be a part of my duty, and that of every true patriot, to assert without reserve, and to insist upon the following positions, that unless the States will suffer Congress to exercise those prerogatives, they are undoubtedly invested with by the Constitution, every thing must very rapidly tend to anarchy and confusion, that it is indispensable to the happiness of the individual States, that there should be lodged somewhere, a Supreme Power to regulate and govern the general concerns of the Confederated Republic, without which the Union cannot be of long duration. That there must be a faithful and pointed compliance on the part of every State, with the late proposals and demands of Congress, or the most fatal consequences will ensue, that whatever measures have a tendency to dissolve the Union, or contribute to violate or lessen the sovereign authority, ought to be considered as hostile to the liberty and independency of America, and the authors of them treated accordingly, and lastly, that unless we can be enabled by the concurrence of the States, to participate of the fruits of the Revolution, and enjoy the essential benefits of civil society, under a form of government so free and uncorrupted, so happily guarded against the danger of oppression, as has been devised and adopted by the Articles of Confederation, it will be a subject of regret, that so much blood and treasure have been lavished for no purpose, that so many sufferings have been encountered without a compensation, and that so many sacrifices have been made in vain. Many other considerations might here be adduced to prove, that without an entire conformity to the spirit of the Union, we cannot exist as an independent power; it will be sufficient for my purpose to mention but one or two which seem to me of the greatest importance. It is only in our united character as an empire, that our independence is acknowledged, that our power can be regarded, or our credit supported among foreign nations. The treaties of the European powers with the United States of America, will have no validity on a dissolution of the Union. We shall be left nearly in a state of nature, or we may find by our own unhappy experience, that there is a natural and necessary progression, from the extreme of anarchy to the extreme of tyranny; and that arbitrary power is most easily established on the ruins of liberty abused to licentiousness.

As to the second Article, which respects the performance of public justice, Congress have, in their late address to the United States, almost exhausted the subject, they have explained their ideas so fully, and have enforced the obligations the States are under, to render compleat justice to all the public creditors, with so much dignity and energy, that in my opinion, no real friend to the honor and independency of America, can hesitate a single moment respecting the propriety of complying with the just and honorable measures proposed; if their arguments do not produce conviction, I know of nothing that will have greater influence; especially when we recollect that the system referred to, being the result of the collected wisdom of the continent, must be esteemed, if not perfect, certainly the least objectionable of any that could be devised; and that if it shall not be carried into immediate execution, a national bankruptcy, with all its deplorable consequences will take place, before any different plan can possibly be proposed and adopted; so pressing are the present circumstances! and such is the alternative now offered to the States!

The ability of the country to discharge the debts which have been incurred in its defence, is not to be doubted, an inclination, I flatter myself, will not be wanting, the path of our duty is plain before us, honesty will be found on every experiment, to be the best and only true policy, let us then as a nation be just, let us fulfil the public contracts, which Congress had undoubtedly a right to make for the purpose of carrying on the War, with the same good faith we suppose ourselves bound to perform our private engagements; in the mean time, let an attention to the chearfull performance of their proper business, as individuals, and as members of society, be earnestly inculcated on the citizens of America, that will they strengthen the hands of government, and be happy under its protection: every one will reap the fruit of his labours, every one will enjoy his own acquisitions without molestation and without danger.

In this state of absolute freedom and perfect security, who will grudge to yield a very little of his property to support the common interest of society, and insure the protection of government? Who does not remember, the frequent declarations, at the commencement of the War, that we should be compleatly satisfied, if at the expence of one half, we could defend the remainder of our possessions? Where is the man to be found, who wishes to remain indebted, for the defence of his own person and property, to the exertions, the bravery, and the blood of others, without making one generous effort to repay the debt of honor and of gratitude? In what part of the continent shall we find any man, or body of men, who would not blush to stand up and propose measures, purposely calculated to rob the soldier of his stipend, and the public creditor of his due? and were it possible that such a flagrant instance of injustice could ever happen, would it not excite the general indignation, and tend to bring down, upon the authors of such measures, the aggravated vengeance of Heaven? If after all, a spirit of disunion or a temper of obstinacy and perverseness, should manifest itself in any of the States, if such an ungracious disposition should attempt to frustrate all the happy effects that might be expected to flow from the Union, if there should be a refusal to comply with the requisitions for funds to discharge the annual interest of the public debts, and if that refusal should revive again all those jealousies and produce all those evils, which are now happily removed, Congress, who have in all their transaction shewn a great degree of magnanimity and justice, will stand justified in the sight of God and man, and the State alone which puts itself in opposition to the aggregate wisdom of the continent, and follows such mistaken and pernicious councils, will be responsible for all the consequences.

For my own part, conscious of having acted while a servant of the public, in the manner I conceived best suited to promote the real interests of my country; having in consequence of my fixed belief in some measure pledged myself to the army, that their country would finally do them compleat and ample justice; and not wishing to conceal any instance of my official conduct from the eyes of the world, I have thought proper to transmit to your Excellency the inclosed collection of papers, relative to the half pay and commutation granted by Congress to the officers of the Army; from these communications, my decided sentiment will be clearly comprehended, together with the conclusive reasons which induced me, at an early period, to recommend the adoption of the measure, in the most earnest and serious manner. As the proceedings of Congress, the Army, and myself are open to all, and contain in my opinion, sufficient information to remove the prejudices and errors which may have been entertained by any; I think it unnecessary to say any thing more, than just to observe, that the resolutions of Congress, now alluded to, are undoubtedly as absolutely binding upon the United States, as the most solemn Acts of Confederation or legislation. As to the idea, which I am informed has in some instances prevailed, that the half pay and commutation are to be regarded merely in the odious light of a pension, it ought to be exploded forever; that provision, should be viewed as it really was, a reasonable compensation offered by Congress, at a time when they had nothing else to give, to the officers of the Army, for services then to be performed. It was the only means to prevent a total dereliction of the service, it was a part of their hire, I may be allowed to say, it was the price of their blood and of your independency, it is therefore more than a common debt, it is a debt of honour, it can never be considered as a pension or gratuity, nor be cancelled until it is fairly discharged.

With regard to a distinction between officers and soldiers, it is sufficient that the uniform experience of every nation of the world, combined with our own, proves the utility and propriety of the discrimination. Rewards in proportion to the aids the public derives from them, are unquestionably due to all its servants; in some lines, the soldiers have perhaps generally had as ample a compensation for their services, by the large bounties which have been paid to them, as their officers will receive in the proposed commutation, in others, if besides the donation of lands, the payment of arrearages of clothing and wages (in which articles all the component parts of the Army must be put upon the same footing) we take into the estimate, the bounties many of the soldiers have received and the gratuity of one year's full pay, which is promised to all, possibly their situation (every circumstance being duly considered) will not be deemed less eligible than that of the officers. Should a farther reward, however, be judged equitable, I will venture to assert, no one will enjoy greater satisfaction than myself, on seeing an exemption from taxes for a limited time (which has been petitioned for in some instances), or any other adequate immunity or compensation, granted to the brave defenders of their country's cause; but neither the adoption or rejection of this proposition will in any manner affect, much less militate against, the Act of Congress, by which they have offered five years full pay, in lieu of the half pay for life, which had been before promised to the officers of the Army.

Before I conclude the subject of public justice, I cannot omit to mention the obligations this country is under, to that meritorious class of veteran non-commissioned officers and privates, who have been discharged for inability, in consequence of the Resolution of Congress of the 23d of April 1782, on an annual pension for life, their peculiar sufferings, their singular merits and claims to that provision need only be known, to interest all the feelings of humanity in their behalf: nothing but a punctual payment of their annual allowance can rescue them from the most complicated misery, and nothing could be a more melancholy and distressing sight, than to behold those who have shed their blood or lost their limbs in the service of their country, without a shelter, without a friend, and without the means of obtaining any of the necessaries or comforts of life; compelled to beg their daily bread from door to door! suffer me to recommend those of this description, belonging to your State, to the warmest patronage of your Excellency and your Legislature.

It is necessary to say but a few words on the third topic which was proposed, and which regards particularly the defence of the Republic, as there can be little doubt but Congress will recommend a proper peace establishment for the United States, in which a due attention will be paid to the importance of placing the militia of the Union upon a regular and respectable footing; if this should be the case, I would beg leave to urge the great advantage of it in the strongest terms. The militia of this country must be considered as the palladium of our security, and the first effectual resort in case of hostility; it is essential therefore, that the same system should pervade the whole; that the formation and discipline of the militia of the continent should be absolutely uniform, and that the same species of arms, accoutrements and military apparatus, should be introduced in every part of the United States; no one, who has not learned it from experience, can conceive the difficulty, expence, and confusion which result from a contrary system, or the vague arrangements which have hitherto prevailed.

If in treating of political points, a greater latitude than usual has been taken in the course of this address, the importance of the crisis, and the magnitude of the objects in discussion, must be my apology: it is, however, neither my wish or expectation, that the preceding observations should claim any regard, except so far as they shall appear to be dictated by a good intention, consonant to the immutable rules of justice; calculated to produce a liberal system of policy, and founded on whatever experience may have been acquired by a long and close attention to public business. Here I might speak with the more confidence from my actual observations, and, if it would not swell this letter (already too prolix) beyond the bounds I had prescribed myself: I could demonstrate to every mind open to conviction, that in less time and with much less expence than has been incurred, the War might have been brought to the same happy conclusion, if the resourses of the continent could have been properly drawn forth, that the distresses and disappointments which have very often occurred, have in too many instances, resulted more from a want of energy, in the Continental government, than a deficiency of means in the particular States. That the inefficiency of measures, arising from the want of an adequate authority in the supreme power, from a partial compliance with the requisitions of Congress in some of the States, and from a failure of punctuality in others, while it tended to damp the zeal of those which were more willing to exert themselves; served also to accumulate the expences of the War, and to frustrate the best concerted plans, and that the discouragement occasioned by the complicated difficulties and embarrassments, in which our affairs were, by this means involved, would have long ago produced the dissolution of any army, less patient, less virtuous and less persevering, than that which I have had the honor to command. But while I mention these things, which are notorious facts, as the defects of our Federal Constitution, particularly in the prosecution of a war, I beg it may be understood, that as I have ever taken a pleasure in gratefully acknowledging the assistance and support I have derived from every class of citizens, so shall I always be happy to do justice to the unparalleled exertion of the individual States, on many interesting occasions.

I have thus freely disclosed what I wished to make known, before I surrendered up my public trust to those who committed it to me, the task is now accomplished, I now bid adieu to your Excellency as the Chief Magistrate of your State, at the same time I bid a last farewell to the cares of office, and all the imployments of public life.

It remains then to be my final and only request, that your Excellency will communicate these sentiments to your Legislature at their next meeting, and that they may be considered as the legacy of one, who has ardently wished, on all occasions, to be useful to his country, and who, even in the shade of retirement, will not fail to implore the divine benediction upon it.

I now make it my earnest prayer, that God would have you, and the State over which you preside, in his holy protection, that he would incline the hearts of the citizens to cultivate a spirit of subordination and obedience to government, to entertain a brotherly affection and love for one another, for their fellow citizens of the United States at large, and particularly for their brethren who have served in the field, and finally, that he would most graciously be pleased to dispose us all, to do justice, to love mercy, and to demean ourselves with that charity, humility and pacific temper of mind, which were the characteristicks of the Divine Author of our blessed religion, and without an humble imitation of whose example in these things, we can never hope to be a happy nation.

PRESIDENTIAL PAPERS

George Washington, twice elected unanimously, served as the President of the United States from 1789 to 1797, from his fifty-seventh to his sixty-fifth year. Included in *Presidential Papers* are Washington's two Inaugurals, eight State of the Union Addresses, and his still timely *Farewell Address*.

FIRST INAUGURAL ADDRESS
APRIL 30, 1789

Fellow-Citizens of the Senate and of the House of Representatives:

Among the vicissitudes incident to life no event could have
filled me with greater anxieties than that of which the noti-
fication was transmitted by your order, and received on the
14th day of the present month. On the one hand, I was sum-
moned by my country, whose voice I can never hear but with
veneration and love, from a retreat which I had chosen with
the fondest predilection, and, in my flattering hopes, with an
immutable decision, as the asylum of my declining years—
a retreat which was rendered every day more necessary as well
as more dear to me by the addition of habit to inclination,
and of frequent interruptions in my health to the gradual
waste committed on it by time. On the other hand, the magnitude and difficulty of the trust to which the voice of my
country called me, being sufficient to awaken in the wisest
and most experienced of her citizens a distrustful scrutiny
into his qualifications, could not but overwhelm with de-
spondence one who (inheriting inferior endowments from nature and unpracticed in the duties of civil administration)
ought to be peculiarly conscious of his own deficiencies. In
this conflict of emotions all I dare aver is that it has been my
faithful study to collect my duty from a just appreciation of
every circumstance by which it might be affected. All I dare
hope is that if, in executing this task, I have been too much
swayed by a grateful remembrance of former instances, or by
an affectionate sensibility to this transcendent proof of the
confidence of my fellow-citizens, and have thence too little
consulted my incapacity as well as disinclination for the
weighty and untried cares before me, my error will be palli-

ated by the motives which mislead me, and its consequences be judged by my country with some share of the partiality in which they originated.

Such being the impressions under which I have, in obedience to the public summons, repaired to the present station, it would be peculiarly improper to omit in this first official act my fervent supplications to that Almighty Being who rules over the universe, who presides in the councils of nations, and whose providential aids can supply every human defect, that His benediction may consecrate to the liberties and happiness of the people of the United States a Government instituted by themselves for these essential purposes, and may enable every instrument employed in its administration to execute with success the functions allotted to his charge. In tendering this homage to the Great Author of every public and private good, I assure myself that it expresses your sentiments not less than my own, nor those of my fellow-citizens at large less than either. No people can be bound to acknowledge and adore the Invisible Hand which conducts the affairs of men more than those of the United States. Every step by which they have been advanced to the character of an independent nation seems to have been distinguished by some token of providential agency; and in the important revolution just accomplished in the system of their united government the tranquil deliberations and voluntary consent of so many distinct communities from which the event has resulted can not be compared with the means by which most governments have been established without some return of pious gratitude, along with an humble anticipation of the future blessings which the past seem to presage. These reflections, arising out of the present crisis, have forced themselves too strongly on my mind to be suppressed. You will join with me, I trust, in thinking that there are none under the influence of which the proceedings of a new and free government can more auspiciously commence.

By the article establishing the executive department it is made the duty of the President "to recommend to your consideration such measures as he shall judge necessary and expedient." The circumstances under which I now meet you will acquit me from entering into that subject further than to refer to the great constitutional charter under which you are assembled, and which, in defining your powers, designates the objects to which your attention is to be given. It will be more consistent with those circumstances, and far more congenial with the feelings which actuate me, to substitute, in place of a recommendation of particular measures, the tribute that is due to the talents, the rectitude, and the patriotism which adorn the characters selected to devise and adopt them. In these honorable qualifications I behold the surest pledges that as on one side no local prejudices or attachments, no separate views nor party animosities, will misdirect the comprehensive and equal eye which ought to watch over this great assemblage of communities and interests, so, on another, that the foundation of our national policy will be laid in the pure and immutable principles of private morality, and the preeminence of free government be exemplified by all the attributes which can win the affections of its citizens and command the respect of the world. I dwell on this prospect with every satisfaction which an ardent love for my country can inspire, since there is no truth more thoroughly established than that there exists in the economy and course of nature an indissoluble union between virtue and happiness; between duty and advantage; between the genuine maxims of an honest and magnanimous policy and the solid rewards of public prosperity and felicity; since we ought to be no less persuaded that the propitious smiles of Heaven can never be expected on a nation that disregards the eternal rules of order and right which Heaven itself has ordained; and since the preservation of the sacred fire of liberty and the destiny of the republican model of government are justly considered, perhaps, as deeply, and finally, staked on the experiment intrusted to the hands of the American people.

Besides the ordinary objects submitted to your care, it will remain with your judgment to decide how far an exercise of the occasional power delegated by the fifth article of the Constitution is rendered expedient at the present juncture by the nature of objections which have been urged against the system, or by the degree of inquietude which has given birth to them. Instead of undertaking particular recommendations on this subject, in which I could be guided by no lights derived from official opportunities, I shall again give way to my entire confidence in your discernment and pursuit of the public good; for I assure myself that whilst you carefully avoid every alteration which might endanger the benefits of an united and effective government, or which ought to await the future lessons of experience, a reverence for the characteristic rights of freemen and a regard for the public harmony will sufficiently influence your deliberations on the question how far the former can be impregnably fortified or the latter be safely and advantageously promoted.

To the foregoing observations I have one to add, which will be most properly addressed to the House of Representatives. It concerns myself, and will therefore be as brief as possible. When I was first honored with a call into the service of my country, then on the eve of an arduous struggle for its liberties, the light in which I contemplated my duty required that I should renounce every pecuniary compensation. From this resolution I have in no instance departed; and being still under the impressions which produced it, I must decline as inapplicable to myself any share in the personal emoluments which may be indispensably included in a permanent provision for the executive department, and must accordingly pray that the pecuniary estimates for the station in which I am placed may during my continuance in it be limited to such actual expenditures as the public good may be thought to require.

Having thus imparted to you my sentiments as they have been awakened by the occasion which brings us together, I shall take my present leave; but not without resorting once more to the benign Parent of the human race in humble supplication that, since He has been pleased to favor the American people with opportunities for deliberating in perfect tranquillity, and dispositions for deciding with unparalleled unanimity on a form of government for the security of their union and the advancement of their happiness, so His divine blessing may be equally conspicuous in the enlarged views, the temperate consultations, and the wise measures on which the success of this Government must depend.

FIRST STATE OF THE UNION ADDRESS
JANUARY 8, 1790

Fellow-citizens of the Senate and House of Representatives,

I embrace with great satisfaction the opportunity, which now presents itself, of congratulating you on the present favorable prospects of our public affairs. The recent accession of the important State of North Carolina to the constitution of the United States (of which official information has been received), the rising credit and respectability of our country, and the general and increasing good will towards the government of the Union, and the concord, peace, and plenty, with which we are blessed, are circumstances auspicious, in an eminent degree, to our national prosperity.

In resuming your consultations for the general good, you cannot but derive encouragement from the reflection, that the measures of the last session have been as satisfactory to your constituents, as the novelty and difficulty of the work allowed you to hope. Still further to realize their expectations, and to secure the blessings, which a gracious Providence has placed within our reach, will, in the course of the present important session, call for the cool and deliberate exertion of your patriotism, firmness, and wisdom.

Among the many interesting objects, which will engage your attention, that of providing for the common defence will merit particular regard. To be prepared for war is one of the most effectual means of preserving peace.

A free people ought not only to be armed, but disciplined; to which end a uniform and well-digested plan is requisite; and their safety and interest require, that they should promote such manufactories as tend to render them independent on others for essential, particularly for military supplies.

The proper establishment of the troops, which may be deemed indispensable, will be entitled to mature consideration. In the arrangements which may be made respecting it, it will be of importance to conciliate the comfortable support of the officers and soldiers with a due regard to economy.

There was reason to hope, that the pacific measures, adopted with regard to certain hostile tribes of Indians, would have relieved the inhabitants of our southern and western frontiers from their depredations. But you will perceive, from the information contained in the papers, which I shall direct to be laid before you (comprehending a communication from the commonwealth of Virginia), that we ought to be prepared to afford protection to those parts of the Union, and, if necessary, to punish aggressors.

The interest of the United States requires, that our intercourse with other nations should be facilitated by such provisions as will enable me to fulfil my duty in that respect, in the manner which circumstances may render most conducive to the public good; and, to this end, that the compensations, to be made to the persons who may be employed, should, according to the nature of their appointments, be defined by law, and a competent fund designated for defraying the expenses incident to the conduct of our foreign affairs.

Various considerations also render it expedient, that the terms, on which foreigners may be admitted to the rights of citizens, should be speedily ascertained by a uniform rule of naturalization.

Uniformity in the currency, weights, and measures of the United States is an object of great importance, and will, I am persuaded, be duly attended to.

The advancement of agriculture, commerce, and manufactures, by all proper means, will not, I trust, need recommendation. But I cannot forbear intimating to you the expediency of giving effectual encouragement, as well to the introduction of new and useful inventions from abroad, as to the exertions of skill and genius in producing them at home; and of facilitating the intercourse between the distant parts of our country by a due attention to the post-office and post-roads.

Nor am I less persuaded, that you will agree with me in opinion, that there is nothing which can better deserve your patronage than the promotion of science and literature. Knowledge is in every country the surest basis of public happiness. In one, in which the measures of government receive their impression so immediately from the sense of the community, as in ours, it is proportionably essential. To the security of a free constitution it contributes in various ways; by convincing those who are intrusted with the public administration, that every valuable end of government is best answered by the enlightened confidence of the people; and by teaching the people themselves to know, and to value their own rights; to discern and provide against invasions of them; to distinguish between oppression and the necessary exercise of lawful authority, between burthens proceeding from a disregard to their convenience and those resulting from the inevitable exigencies of society; to discriminate the spirit of liberty from that of licentiousness, cherishing the first, avoiding the last, and uniting a speedy but temperate vigilance against encroachments, with an inviolable respect to the laws.

Whether this desirable object will be the best promoted by affording aids to seminaries of learning already established, by the institution of a national university, or by any other expedients, will be well worthy of a place in the deliberations of the legislature.

Gentlemen of the House of Representatives,

I saw with peculiar pleasure, at the close of the last session, the resolution entered into by you, expressive of your opinion, that an adequate provision for the support of the public credit is a matter of high importance to the national honor and prosperity. In this sentiment I entirely concur. And to a perfect confidence in your best endeavours to devise such a provision as will be truly consistent with the end, I add an equal reliance on the cheerful cooperation of the other branch of the legislature. It would be superfluous to specify inducements to a measure, in which the character and permanent interests of the United States are so obviously and so deeply concerned, and which has received so explicit a sanction from your declaration.

Gentlemen of the Senate and House of Representatives,

I have directed the proper officers to lay before you respectively such papers and estimates as regard the affairs particularly recommended to your consideration, and necessary to convey to you that information of the state of the Union, which it is my duty to afford.

The welfare of our country is the great object to which our cares and efforts ought to be directed; and I shall derive great satisfaction from a cooperation with you in the pleasing though arduous task of insuring to our fellow-citizens the blessings, which they have a right to expect from a free, efficient, and equal government.

SECOND STATE OF THE UNION ADDRESS
DECEMBER 8, 1790

Fellow-citizens of the Senate and House of Representatives,

In meeting you again, I feel much satisfaction in being able to repeat my congratulations on the favorable prospects, which continue to distinguish our public affairs. The abundant fruits of another year have blessed our country with plenty, and with the means of a flourishing commerce. The progress of public credit is witnessed by a considerable rise of American stock abroad, as well as at home; and the revenues allotted for this and other national purposes have been productive beyond the calculations by which they were regulated. This latter circumstance is the more pleasing, as it is not only a proof of the fertility of our resources, but as it assures us of a further increase of the national respectability and credit, and, let me add, as it bears an honorable testimony to the patriotism and integrity of the mercantile and marine part of our citizens. The punctuality of the former in discharging their engagements has been exemplary.

In conformity to the powers vested in me by acts of the last session, a loan of three millions of florins, towards which some provisional measures had previously taken place, has been completed in Holland. As well the celerity with which it has been filled, as the nature of the terms (considering the more than ordinary demand for borrowing, created by the situation of Europe), gives a reasonable hope, that the further execution of those powers may proceed with advantage and success. The Secretary of the Treasury has my directions to communicate such further particulars as may be requisite for more precise information.

Since your last sessions, I have received communications by

which it appears, that the district of Kentucky, at present a part of Virginia, has concurred in certain propositions contained in a law of that State, in consequence of which the district is to become a distinct member of the Union, in case the requisite sanction of Congress be added. For this sanction application is now made. I shall cause the papers on this very important transaction to be laid before you. The liberality and harmony, with which it has been conducted, will be found to do great honor to both the parties; and the sentiments of warm attachment to the Union and its present government, expressed by our fellow-citizens of Kentucky, cannot fail to add an affectionate concern for their particular welfare to the great national impressions under which you will decide on the case submitted to you.

It has been heretofore known to Congress, that frequent incursions have been made on our frontier settlements by certain banditti of Indians from the northwest side of the Ohio. These, with some of the tribes dwelling on and near the Wabash, have of late been particularly active in their depredations; and, being emboldened by the impunity of their crimes, and aided by such parts of the neighbouring tribes as could be seduced to join in their hostilities or afford them a retreat for their prisoners and plunder, they have, instead of listening to the humane invitations and overtures made on the part of the United States, renewed their violences with fresh alacrity and greater effect. The lives of a number of valuable citizens have thus been sacrified, and some of them under circumstances peculiarly shocking, whilst others have been carried into a deplorable captivity.

These aggravated provocations rendered it essential to the safety of the western settlements, that the aggressors should be made sensible, that the government of the Union is not less capable of punishing their crimes, than it is disposed to respect their rights and reward their attachments. As this object could not be effected by defensive measures, it became necessary to put in force the act, which empowers the President to call out the militia for the protection of the frontiers; and I have accordingly authorized an expedition, in which the regular troops in that quarter are combined with such drafts of militia as were deemed sufficient. The event of the measure is yet unknown to me. The Secretary of War is directed to lay before you a statement of the information on which it is founded, as well as an estimate of the expense with which it will be attended.

The disturbed situation of Europe, and particularly the critical posture of the great maritime powers, whilst it ought to make us more thankful for the general peace and security enjoyed by the United States, reminds us at the same time of the circumspection with which it becomes us to preserve these blessings. It requires also, that we should not overlook the tendency of a war, and even of preparations for a war, among the nations most concerned in active commerce with this country, to abridge the means, and thereby at least enhance the price, of transporting its valuable productions to their proper markets. I recommend it to your serious reflection, how far and in what mode it may be expedient to guard against embarrassments from these contingencies, by such encouragements to our own navigation as will render our commerce and agriculture less dependent on foreign bottoms, which may fail us in the very moments most interesting to both of these great objects. Our fisheries, and the transportation of our own produce, offer us abundant means for guarding ourselves against this evil.

Your attention seems to be not less due to that particular branch of our trade, which belongs to the Mediterranean. So many circumstances unite in rendering the present state of it distressful to us, that you will not think any deliberations misemployed, which may lead to its relief and protection.

The laws you have already passed for the establishment of a judiciary system, have opened the doors of justice to all descriptions of persons. You will consider in your wisdom, whether improvements in that system may yet be made, and particularly whether a uniform process of execution on sentences issuing from the federal courts be not desirable through all the States.

The patronage of our commerce, of our merchants and seamen, has called for the appointment of consuls in foreign countries. It seems expedient to regulate by law the exercise of that jurisdiction and those functions, which are permitted them, either by express convention, or by a friendly indulgence in the places of their residence. The consular convention, too, with his Most Christian Majesty has stipulated, in certain cases, the aid of the national authority to his consuls established here. Some legislative provision is requisite to carry these stipulations into full effect.

The establishment of the militia, of a mint, of standards of weights and measures, of the post-office and post-roads, are subjects which (I presume) you will resume of course, and which are abundantly urged by their own importance.

Gentlemen of the House of Representatives,

The sufficiency of the revenues you have established, for the objects to which they are appropriated, leaves no doubt that the residuary provisions will be commensurate to the other objects for which the public faith stands now pledged. Allow me, moreover, to hope, that it will be a favorite policy with you, not merely to secure a payment of the interest of the debt funded, but, as far and as fast as the growing resources of the country will permit, to exonerate it of the principal itself. The appropriation you have made of the western lands explains your dispositions on this subject; and I am persuaded the sooner that valuable fund can be made to contribute, along with other means, to the actual reduction of the public debt, the more salutary will the measure be to every public interest, as well as the more satisfactory to our constituents.

Gentlemen of the Senate and House of Representatives,

In pursuing the various and weighty business of the present session, I indulge the fullest persuasion, that your consultations will be equally marked with wisdom and animated by the love of your country. In whatever belongs to my duty, you shall have all the cooperation, which an undiminished zeal for its welfare can inspire. It will be happy for us both, and our best reward, if, by a successful administration of our respective trusts, we can make the established government more and more instrumental in promoting the good of our fellow-citizens, and more and more the object of their attachment and confidence.

THIRD STATE OF THE UNION ADDRESS
OCTOBER 25, 1791

Fellow-citizens of the Senate and House of Representatives,

I meet you upon the present occasion with the feelings, which are naturally inspired by a strong impression of the prosperous situation of our common country, and by a persuasion equally strong, that the labors of the session which has just commenced will, under the guidance of a spirit no less prudent than patriotic, issue in measures conducive to the stability and increase of national prosperity.

Numerous as are the providential blessings, which demand our grateful acknowledgments, the abundance, with which another year has again rewarded the industry of the husbandman, is too important to escape recollection.

Your own observations, in your respective situations, will have satisfied you of the progressive state of agriculture, manufactures, commerce, and navigation. In tracing their causes, you will have remarked, with particular pleasure, the happy effects of that revival of confidence, public as well as private, to which the constitution and laws of the United States have so eminently contributed; and you will have observed, with no less interest, new and decisive proofs of the increasing reputation and credit of the nation. But you, nevertheless, cannot fail to derive satisfaction from the confirmation of these circumstances, which will be disclosed in the several official communications, that will be made to you in the course of your deliberations.

The rapid subscriptions to the Bank of the United States, which completed the sum allowed to be subscribed in a single day, is among the striking and pleasing evidences which present themselves, not only of confidence in the government, but of resource in the community.

In the interval of your recess, due attention has been paid to the execution of the different objects, which were specially provided for by the laws and resolutions of the last session.

Among the most important of these, is the defence and security of the western frontiers. To accomplish it on the most humane principles was a primary wish.

Accordingly, at the same time that treaties have been provisionally concluded, and other proper means used to attach the wavering, and to confirm in their friendship the well-disposed tribes of Indians, effectual measures have been adopted to make those of a hostile description sensible, that a pacification was desired upon terms of moderation and justice.

These measures having proved unsuccessful, it became necessary to convince the refractory of the power of the United States to punish their depredations. Offensive operations have, therefore, been directed; to be conducted, however, as consistently as possible with the dictates of humanity. Some of these have been crowned with full success, and others are yet depending. The expeditions, which have been completed, were carried on, under the authority and at the expense of the United States, by the militia of Kentucky; whose enterprise, intrepidity, and good conduct are entitled to peculiar commendation.

Overtures of peace are still continued to the deluded tribes, and considerable numbers of individuals belonging to them have lately renounced all further opposition, removed from their former situations, and placed themselves under the immediate protection of the United States.

It is sincerely to be desired, that all need of coercion in future may cease; and that an intimate intercourse may succeed, calculated to advance the happiness of the Indians, and to attach them firmly to the United States.

In order to do this, it seems necessary, that they should experience the benefits of an impartial dispensation of justice; that the mode of alienating their lands, the main source of discontent and war, should be so defined and regulated as to obviate imposition, and, as far as may be practicable, controversy concerning the reality and extent of the alienations which are made; that commerce with them should be promoted under regulations tending to secure an equitable deportment towards them, and that such rational experiments should be made for imparting to them the blessings of civilization, as may from time to time suit their condition; that the executive of the United States should be enabled to employ the means, to which the Indians have been long accustomed, for uniting their immediate interests with the preservation of peace; and that efficacious provision should be made for inflicting adequate penalties upon all those, who, by violating their rights, shall infringe the treaties and endanger the peace of the Union.

A system corresponding with the mild principles of religion and philanthropy towards an unenlightened race of men, whose happiness materially depends on the conduct of the United States, would be as honorable to the national character as conformable to the dictates of sound policy.

The powers specially vested in me by the act laying certain duties on distilled spirits, which respect the subdivisions of the districts into surveys, the appointment of officers, and the assignment of compensations, have likewise been carried into effect. In a matter, in which both materials and experience were wanting to guide the calculation, it will be readily conceived, that there must have been difficulty in such an adjustment of the rates of compensation, as would conciliate a reasonable competency with a proper regard to the limits prescribed by the law. It is hoped that the circumspection, which has been used, will be found in the result to have secured the last of the two objects; but it is probable, that, with a view to the first, in some instances a revision of the provision will be found advisable.

The impressions, with which this law has been received by the community, have been, upon the whole, such as were to be expected among enlightened and well-disposed citizens, from the propriety and necessity of the measure. The novelty, however, of the tax, in a considerable part of the United States, and a misconception of some of its provisions, have given occasion in particular places to some degree of discontent. But it is satisfactory to know, that this disposition yields to proper explanations and more just apprehensions of the true nature of the law. And I entertain a full confidence, that it will, in all, give way to motives, which arise out of a just sense of duty and a virtuous regard to the public welfare.

If there are any circumstances in the law, which, consistently with its main design, may be so varied as to remove any well-intentioned objections that may happen to exist, it will consist with a wise moderation to make the proper variations. It is desirable, on all occasions, to unite with a steady and firm adherence to constitutional and necessary acts of government, the fullest evidence of a disposition, as far as may be practicable, to consult the wishes of every part of the community, and to lay the foundations of the public administration in the affections of the people.

Pursuant to the authority contained in the several acts on that subject, a district of ten miles square, for the permanent seat of the government of the United States, has been fixed, and announced by proclamation; which district will comprehend lands on both sides of the river Potomac, and the towns of Alexandria and Georgetown. A city has also been laid out agreeably to a plan which will be placed before Congress; and, as there is a prospect, favored by the rate of sales which have already taken place, of ample funds for carrying on the necessary public buildings, there is every expectation of their due progress.

The completion of the census of the inhabitants, for which provision was made by law, has been duly notified (excepting in one instance, in which the return has been informal, and another, in which it has been omitted or miscarried); and the returns of the officers who were charged with this duty, which will be laid before you, will give you the pleasing assurance, that the present population of the United States borders on four millions of persons.

It is proper also to inform you, that a further loan of two millions and a half of florins has been completed in Holland; the terms of which are similar to those of the one last announced, except as to a small reduction of charges. Another, on like terms, for six millions of florins had been set on foot, under circumstances that assured immediate completion.

Gentlemen of the Senate,

Two treaties, which have been provisionally concluded with the Cherokees, and Six Nations of Indians, will be laid before you for your consideration and ratification.

Gentlemen of the House of Representatives,

In entering upon the discharge of your legislative trust, you must anticipate with pleasure, that many of the difficulties, necessarily incident to the first arrangements of a new government for an extensive country, have been happily surmounted by the zealous and judicious exertions of your predecessors in cooperation with the other branch of the legislature. The important objects, which remain to be accomplished, will, I am persuaded, be conducted upon principles equally comprehensive, and equally well calculated for the advancement of the general weal.

The time limited for receiving subscriptions to the loans proposed by the act making provision for the debt of the United States having expired, statements from the proper department will as soon as possible apprize you of the exact result. Enough, however, is known already to afford an assurance, that the views of that act have been substantially fulfilled. The subscription in the domestic debt of the United States has embraced by far the greatest proportion of that debt; affording at the same time proof of the general satisfaction of the public creditors with the system which has been proposed to their acceptance, and of the spirit of accommodation to the convenience of the government with which they are actuated. The subscriptions in the debts of the respective States, as far as the provisions of the law have permitted, may be said to be yet more general. The part of the debt of the United States, which remains unsubscribed, will naturally engage your further deliberations.

It is particularly pleasing to me to be able to announce to you, that the revenues which have been established promise to be adequate to their objects, and may be permitted, if no unforeseen exigency occurs, to supersede for the present the necessity of any new burthens upon our constituents.

An object which will claim your early attention is a provision for the current service of the ensuing year, together with such ascertained demands upon the treasury as require to be immediately discharged, and such casualties as may have arisen in the execution of the public business, for which no specific appropriation may have yet been made; of all which a proper estimate will be laid before you.

Gentlemen of the Senate and House of Representatives,

I shall content myself with a general reference to former communications for several objects, upon which the urgency of other affairs has hitherto postponed any definitive resolution. Their importance will recall them to your attention; and I trust, that the progress already made in the most arduous arrangements of the government will afford you leisure to resume them with advantage.

There are, however, some of them, of which I cannot forbear a more particular mention. These are, the militia; the post-office and post-roads; the mint; weights and measures; a provision for the sale of the vacant lands of the United States.

The first is certainly an object of primary importance, whether viewed in reference to the national security, to the satisfaction of the community, or to the preservation of order. In connexion with this, the establishment of competent magazines and arsenals, and the fortification of such places as are peculiarly important and vulnerable, naturally present themselves to consideration. The safety of the United States, under divine protection, ought to rest on the basis of systematic and solid arrangements, exposed as little as possible to the hazards of fortuitous circumstances.

The importance of the post-office and post-roads on a plan sufficiently liberal and comprehensive, as they respect the expedition, safety, and facility of communication, is increased by the instrumentality in diffusing a knowledge of the laws and proceedings of the government; which, while it contributes to the security of the people, serves also to guard them against the effects of misrepresentation and misconception. The establishment of additional cross posts, especially to some of the important points in the western and northern parts of the Union, cannot fail to be of material utility.

The disorders in the existing currency, and especially the scarcity of small change, a scarcity so peculiarly distressing to the poorer classes, strongly recommend the carrying into immediate effect the resolution already entered into concerning the establishment of a mint. Measures have been taken, pursuant to that resolution, for procuring some of the most necessary articles, together with the requisite apparatus.

A uniformity in the weights and measures of the country is among the important objects submitted to you by the constitution; and, if it can be derived from a standard at once invariable and universal, must be no less honorable to the public councils, than conducive to the public convenience.

A provision for the sale of the vacant lands of the United States is particularly urged, among other reasons, by the important considerations, that they are pledged as a fund for reimbursing the public debt; that, if timely and judiciously applied, they may save the necessity of burthening our citizens with new taxes for the extinguishment of the principal; and that, being free to discharge the principal but in a limited proportion, no opportunity ought to be lost for availing the public of its rights.

FOURTH STATE OF THE UNION ADDRESS
NOVEMBER 6, 1792

Fellow-citizens of the Senate and House of Representatives,

It is some abatement of the satisfaction, with which I meet you on the present occasion, that, in felicitating you on a continuance of the national prosperity generally, I am not able to add to it information, that the Indian hostilities, which have for some time past distressed our northwestern frontier, have terminated.

You will, I am persuaded, learn, with no less concern than I communicate it, that reiterated endeavours towards effecting a pacification have hitherto issued only in new and outrageous proofs of persevering hostility on the part of the tribes with whom we are in contest. An earnest desire to procure tranquillity to the frontiers, to stop the further effusion of blood, to arrest the progress of expense, to forward the prevalent wish of the nation for peace, has led to strenuous efforts through various channels to accomplish these desirable purposes; in making which efforts I consulted less my own anticipations of the event, or the scruples which some considerations were calculated to inspire, than the wish to find the object attainable, or, if not attainable, to ascertain unequivocally, that such is the case.

A detail of the measures which have been pursued, and of their consequences, which will be laid before you, while it will confirm to you the want of success thus far, will, I trust, evince that means, as proper and as efficacious as could have been devised, have been employed. The issue of some of them, indeed, is still depending; but a favorable one, though not to be despaired of, is not promised by any thing that has yet happened.

In the course of the attempts which have been made, some valuable citizens have fallen victims to their zeal for the public service. A sanction commonly respected, even among savages, has been found, in this instance, insufficient to protect from massacre the emissaries of peace; it will, I presume, be duly considered, whether the occasion does not call for an exercise of liberality towards the families of the deceased.

It must add to your concern to be informed, that, besides the continuation of hostile appearances among the tribes north of the Ohio, some threatening symptoms have of late been revived among some of those south of it.

A part of the Cherokees, known by the name of Chickamagas, inhabiting five villages on the Tennessee River, have long been in the practice of committing depredations on the neighbouring settlements.

It was hoped, that the treaty of Holston, made with the Cherokee nation in July, 1791, would have prevented a repetition of such depredations; but the event has not answered this hope. The Chickamagas, aided by some banditti of another tribe in their vicinity, have recently perpetrated wanton and unprovoked hostilities upon the citizens of the United States in that quarter. The information which has been received on this subject will be laid before you. Hitherto, defensive precautions only have been strictly enjoined and observed.

It is not understood that any breach of treaty, or aggression whatsoever, on the part of the United States, or their citizens, is even alleged as a pretext for the spirit of hostility in this quarter.

I have reason to believe, that every practicable exertion has been made (pursuant to the provision by law for that purpose) to be prepared for the alternative of a prosecution of the war, in the event of a failure of pacific overtures. A large proportion of the troops authorized to be raised have been recruited, though the number is still incomplete; and pains have been taken to discipline and put them in condition for the particular kind of service to be performed. A delay of operations (besides being dictated by the measures which were pursuing towards a pacific termination of the war) has been in itself deemed preferable to immature efforts. A statement, from the proper department, with regard to the number of troops raised, and some other points which have been suggested, will afford more precise information as a guide to the legislative consultations; and, among other things, will enable Congress to judge whether some additional stimulus to the recruiting service may not be advisable.

In looking forward to the future expense of the operations, which may be found inevitable, I derive consolation from the information I receive, that the product of the revenues for the present year is likely to supersede the necessity of additional burthens on the community for the service of the ensuing year. This, however, will be better ascertained in the course of the session; and it is proper to add, that the information alluded to proceeds upon the supposition of no material extension of the spirit of hostility.

I cannot dismiss the subject of Indian affairs, without again recommending to your consideration the expediency of more adequate provision for giving energy to the laws throughout our interior frontier, and for restraining the commission of outrages upon the Indians; without which all pacific plans must prove nugatory. To enable, by competent rewards, the employment of qualified and trusty persons to reside among them as agents, would also contribute to the preservation of peace and good neighbourhood. If, in addition to these expedients, an eligible plan could be devised for promoting civilization among the friendly tribes, and for carrying on trade with them upon a scale equal to their wants, and under regulations calculated to protect them from imposition and extortion, its influence in cementing their interests with ours could not but be considerable.

The prosperous state of our revenue has been intimated. This would be still more the case, were it not for the impediments, which in some places continue to embarrass the collection of the duties on spirits distilled within the United States. These impediments have lessened, and are lessening, in local extent; and, as applied to the community at large, the contentment with the law appears to be progressive.

But, symptoms of increased opposition having lately manifested themselves in certain quarters, I judged a special interposition on my part proper and advisable; and under this impression have issued a proclamation, warning against all unlawful combinations and proceedings having for their object, or tending, to obstruct the operation of the law in question, and announcing that all lawful ways and means would be strictly put in execution for bringing to justice the infractors thereof, and securing obedience thereto.

Measures have also been taken for the prosecution of offenders. And Congress may be assured, that nothing within constitutional and legal limits, which may depend on me, shall be wanting to assert and maintain the just authority of the laws. In fulfilling this trust, I shall count entirely upon the full cooperation of the other departments of government, and upon the zealous support of all good citizens.

I cannot forbear to bring again into the view of the legislature the subject of a revision of the judiciary system. A representation from the judges of the Supreme Court, which will be laid before you, points out some of the inconveniences that are experienced. In the course of the execution of the laws, considerations rise out of the structure of that system, which in some measure tend to relax their efficacy. As connected with this subject, provisions to facilitate the taking of bail upon processes out of the courts of the United States, and supplementary definition of offences against the constitution and laws of the Union, and of the punishment for such offences, will, it is presumed, be found worthy of particular attention.

Observations on the value of peace with other nations are unnecessary. It would be wise, however, by timely provisions, to guard against those acts of our own citizens, which might tend to disturb it, and to put ourselves in a condition to give that satisfaction to foreign nations, which we may sometimes have occasion to require from them. I particularly recommend to your consideration the means of preventing those aggressions by our citizens on the territory of other nations, and other infractions of the law of nations, which, furnishing just subject of complaint, might endanger our peace with them. And, in general, the maintenance of a friendly intercourse with foreign powers will be presented to your attention by the expiration of the law for that purpose, which takes place, if not renewed, at the close of the present session.

In execution of the authority given by the legislature, measures have been taken for engaging some artists from abroad to aid in the establishment of our mint; others have been employed at home. Provision has been made of the requisite buildings, and these are now putting into proper condition for the purposes of the establishment. There has also been a small beginning in the coinage of half-dimes, the want of small coins in circulation calling the first attention to them.

The regulation of foreign coins, in correspondency with the principles of our national coinage, as being essential to their due operation, and to order in our money concerns, will, I doubt not, be resumed and completed.

It is represented that some provisions in the law, which establishes the post-office, operate, in experiment, against the transmission of newspapers to distant parts of the country. Should this, upon due inquiry, be found to be the fact, a full conviction of the importance of facilitating the circulation of political intelligence and information will, I doubt not, lead to the application of a remedy.

The adoption of a constitution for the State of Kentucky has been notified to me. The legislature will share with me in the satisfaction, which arises from an event, interesting to the happiness of the part of the nation to which it relates, and conducive to the general order.

It is proper likewise to inform you, that, since my last communication on the subject, and in further execution of the acts, severally making provision for the public debt, and for the reduction thereof, three new loans have been effected, each for three millions of florins; one at Antwerp at the annual interest of four and one half per cent, with an allowance of four per cent in lieu of all charges; and the other two at Amsterdam, at the annual interest of four per cent, with an allowance of five and one half per cent in one case and of five per cent in the other, in lieu of all charges. The rates of these loans, and the circumstances under which they have been made, are confirmations of the high state of our credit abroad.

Among the objects to which these funds have been directed to be applied, the payment of the debts due to certain foreign officers, according to the provision made during the last session, has been embraced.

Gentlemen of the House of Representatives,

I entertain a strong hope, that the state of the national finances is now sufficiently matured to enable you to enter upon a systematic and effectual arrangement for the regular redemption and discharge of the public debt, according to the right which has been reserved to the government. No measure can be more desirable, whether viewed with an eye to its intrinsic importance, or to the general sentiment and wish of the nation.

Provision is likewise requisite for the reimbursement of the loan, which has been made for the Bank of the United States, pursuant to the eleventh section of the act by which it is incorporated. In fulfilling the public stipulations in this particular, it is expected a valuable saving will be made.

Appropriations for the current service of the ensuing year, and for such extraordinaries as may require provision, will demand, and I doubt not will engage, your early attention.

Gentlemen of the Senate and House of Representatives,

I content myself with recalling your attention, generally, to such objects not particularized in my present, as have been suggested in my former communications to you.

Various temporary laws will expire during the present session. Among these, that which regulates trade and intercourse with the Indian tribes will merit particular notice.

The results of your common deliberations hitherto will, I trust, be productive of solid and durable advantages to our constituents; such as, by conciliating more and more their ultimate suffrage, will tend to strengthen and confirm their attachment to that constitution of government, upon which, under Divine Providence, materially depend their union, their safety, and their happiness.

Still further to promote and secure these inestimable ends, there is nothing which can have a more powerful tendency, than the careful cultivation of harmony, combined with a due regard to stability in the public councils.

SECOND INAUGURAL ADDRESS
MARCH 4, 1793

Fellow Citizens:

I am again called upon by the voice of my country to execute
the functions of its Chief Magistrate. When the occasion
proper for it shall arrive, I shall endeavor to express the high
sense I entertain of this distinguished honor, and of the confidence which has been reposed in me by the people of
united America.

Previous to the execution of any official act of the President
the Constitution requires an oath of office. This oath I am
now about to take, and in your presence: That if it shall be
found during my administration of the Government I have
in any instance violated willingly or knowingly the injunc-
tions thereof, I may (besides incurring Constitutional punishment) be subject to the upbraidings of all who are now
witnesses of the present solemn ceremony.

FIFTH STATE OF THE UNION ADDRESS
DECEMBER 3, 1793

Fellow-citizens of the Senate and House of Representatives,

Since the commencement of the term, for which I have been again called into office, no fit occasion has arisen for expressing to my fellow-citizens at large, the deep and respectful sense, which I feel, of the renewed testimony of public approbation. While, on the one hand, it awakened my gratitude for all those instances of affectionate partiality, with which I have been honored by my country; on the other, it could not prevent an earnest wish for that retirement, from which no private consideration should ever have torn me. But influenced by the belief; that my conduct would be estimated according to its real motives, and that the people, and the authorities derived from them, would support exertions having nothing personal for their object, I have obeyed the suffrage, which commanded me to resume the executive power; and I humbly implore that Being, on whose will the fate of nations depends, to crown with success our mutual endeavours for the general happiness.

As soon as the war in Europe had embraced those powers, with whom the United States have the most extensive relations, there was reason to apprehend, that our intercourse with them might be interrupted, and our disposition for peace drawn into question, by the suspicions too often entertained by belligerent nations. It seemed, therefore, to be my duty to admonish our citizens of the consequences of a contraband trade, and of hostile acts to any of the parties; and to obtain, by a declaration of the existing legal state of things, an easier admission of our right to the immunities belonging to our situation. Under these impressions, the Proclamation, which will be laid before you, was issued.

In this posture of affairs, both new and delicate, I resolved to adopt general rules, which should conform to the treaties and assert the privileges of the United States. These were reduced into a system, which will be communicated to you. Although I have not thought myself at liberty to forbid the sale of the prizes, permitted by our treaty of commerce with France to be brought into our ports, I have not refused to cause them to be restored, when they were taken within the protection of our territory, or by vessels commissioned or equipped in a warlike form within the limits of the United States.

It rests with the wisdom of Congress to correct, improve, or enforce this plan of procedure; and it will probably be found expedient to extend the legal code, and the jurisdiction of the courts of the United States, to many cases, which, though dependent on principles already recognised, demand some further provisions.

Where individuals shall within the United States array themselves in hostility against any of the powers at war; or enter upon military expeditions or enterprises within the jurisdiction of the United States; or usurp and exercise judicial authority within the United States; or where the penalties on violations of the law of nations may have been indistinctly marked, or are inadequate; these offences cannot receive too early and close an attention, and require prompt and decisive remedies.

Whatsoever those remedies may be, they will be well administered by the judiciary, who possess a long-established course of investigation, effectual process, and officers in the habit of executing it.

In like manner, as several of the courts have doubted, under particular circumstances, their power to liberate the vessels

of a nation at peace, and even of a citizen of the United
States, although seized under a false color of being hostile
property, and have denied their power to liberate certain captures within the protection of our territory, it would seem
proper to regulate their jurisdiction in these points. But if
the Executive is to be the resort in either of the two last-
mentioned cases, it is hoped that he will be authorized by
law to have facts ascertained by the courts when for his own
information he shall request it.

I can not recommend to your notice measures for the fulfillment of our duties to the rest of the world without again
pressing upon you the necessity of placing ourselves in a condition of complete defense and of exacting from them the
fulfillment of their duties toward us. The United States
ought not to indulge a persuasion that, contrary to the order
of human events, they will forever keep at a distance those
painful appeals to arms with which the history of every other
nation abounds. There is a rank due to the United States
among nations which will be withheld, if not absolutely lost,
by the reputation of weakness. If we desire to avoid insult,
we must be able to repel it; if we desire to secure peace, one
of the most powerful instruments of our rising prosperity, it
must be known that we are at all times ready for war. The
documents which will be presented to you will shew the
amount and kinds of arms and military stores now in our
magazines and arsenals; and yet an addition even to these
supplies can not with prudence be neglected, as it would
leave nothing to the uncertainty of procuring of warlike apparatus in the moment of public danger.

Nor can such arrangements, with such objects, be exposed to
the censure or jealousy of the warmest friends of republican
government. They are incapable of abuse in the hands of the
militia, who ought to possess a pride in being the depository

of the force of the Republic, and may be trained to a degree of energy equal to every military exigency of the United States. But it is an inquiry which can not be too solemnly pursued, whether the act "more effectually to provide for the national defense by establishing an uniform militia throughout the United States" has organized them so as to produce their full effect; whether your own experience in the several States has not detected some imperfections in the scheme, and whether a material feature in an improvement of it ought not to be to afford an opportunity for the study of those branches of the military art which can scarcely ever be attained by practice alone.

The connection of the United States with Europe has become extremely interesting. The occurrences which relate to it and have passed under the knowledge of the Executive will be exhibited to Congress in a subsequent communication.

When we contemplate the war on our frontiers, it may be truly affirmed that every reasonable effort has been made to adjust the causes of dissension with the Indians north of the Ohio. The instructions given to the commissioners evince a moderation and equity proceeding from a sincere love of peace, and a liberality having no restriction but the essential interests and dignity of the United States. The attempt, however, of an amicable negotiation having been frustrated, the troops have marched to act offensively. Although the proposed treaty did not arrest the progress of military preparation, it is doubtful how far the advance of the season, before good faith justified active movements, may retard them during the remainder of the year. From the papers and intelligence, which relate to this important subject, you will determine, whether the deficiency in the number of troops, granted by law, shall be compensated by succours of militia; or additional encouragements shall be proposed to recruits.

An anxiety has been also demonstrated by the executive for peace with the Creeks and the Cherokees. The former have been relieved with corn and with clothing, and offensive measures against them prohibited, during the recess of Congress. To satisfy the complaints of the latter, prosecutions have been instituted for the violences committed upon them. But the papers, which will be delivered to you, disclose the critical footing on which we stand in regard to both those tribes; and it is with Congress to pronounce what shall be done.

After they shall have provided for the present emergency, it will merit their most serious labors, to render tranquillity with the savages permanent by creating ties of interest. Next to a rigorous execution of justice on the violators of peace, the establishment of commerce with the Indian nations on behalf of the United States is most likely to conciliate their attachment. But it ought to be conducted without fraud, without extortion, with constant and plentiful supplies, with a ready market for the commodities of the Indians, and a stated price for what they give in payment, and receive in exchange. Individuals will not pursue such a traffic, unless they are allured by the hope of profit; but it will be enough for the United States to be reimbursed only. Should this recommendation accord with the opinion of Congress, they will recollect, that it cannot be accomplished by any means yet in the hands of the Executive.

Gentlemen of the House of Representatives,

The commissioners, charged with the settlement of accounts between the United and individual States, concluded their important functions within the time limited by law; and the balances, struck in their report, which will be laid before Congress, have been placed on the books of the treasury.

On the first day of June last, an installment of one million of florins became payable on the loans of the United States in Holland. This was adjusted by a prolongation of the period of reimbursement, in the nature of a new loan, at interest at five per cent for the term of ten years; and the expenses of this operation were a commission of three per cent.

The first installment of the loan of two millions of dollars from the Bank of the United States has been paid, as was directed by law. For the second, it is necessary that provision should be made.

No pecuniary consideration is more urgent than the regular redemption and discharge of the public debt; on none can delay be more injurious, or an economy of time more valuable.

The productiveness of the public revenues hitherto has continued to equal the anticipations which were formed of it; but it is not expected to prove commensurate with all the objects, which have been suggested. Some auxiliary provisions will, therefore, it is presumed, be requisite; and it is hoped that these may be made, consistently with a due regard to the convenience of our citizens, who cannot but be sensible of the true wisdom of encountering a small present addition to their contributions, to obviate a future accumulation of burdens.

But here I cannot forbear to recommend a repeal of the tax on the transportation of public prints. There is no resource so firm for the government of the United States, as the affections of the people, guided by an enlightened policy; and to this primary good, nothing can conduce more than a faithful representation of public proceedings, diffused without restraint throughout the United States.

An estimate of the appropriations necessary for the current service of the ensuing year, and a statement of a purchase of arms and military stores made during the recess, will be presented to Congress.

Gentlemen of the Senate and House of Representatives,

The several subjects, to which I have now referred, open a wide range to your deliberations, and involve some of the choicest interests of our common country. Permit me to bring to your remembrance the magnitude of your task. Without an unprejudiced coolness, the welfare of the government may be hazarded; without harmony, as far as consists with freedom of sentiment, its dignity may be lost. But as the legislative proceedings of the United States will never, I trust, be reproached for the want of temper or candor; so shall not the public happiness languish from the want of my strenuous and warmest cooperations.

SIXTH STATE OF THE UNION ADDRESS
NOVEMBER 19, 1794

Fellow-citizens of the Senate and House of Representatives,

When we call to mind the gracious indulgence of Heaven, by which the American people became a nation; when we survey the general prosperity of our country, and look forward to the riches, power, and happiness, to which it seems destined; with the deepest regret do I announce to you, that, during your recess, some of the citizens of the United States have been found capable of an insurrection [the Whiskey Rebellion]. It is due, however, to the character of our government, and to its stability, which cannot be shaken by the enemies of order, freely to unfold the course of this event.

During the session of the year 1790, it was expedient to exercise the legislative power, granted by the constitution of the United States, "to lay and collect excises." In a majority of the States, scarcely an objection was made to this mode of taxation. In some, indeed, alarms were at first conceived, until they were banished by reason and patriotism. In the four western counties of Pennsylvania, a prejudice, fostered and embittered by the artifice of men, who labored for an ascendency over the will of others by the guidance of their passions, produced symptoms of riot and violence. It is well known, that Congress did not hesitate to examine the complaints which were presented, and to relieve them, as far as justice dictated, or general convenience would permit. But the impression, which this moderation made on the discontented, did not correspond with what it deserved; the arts of delusion were no longer confined to the efforts of designing individuals.

The very forbearance to press prosecutions was misinterpreted into a fear of urging the execution of the laws; and associations of men began to denounce threats against the officers employed. From a belief, that, by a more formal concert, their operation might be defeated, certain self-created societies assumed the tone of condemnation. Hence, while the greater part of Pennsylvania itself were conforming themselves to the acts of excise, a few counties were resolved to frustrate them. It was now perceived, that every expectation from the tenderness, which had hitherto been pursued, was unavailing, and that further delay could only create an opinion of impotency or irresolution in the government. Legal process was, therefore, delivered to the marshal, against the rioters and delinquent distillers.

No sooner was he understood to be engaged in this duty, than the vengeance of armed men was aimed at *his* person, and the person and property of the inspector of the revenue. They fired upon the marshal, arrested him, and detained him for some time as a prisoner. He was obliged, by the jeopardy of his life, to renounce the service of other process on the west side of the Allegany Mountain; and a deputation was afterwards sent to him to demand a surrender of that which he *had* served. A numerous body repeatedly attacked the house of the inspector, seized his papers of office, and finally destroyed, by fire, his buildings, and whatsoever they contained. Both of these officers, from a just regard to their safety, fled to the seat of government; it being avowed, that the motives to such outrages were to compel the resignation of the inspector, to withstand, by force of arms, the authority of the United States, and thereby to extort a repeal of the laws of excise, and an alteration in the conduct of government.

Upon the testimony of these facts, an associate justice of the Supreme Court of the United States notified to me, that "in the counties of Washington and Allegany, in Pennsylvania, laws of the United States were opposed, and the execution thereof obstructed, by combinations too powerful to be suppressed by the ordinary course of judicial proceedings, or by the powers vested in the marshal of that district." On this call, momentous in the extreme, I sought and weighed what might best subdue the crisis. On the one hand, the judiciary was pronounced to be stripped of its capacity to enforce the laws; crimes, which reached the very existence of social order, were perpetrated without control; the friends of government were insulted, abused, and overawed into silence or an apparent acquiescence; and to yield to the treasonable fury of so small a portion of the United States would be to violate the fundamental principle of our constitution, which enjoins, that the will of the majority shall prevail. On the other, to array citizen against citizen, to publish the dishonor of such excesses, to encounter the expense and other embarrassments of so distant an expedition, were steps too delicate, too closely interwoven with many affecting considerations, to be lightly adopted. I postponed, therefore, the summoning of the militia immediately into the field; but I required them to be held in readiness, that, if my anxious endeavours to reclaim the deluded, and to convince the malignant of their danger, should be fruitless, military force might be prepared to act, before the season should be too far advanced.

My proclamation of the 7th of August last was accordingly issued, and accompanied by the appointment of commissioners, who were charged to repair to the scene of insurrection. They were authorized to confer with any bodies of men, or individuals. They were instructed to be candid and explicit, in stating the sensations which had been excited in the executive, and his earnest wish to avoid a resort to coercion; to represent, however, that, without submission, coercion *must* be the resort; but to invite them, at the same time, to return to the demeanor of faithful citizens, by such accommodations as lay within the sphere of the executive power. Pardon, too, was tendered to them by the government of the United States, and that of Pennsylvania, upon no other condition, than a satisfactory assurance of obedience to the laws.

Although the report of the commissioners marks their firmness and abilities, and must unite all virtuous men, by showing that the means of conciliation have been exhausted; all of those, who had committed or abetted the tumults, did not subscribe the mild form, which was proposed as the atonement; and the indications of a peaceable temper were neither sufficiently general nor conclusive to recommend or warrant a further suspension of the march of the militia.

Thus the painful alternative could not be discarded. I ordered the militia to march, after once more admonishing the insurgents, in my proclamation of the 25th of September last.

It was a task too difficult to ascertain, with precision, the lowest degree of force competent to the quelling of the insurrection. From a respect, indeed, to economy and the ease of my fellow-citizens belonging to the militia, it would have gratified me to accomplish such an estimate. My very reluctance to ascribe too much importance to the opposition, had its extent been accurately seen, would have been a decided inducement to the smallest efficient numbers. In this uncertainty, therefore, I put in motion fifteen thousand men, as being an army, which, according to all human calculation, would be prompt, and adequate in every view, and might perhaps, by rendering resistance desperate, prevent the effusion of blood. Quotas had been assigned to the States of New Jersey, Pennsylvania, Maryland, and Virginia; the governor of Pennsylvania having declared on this occasion an opinion, which justified a requisition to the other States.

As Commander-in-chief of the militia, when called into the actual service of the United States, I have visited the places of general rendezvous, to obtain more exact information, and to direct a plan for ulterior movements. Had there been room for a persuasion, that the laws were secure from obstruction; that the civil magistrate was able to bring to justice such of the most culpable, as have not embraced the proffered terms of amnesty, and may be deemed fit objects of example; that the friends of peace and good government were not in need of that aid and countenance, which they ought always to receive, and I trust ever will receive, against the vicious and turbulent, I should have caught with avidity the opportunity of restoring the militia to their families and home. But succeeding intelligence has tended to manifest the necessity of what has been done; it being now confessed, by those who were not inclined to exaggerate the ill conduct of the insurgents, that their malevolence was not pointed merely to a particular law, but that a spirit inimical to all order has actuated many of the offenders. If the state of things had afforded reason for the continuance of my presence with the army, it would not have been withholden; but, every appearance assuring such an issue as will redound to the reputation and strength of the United States, I have judged it most proper to resume my duties at the seat of government, leaving the chief command with the governor of Virginia.

Still, however, as it is probable, that, in a commotion like the present, whatsoever may be the pretence, the purposes of mischief and revenge may not be laid aside; the stationing of a small force for a certain period, in the four western counties of Pennsylvania, will be indispensable, whether we contemplate the situation of those who are connected with the execution of the laws, or of others, who may have exposed themselves by an honorable attachment to them.

Thirty days from the commencement of this session being the legal limitation of the employment of the militia, Congress cannot be too early occupied with this subject.

Among the discussions, which may arise from this aspect of our affairs, and from the documents which will be submitted to Congress, it will not escape their observation, that not only the inspector of the revenue, but other officers of the United States in Pennsylvania, have, from their fidelity in the discharge of their functions, sustained material injuries to their property. The obligation and policy of indemnifying them are strong and obvious. It may also merit attention, whether policy will not enlarge this provision to the retribution of other citizens, who, though not under the ties of office, may have suffered damage by their generous exertions for upholding the constitution and the laws. The amount, even if all the injured were included, would not be great; and, on future emergencies, the government would be amply repaid by the influence of an example, that he who incurs a loss in its defence shall find a recompense in its liberality.

While there is cause to lament, that occurrences of this nature should have disgraced the name, or interrupted the tranquillity, of any part of our community, or should have diverted to a new application any portion of the public resources, there are not wanting real and substantial consolations for the misfortune. It has demonstrated, that our prosperity rests on solid foundations; by furnishing an additional proof that my fellow-citizens understand the true principles of government and liberty; that they feel their inseparable union; that, notwithstanding all the devices, which have been used to sway them from their interest and duty, they are now as ready to maintain the authority of the laws against licentious invasions, as they were to defend their rights against usurpation. It has been a spectacle, displaying to the highest advantage the value of republican government, to behold the most and least wealthy of our citizens standing in the same ranks as private soldiers; preeminently distinguished by being the army of the constitution; undeterred by a march of three hundred miles over rugged mountains, by the approach of an inclement season, or by any other discouragement. Nor ought I to omit to acknowledge the efficacious and patriotic cooperation, which I have experienced from the chief magistrates of the States to which my requisitions have been addressed.

To every description, indeed, of citizens, let praise be given; but let them persevere in their affectionate vigilance over that precious depository of American happiness, the Constitution of the United States. Let them cherish it, too, for the sake of those, who, from every clime, are daily seeking a dwelling in our land. And when, in the calm moments of reflection, they shall have retraced the origin and progress of the insurrection, let them determine, whether it has not been fomented by combinations of men, who, careless of consequences, and disregarding the unerring truth, that those who rouse, cannot always appease, a civil convulsion, have disseminated, from an ignorance or perversion of facts, suspicions, jealousies, and accusations of the whole government.

Having thus fulfilled the engagement, which I took, when I entered into office, "to the best of my ability to preserve, protect, and defend the constitution of the United States," on you, Gentlemen, and the people by whom you are deputed, I rely for support.

In the arrangements, to which the possibility of a similar contingency will naturally draw your attention, it ought not to be forgotten, that the militia laws have exhibited such striking defects, as could not have been supplied but by the zeal of our citizens. Besides the extraordinary expense and waste, which are not the least of the defects, every appeal to those laws is attended with a doubt of its success.

The devising and establishing of a well-regulated militia would be a genuine source of legislative honor; and a perfect title to public gratitude. I therefore entertain a hope, that the present session will not pass, without carrying to its full energy the power of organizing, arming, and disciplining the militia, and thus providing, in the language of the Constitution, for calling them forth to execute the laws of the Union, suppress insurrections, and repel invasions.

As auxiliary to the state of our defence, to which Congress can never too frequently recur, they will not omit to inquire whether the fortifications, which have been already licensed by law, be commensurate with our exigences.

The intelligence from the army, under the command of General Wayne, is a happy presage to our military operations against the hostile Indians north of the Ohio. From the advices which have been forwarded, the advance which he has made must have damped the ardor of the savages, and weakened their obstinacy in waging war against the United States; and yet, even at this late hour, when our power to punish them cannot be questioned, we shall not be unwilling to cement a lasting peace, upon terms of candor, equity, and good neighbourhood.

Towards none of the Indian tribes have overtures of friendship been spared. The Creeks in particular are covered from encroachment by the interposition of the general government, and that of Georgia. From a desire also to remove the discontents of the Six Nations, a settlement, meditated at Presque Isle, on Lake Erie, has been suspended; and an agent is now endeavouring to rectify any misconception into which they may have fallen. But I cannot refrain from again pressing upon your deliberations the plan, which I recommended at the last session, for the improvement of harmony with all the Indians within our limits, by the fixing and conducting of trading-houses, upon the principles then expressed.

Gentlemen of the House of Representatives,

The time, which has elapsed since the commencement of our fiscal measures, has developed our pecuniary resources, so as to open a way for a definitive plan for the redemption of the public debt. It is believed, that the result is such as to encourage Congress to consummate this work without delay. Nothing can more promote the permanent welfare of the nation, and nothing would be more grateful to our constituents. Indeed, whatsoever is unfinished of our system of public credit, cannot be benefited by procrastination; and, as far as may be practicable, we ought to place that credit on grounds which cannot be disturbed, and to prevent that progressive accumulation of debt, which must ultimately endanger all governments.

An estimate of the necessary appropriations, including the expenditures into which we have been driven by the insurrection, will be submitted to Congress.

Gentlemen of the Senate and House of Representatives,

The mint of the United States has entered upon the coinage of the precious metals, and considerable sums of defective coins and bullion have been lodged with the director by individuals. There is a pleasing prospect, that the institution will, at no remote day, realize the expectation which was originally formed of its utility.

In subsequent communications, certain circumstances of our intercourse with foreign nations will be transmitted to Congress; however, it may not be unreasonable to announce, that my policy, in our foreign transactions, has been, to cultivate peace with all the world; to observe treaties with pure and absolute faith; to check every deviation from the line of impartiality; to explain what may have been misapprehended, and correct what may have been injurious to any nation; and, having thus acquired the right, to lose no time in acquiring the ability, to insist upon justice being done to ourselves.

Let us unite, therefore, in imploring the Supreme Ruler of nations to spread his holy protection over these United States; to turn the machinations of the wicked to the confirming of our constitution; to enable us at all times to root out internal sedition, and put invasion to flight; to perpetuate to our country that prosperity, which His goodness has already conferred; and to verify the anticipations of this government being a safeguard to human rights.

SEVENTH STATE OF THE
UNION ADDRESS
DECEMBER 8, 1795

Fellow-citizens of the Senate and House of Representatives,

I trust I do not deceive myself, while I indulge the persuasion, that I have never met you at any period, when, more than at the present, the situation of our public affairs has afforded just cause for mutual congratulation, and for inviting you to join with me in profound gratitude to the Author of all good, for the numerous and extraordinary blessings we enjoy.

The termination of the long, expensive, and distressing war, in which we have been engaged with certain Indians, northwest of the Ohio, is placed in the option of the United States, by a treaty, which the commander of our army has concluded provisionally with the hostile tribes in that region.

In the adjustment of the terms, the satisfaction of the Indians was deemed an object worthy no less of the policy, than of the liberality of the United States, as the necessary basis of durable tranquillity. This object, it is believed, has been fully attained. The articles agreed upon will immediately be laid before the Senate for their consideration.

The Creek and Cherokee Indians, who alone of the southern tribes had annoyed our frontier, have lately confirmed their preexisting treaties with us; and were giving evidence of a sincere disposition to carry them into effect, by the surrender of the prisoners and property they had taken. But we have to lament, that the fair prospect in this quarter has been once more clouded by wanton murders, which some citizens of Georgia are represented to have recently perpetrated on hunting parties of the Creeks, which have again subjected that frontier to disquietude and danger; which will be productive of further expense, and may occasion more effusion of blood. Measures are pursuing to prevent or mitigate the usual consequences of such outrages, and with the hope of their succeeding, at least to avert general hostility.

A letter from the Emperor of Morocco announces to me his recognition of our treaty made with his father the late Emperor; and, consequently, the continuance of peace with that power. With peculiar satisfaction I add, that information has been received from an agent deputed on our part to Algiers, importing, that the terms of a treaty with the Dey and Regency of that country had been adjusted in such a manner, as to authorize the expectation of a speedy peace, and the restoration of our unfortunate fellow-citizens from a grievous captivity.

The latest advices from our envoy at the court of Madrid give, moreover, the pleasing information, that he had received assurances of a speedy and satisfactory conclusion of his negotiation. While the event, depending upon unadjusted particulars, cannot be regarded as ascertained, it is agreeable to cherish the expectation of an issue, which, securing amicably very essential interests of the United States, will at the same time lay the foundation of lasting harmony with a power, whose friendship we have uniformly and sincerely desired to cultivate.

Though not before officially disclosed to the House of Representatives, you, gentlemen, are all apprized, that a treaty of amity, commerce, and navigation has been negotiated with

Great Britain; and that the Senate have advised and consented to its ratification, upon a condition which excepts part of one article. Agreeably thereto, and to the best judgment I was able to form of the public interest, after full and mature deliberation, I have added my sanction. The result on the part of his Britannic Majesty is unknown. When received, the subject will, without delay, be placed before Congress.

This interesting summary of our affairs, with regard to the foreign powers, between whom and the United States controversies have subsisted; and with regard also to those of our Indian neighbours, with whom we have been in a state of enmity or misunderstanding, opens a wide field for consoling and gratifying reflections. If, by prudence and moderation on every side, the extinguishment of all the causes of external discord, which have heretofore menaced our tranquillity, on terms compatible with our national rights and honor, shall be the happy result; how firm and how precious a foundation will have been laid for accelerating, maturing, and establishing the prosperity of our country.

Contemplating the internal situation, as well as the external relations, of the United States, we discover equal cause for contentment and satisfaction. While many of the nations of Europe, with their American dependencies, have been involved in a contest unusually bloody, exhausting, and calamitous; in which the evils of foreign war have been aggravated by domestic convulsion and insurrection; in which many of the arts most useful to society have been exposed to discouragement and decay; in which scarcity of subsistence has embittered other sufferings; while even the anticipations of a return of the blessings of peace and repose are alloyed by the sense of heavy and accumulating burthens, which press upon all the departments of industry, and threaten to clog the future springs of government; our favored country, happy in a striking contrast, has enjoyed general tranquillity; a tranquillity the more satisfactory, because maintained at the expense of no duty. Faithful to ourselves, we have violated no obligation to others. Our agriculture, commerce, and manufactures prosper beyond former example; the molestations of our trade (to prevent a continuance of which, however, very pointed remonstrances have been made) being overbalanced by the aggregate benefits which it derives from a neutral position. Our population advances with a celerity, which, exceeding the most sanguine calculations, proportionally augments our strength and resources, and guaranties our future security. Every part of the Union displays indications of rapid and various improvement; and with burthens so light as scarcely to be perceived, with resources fully adequate to our present exigences, with governments founded on the genuine principles of rational liberty, and with mild and wholesome laws, is it too much to say, that our country exhibits a spectacle of national happiness never surpassed, if ever before equalled?

Placed in a situation every way so auspicious, motives of commanding force impel us, with sincere acknowledgment to Heaven, and pure love to our country, to unite our efforts to preserve, prolong, and improve our immense advantages. To cooperate with you in this desirable work is a fervent and favorite wish of my heart.

It is a valuable ingredient in the general estimate of our welfare, that the part of our country, which was lately the scene of disorder and insurrection, now enjoys the blessings of quiet and order. The misled have abandoned their errors, and pay the respect to our Constitution and laws, which is due from good citizens to the public authorities of the society. These circumstances have induced me to pardon, generally, the offenders here referred to; and to extend forgiveness to those, who had been adjudged to capital punishment. For, though I shall always think it a sacred duty, to exercise with firmness and energy the constitutional powers with which I am vested, yet it appears to me no less consistent with the public good, than it is with my personal feelings, to mingle in the operations of government every degree of moderation and tenderness, which the national justice, dignity, and safety may permit.

Gentlemen,

Among the objects, which will claim your attention in the course of the session, a review of our military establishment is not the least important. It is called for by the events which have changed, and may be expected still further to change, the relative situation of our frontiers. In this review, you will doubtless allow due weight to the considerations, that the questions between us and certain foreign powers are not yet finally adjusted; that the war in Europe is not yet terminated; and that our western posts, when recovered, will demand provision for garrisoning and securing them. A statement of our present military force will be laid before you by the department of war.

With the review of our army establishment is naturally connected that of the militia. It will merit inquiry, what imperfections in the existing plan further experience may have unfolded. The subject is of so much moment in my estimation, as to excite a constant solicitude, that the consideration of it may be renewed, till the greatest attainable perfection shall be accomplished. Time is wearing away some advantages for forwarding the object, while none better deserves the persevering attention of the public councils.

While we indulge the satisfaction, which the actual condition of our western borders so well authorizes, it is necessary that we should not lose sight of an important truth, which continually receives new confirmations, namely, that the provisions heretofore made with a view to the protection of the Indians from the violences of the lawless part of our frontier inhabitants are insufficient. It is demonstrated that these violences can now be perpetrated with impunity; and it can need no argument to prove, that, unless the murdering of Indians can be restrained by bringing the murderers to condign punishment, all the exertions of the government to prevent destructive retaliations by the Indians will prove fruitless, and all our present agreeable prospects illusory. The frequent destruction of innocent women and children, who are chiefly the victims of retaliation, must continue to shock humanity; and an enormous expense, to drain the treasury of the Union.

To enforce upon the Indians the observance of justice, it is indispensable that there shall be competent means of rendering justice to them. If these means can be devised by the wisdom of Congress, and especially if there can be added an adequate provision for supplying the necessities of the Indians on reasonable terms (a measure, the mention of which I the more readily repeat, as in all the conferences with them they urge it with solicitude), I should not hesitate to entertain a strong hope of rendering our tranquillity permanent. I add, with pleasure, that the probability even of their civilization is not diminished by the experiments which have been thus far made, under the auspices of government. The accomplishment of this work, if practicable, will reflect undecaying lustre on our national character, and administer the most grateful consolations that virtuous minds can know.

Gentlemen of the House of Representatives,

The state of our revenue, with the sums which have been borrowed and reimbursed, pursuant to different acts of Congress, will be submitted from the proper department; together with an estimate of the appropriations necessary to be made for the service of the ensuing year.

Whether measures may not be advisable to reinforce the provision for the redemption of the public debt, will naturally engage your examination. Congress have demonstrated their sense to be, and it were superfluous to repeat mine, that whatsoever will tend to accelerate the honorable extinction of our public debt, accords as much with the true interest of our country as with the general sense of our constituents.

Gentlemen of the Senate and House of Representatives,

The statements, which will be laid before you, relative to the mint, will show the situation of that institution, and the necessity of some further legislative provisions for carrying the business of it more completely into effect, and for checking abuses which appear to be arising in particular quarters.

The progress in providing materials for the frigates, and in building them; the state of the fortifications of our harbours; the measures which have been pursued for obtaining proper sites for arsenals, and for replenishing our magazines with military stores; and the steps which have been taken towards the execution of the law for opening a trade with the Indians, will likewise be presented for the information of Congress.

Temperate discussion of the important subjects, which may arise in the course of the session, and mutual forbearance where there is a difference of opinion, are too obvious and necessary for the peace, happiness, and welfare of our country, to need any recommendation of mine.

EIGHTH STATE OF THE UNION ADDRESS
DECEMBER 7, 1796

Fellow-citizens of the Senate and House of Representatives,

In recurring to the internal situation of our country, since I had last the pleasure to address you, I find ample reason for a renewed expression of that gratitude to the Ruler of the Universe, which a continued series of prosperity has so often and so justly called forth.

The acts of the last session, which required special arrangements, have been, as far as circumstances would admit, carried into operation.

Measures calculated to insure a continuance of the friendship of the Indians, and to preserve peace along the extent of our interior frontier, have been digested and adopted. In the framing of these, care has been taken to guard, on the one hand, our advanced settlements from the predatory incursions of those unruly individuals, who cannot be restrained by their tribes; and, on the other hand, to protect the rights secured to the Indians by treaty; to draw them nearer to the civilized state; and inspire them with correct conceptions of the power, as well as justice, of the government.

The meeting of the deputies from the Creek nation at Colerain, in the State of Georgia, which had for a principal object the purchase of a parcel of their land by that State, broke up without its being accomplished; the nation having, previous to their departure, instructed them against making any sale. The occasion, however, has been improved, to confirm, by a new treaty with the Creeks, their preexisting engagements with the United States, and to obtain their consent to the establishment of trading-houses and military posts within their boundary; by means of which their friendship, and the general peace, may be more effectually secured.

The period, during the late session, at which the appropriation was passed for carrying into effect the treaty of amity, commerce, and navigation between the United States and his Britannic Majesty, necessarily procrastinated the reception of the posts stipulated to be delivered, beyond the date assigned for that event. As soon, however, as the governor-general of Canada could be addressed with propriety on the subject, arrangements were cordially and promptly concluded for their evacuation, and the United States took possession of the principal of them, comprehending Oswego, Niagara, Detroit, Michilimakinac, and Fort Miami, where such repairs and additions have been ordered to be made, as appeared indispensable.

The commissioners, appointed on the part of the United States and of Great Britain, to determine which is the river St. Croix mentioned in the treaty of peace of 1783, agreed in the choice of Egbert Benson, Esquire, of New York, for the third commissioner. The whole met at St. Andrew's, in Passamaquoddy Bay, in the beginning of October, and directed surveys to be made of the rivers in dispute; but, deeming it impracticable to have these surveys completed before the next year, they adjourned, to meet at Boston in August, 1797, for the final decision of the question.

Other commissioners, appointed on the part of the United States, agreeably to the seventh article of the treaty with Great Britain, relative to captures and condemnations of vessels and other property, met the commissioners of his Britannic Majesty, in London, in August last, when John Trumbull, Esquire, was chosen by lot for the fifth commissioner. In October following, the board were to proceed to business. As yet, there has been no communication of commissioners on the part of Great Britain, to unite with those who have been appointed on the part of the United States, for carrying into effect the sixth article of the treaty.

The treaty with Spain required, that the commissioners for running the boundary line between the territory of the United States and his Catholic Majesty's provinces of East and West Florida should meet at the Natchez, before the expiration of six months after the exchange of the ratifications, which was effected at Aranjuez on the 25th day of April; and the troops of his Catholic Majesty, occupying any posts within the limits of the United States, were, within the same period, to be withdrawn. The commissioner of the United States, therefore, commenced his journey for the Natchez in September, and troops were ordered to occupy the posts from which the Spanish garrisons should be withdrawn. Information has been recently received of the appointment of a commissioner on the part of his Catholic Majesty for running the boundary line; but none of any appointment for the adjustment of the claims of our citizens, whose vessels were captured by the armed vessels of Spain.

In pursuance of the act of Congress, passed in the last session, for the protection and relief of American seamen, agents were appointed, one to reside in Great Britain, and the other in the West Indies. The effects of the agency in the West Indies are not yet fully ascertained; but those, which have been communicated, afford grounds to believe the measure will be beneficial. The agent destined to reside in Great Britain declining to accept the appointment, the business has consequently devolved on the minister of the United States in London, and will command his attention until a new agent shall be appointed.

After many delays and disappointments, arising out of the European war, the final arrangements for fulfilling the engagements made to the Dey and Regency of Algiers will, in all present appearance, be crowned with success; but under great, though inevitable disadvantages in the pecuniary transactions, occasioned by that war, which will render a further provision necessary. The actual liberation of all our citizens, who were prisoners in Algiers, while it gratifies every feeling heart, is itself an earnest of a satisfactory termination of the whole negotiation. Measures are in operation for effecting treaties with the Regencies of Tunis and Tripoli.

To an active external commerce, the protection of a naval force is indispensable. This is manifest with regard to wars, in which a state itself is a party. But, besides this, it is in our own experience, that the most sincere neutrality is not a sufficient guard against the depredations of nations at war. To secure respect to a neutral flag requires a naval force, organized and ready to vindicate it from insult or aggression. This may even prevent the necessity of going to war, by discouraging belligerent powers from committing such violations of the rights of the neutral party, as may, first or last, leave no other option. From the best information I have been able to obtain, it would seem as if our trade to the Mediterranean, without a protecting force, will always be insecure, and our citizens exposed to the calamities from which numbers of them have but just been relieved.

These considerations invite the United States to look to the means, and to set about the gradual creation of a navy. The increasing progress of their navigation promises them, at no distant period, the requisite supply of seamen; and their means, in other respects, favor the undertaking. It is an encouragement, likewise, that their particular situation will give weight and influence to a moderate naval force in their hands. Will it not then be advisable to begin, without delay, to provide and lay up the materials for the building and equipping of ships of war; and to proceed in the work by degrees, in proportion as our resources shall render it practicable without inconvenience; so that a future war of Europe may not find our commerce in the same unprotected state in which it was found by the present?

Congress have repeatedly, and not without success, directed their attention to the encouragement of manufactures. The object is of too much consequence not to insure a continuance of their efforts in every way which shall appear eligible. As a general rule, manufactures on public account are inexpedient. But, where the state of things in a country leaves little hope, that certain branches of manufacture will, for a great length of time, obtain; when these are of a nature essential to the furnishing and equipping of the public force in time of war; are not establishments for procuring them on public account, to the extent of the ordinary demand for the public service, recommended by strong considerations of national policy, as an exception to the general rule? Ought our country to remain in such cases dependent on foreign supply, precarious, because liable to be interrupted? If the necessary articles should, in this mode, cost more in time of peace, will not the security and independence, thence arising, form an ample compensation? Establishments of this sort, commensurate only with the calls of the public service in time of peace, will, in time of war, easily be extended in proportion to the exigencies of the government; and may even, perhaps, be made to yield a surplus for the supply of our citizens at large, so as to mitigate the privations from the interruption of their trade. If adopted, the plan ought to exclude all those branches which are already, or likely soon to be, established in the country, in order that there may be no danger of interference with pursuits of individual industry.

It will not be doubted, that, with reference either to individual or national welfare, agriculture is of primary importance. In proportion as nations advance in population and other circumstances of maturity, this truth becomes more apparent, and renders the cultivation of the soil more and more an object of public patronage. Institutions for promoting it grow up, supported by the public purse; and to what object can it be dedicated with greater propriety? Among the means, which have been employed to this end, none have been attended with greater success than the establishment of boards, composed of proper characters, charged with collecting and diffusing information, and enabled by premiums, and small pecuniary aids, to encourage and assist a spirit of discovery and improvement. This species of establishment contributes doubly to the increase of improvement, by stimulating to enterprise and experiment, and by drawing to a common centre the results everywhere of individual skill and observation, and spreading them thence over the whole nation. Experience accordingly has shown, that they are very cheap instruments of immense national benefits.

I have heretofore proposed to the consideration of Congress, the expediency of establishing a national university, and also a military academy. The desirableness of both these institutions has so constantly increased with every new view I have taken of the subject, that I cannot omit the opportunity of once for all recalling your attention to them.

The assembly to which I address myself, is too enlightened not to be fully sensible how much a flourishing state of the arts and sciences contributes to national prosperity and reputation. True it is, that our country, much to its honor, contains many seminaries of learning highly respectable and useful; but the funds upon which they rest are too narrow to command the ablest professors, in the different departments of liberal knowledge, for the institution contemplated, though they would be excellent auxiliaries.

Amongst the motives to such an institution, the assimilation of the principles, opinions, and manners of our countrymen, by the common education of a portion of our youth from every quarter, well deserves attention. The more homogeneous our citizens can be made in these particulars, the greater will be our prospect of permanent union; and a primary object of such a national institution should be, the education of our youth in the science of government. In a republic, what species of knowledge can be equally important, and what duty more pressing on its legislature, than to patronize a plan for communicating it to those, who are to be the future guardians of the liberties of the country?

The institution of a military academy is also recommended by cogent reasons. However pacific the general policy of a nation may be, it ought never to be without an adequate stock of military knowledge for emergencies. The first would impair the energy of its character, and both would hazard its safety, or expose it to greater evils when war could not be avoided. Besides that war might often not depend upon its own choice. In proportion as the observance of pacific maxims might exempt a nation from the necessity of practising the rules of the military art, ought to be its care in preserving and transmitting, by proper establishments, the knowledge of that art. Whatever argument may be drawn from particular examples, superficially viewed, a thorough examination of the subject will evince, that the art of war is at once comprehensive and complicated; that it demands much previous study; and that the possession of it, in its most improved and perfect state, is always of great moment to the security of a nation. This, therefore, ought to be a serious care of every government; and for this purpose, an academy, where a regular course of instruction is given, is an obvious expedient, which different nations have successfully employed.

The compensations to the officers of the United States, in various instances, and in none more than in respect to the most important stations, appear to call for legislative revision. The consequences of a defective provision are of serious import to the government. If private wealth is to supply the defect of public retribution, it will greatly contract the sphere within which the selection of characters for office is to be made, and will proportionally diminish the probability of a choice of men able as well as upright. Besides that it would be repugnant to the vital principles of our government virtually to exclude, from public trusts, talents and virtue, unless accompanied by wealth.

While, in our external relations, some serious inconveniences and embarrassments have been overcome, and others lessened, it is with much pain and deep regret I mention, that circumstances of a very unwelcome nature have lately occurred. Our trade has suffered, and is suffering, extensive injuries in the West Indies from the cruisers and agents of the French Republic; and communications have been received from its minister here, which indicate the danger of a further disturbance of our commerce by its authority; and which are, in other respects, far from agreeable.

It has been my constant, sincere, and earnest wish, in conformity with that of our nation, to maintain cordial harmony, and a perfectly friendly understanding with that Republic. This wish remains unabated; and I shall persevere in the endeavour to fulfil it, to the utmost extent of what shall be consistent with a just and indispensable regard to the rights and honor of our country; nor will I easily cease to cherish the expectation, that a spirit of justice, candor, and friendship, on the part of the Republic, will eventually insure success.

In pursuing this course, however, I cannot forget what is due to the character of our government and nation; or to a full and entire confidence in the good sense, patriotism, self-respect, and fortitude of my countrymen.

I reserve for a special message a more particular communication on this interesting subject.

Gentlemen of the House of Representatives,

I have directed an estimate of the appropriations necessary for the service of the ensuing year to be submitted from the proper department, with a view of the public receipts and expenditures to the latest period to which an account can be prepared.

It is with satisfaction I am able to inform you, that the revenues of the United States continue in a state of progressive improvement.

A reinforcement of the existing provisions for discharging our public debt was mentioned in my address at the opening of the last session. Some preliminary steps were taken towards it, the maturing of which will, no doubt, engage your zealous attention during the present. I will only add, that it will afford me heart-felt satisfaction to concur in such further measures as will ascertain to our country the prospect of a speedy extinguishment of the debt. Posterity may have cause to regret, if, from any motive, intervals of tranquillity are left unimproved for accelerating this valuable end.

Gentlemen of the Senate and House of Representatives,

My solicitude to see the militia of the United States placed on an efficient establishment has been so often and so ardently expressed, that I shall but barely recall the subject to your view on the present occasion; at the same time, that I shall submit to your inquiry, whether our harbours are yet sufficiently secured.

The situation in which I now stand, for the last time, in the midst of the representatives of the people of the United States, naturally recalls the period when the administration of the present form of government commenced; and I cannot omit the occasion to congratulate you and my country, on the success of the experiment, nor to repeat my fervent supplications to the Supreme Ruler of the Universe and Sovereign Arbiter of Nations, that his providential care may still be extended to the United States; that the virtue and happiness of the people may be preserved; and that the government, which they have instituted for the protection of their liberties, may be perpetual.

FAREWELL ADDRESS
SEPTEMBER 19, 1796

To the people of the United States,

Friends, and fellow-citizens:

The period for a new election of a citizen, to administer the Executive Government of the United States, being not far distant, and the time actually arrived, when your thoughts must be employed in designating the person, who is to be clothed with that important trust, it appears to me proper, especially as it may conduce to a more distinct expression of the public voice, that I should now apprise you of the resolution I have formed, to decline being considered among the number of those, out of whom a choice is to be made.

I beg you, at the same time, to do me the justice to be assured, that this resolution has not been taken, without a strict regard to all the considerations appertaining to the relation, which binds a dutiful citizen to his country—and that, in withdrawing the tender of service which silence in my situation might imply, I am influenced by no diminution of zeal for your future interest, no deficiency of grateful respect for your past kindness; but am supported by a full conviction that the step is compatible with both.

The acceptance of, and continuance hitherto in, the office to which your suffrages have twice called me, have been a uniform sacrifice of inclination to the opinion of duty, and to a deference for what appeared to be your desire. I constantly hoped, that it would have been much earlier in my power, consistently with motives, which I was not at liberty to disregard, to return to that retirement, from which I had been reluctantly drawn. The strength of my inclination to do this, previous to the last election, had even led to the preparation of an address to declare it to you; but mature reflection on the then perplexed and critical posture of our affairs with foreign nations, and the unanimous advice of persons entitled to my confidence, impelled me to abandon the idea.

I rejoice that the state of your concerns, external as well as internal, no longer renders the pursuit of inclination incompatible with the sentiment of duty, or propriety; and am persuaded, whatever partiality may be retained for my services, that in the present circumstances of our country, you will not disapprove my determination to retire.

The impressions, with which I first undertook the arduous trust, were explained on the proper occasion. In the discharge of this trust, I will only say, that I have, with good intentions, contributed towards the organization and administration of the government, the best exertions of which a very fallible judgment was capable. Not unconscious, in the outset, of the inferiority of my qualifications, experience in my own eyes, perhaps still more in the eyes of others, has strengthened the motives to diffidence of myself; and every day the increasing weight of years admonishes me more and more, that the shade of retirement is as necessary to me as it will be welcome. Satisfied, that, if any circumstances have given peculiar value to my services, they were temporary, I have the consolation to believe, that, while choice and prudence invite me to quit the political scene, patriotism does not forbid it.

In looking forward to the moment, which is intended to terminate the career of my public life, my feelings do not permit me to suspend the deep acknowledgment of that debt of gratitude, which I owe to my beloved country—for the many honors it has conferred upon me; still more for the steadfast confidence with which it has supported me; and for the opportunities I have thence enjoyed of manifesting my inviolable attachment, by services faithful and persevering, though in usefulness unequal to my zeal. If benefits have resulted to our country from these services, let it always be remembered to your praise, and as an instructive example in our annals, that under circumstances in which the passions agitated in every direction were liable to mislead, amidst appearances sometimes dubious—vicissitudes of fortune often discouraging—in situations in which not unfrequently want of success has countenanced the spirit of criticism, the constancy of your support was the essential prop of the efforts and a guarantee of the plans by which they were effected. Profoundly penetrated with this idea, I shall carry it with me to the grave, as a strong incitement to unceasing vows that Heaven may continue to you the choicest tokens of its beneficence—that your union and brotherly affection may be perpetual—that the free Constitution, which is the work of your hands, may be sacredly maintained—that its administration in every department may be stamped with wisdom and virtue—that, in fine, the happiness of the people of these States, under the auspices of liberty, may be made complete, by so careful a preservation and so prudent a use of this blessing as will acquire to them the glory of recommending it to the applause, the affection, and adoption of every nation, which is yet a stranger to it.

Here, perhaps, I ought to stop. But a solicitude for your welfare, which cannot end but with my life, and the apprehension of danger, natural to that solicitude, urge me on an occasion like the present, to offer to your solemn contemplation, and to recommend to your frequent review, some sentiments; which are the result of much reflection, of no inconsiderable observation, and which appear to me all-important to the permanency of your felicity as a people. These will be offered to you with the more freedom, as you can only see in them the disinterested warnings of a parting friend, who can possibly have no personal motive to bias his counsels. Nor can I forget, as an encouragement to it your indulgent reception of my sentiments on a former and not dissimilar occasion.

Interwoven as is the love of liberty with every ligament of your hearts, no recommendation of mine is necessary to fortify or confirm the attachment.

The unity of Government which constitutes you one people, is also now dear to you. It is justly so; for it is a main pillar in the edifice of your real independence; the support of your tranquillity at home; your peace abroad; of your safety; of your prosperity; of that very liberty, which you so highly prize. But as it is easy to foresee, that from different causes, and from different quarters, much pains will be taken, many artifices employed, to weaken in your minds the conviction of this truth; as this is the point in your political fortress against which the batteries of internal and external enemies will be most constantly and actively (though often covertly and insidiously) directed, it is of infinite moment, that you should properly estimate the immense value of your national Union to your collective and individual happiness; that you should cherish a cordial, habitual, and immoveable attachment to it; accustoming yourselves to think and speak of it as of the palladium of your political safety and prosperity; watching for its preservation with jealous anxiety; discountenancing whatever may suggest even a suspicion that it can in any event be abandoned, and indignantly frowning upon the first dawning of every attempt to alienate any portion of our Country from the rest, or to enfeeble the sacred ties which now link together the various parts.

For this you have every inducement of sympathy and interest. Citizens by birth or choice of a common country, that country has a right to concentrate your affections. The name of American, which belongs to you, in your national capacity, must always exalt the just pride of patriotism, more than any appellation derived from local discriminations. With slight shades of difference, you have the same religion, manners, habits, and political principles. You have in a common cause fought and triumphed together. The independence and liberty you possess are the work of joint councils, and joint efforts—of common dangers, sufferings and successes.

But these considerations, however powerfully they address themselves to your sensibility, are greatly outweighed by those which apply more immediately to your interest. Here every portion of our country finds the most commanding motives for carefully guarding and preserving the Union of the whole.

The North in an unrestrained intercourse with the South, protected by the equal laws of a common government, finds in the productions of the latter great additional resources of maritime and commercial enterprise—and precious materials of manufacturing industry. The South in the same intercourse, benefiting by the agency of the North, sees its agriculture grow and its commerce expand. Turning partly into its own channels the seamen of the North, it finds its particular navigation envigorated; and, while it contributes, in different ways, to nourish and increase the general mass of the national navigation, it looks forward to the protection of a maritime strength to which itself is unequally adapted. The East, in a like intercourse with the West, already finds, and in the progressive improvement of interior communications, by land and water, will more and more find, a valuable vent for the commodities which it brings from abroad, or manufactures at home. The West derives from the East supplies requisite to its growth and comfort, and what is perhaps of still greater consequence, it must of necessity owe the secure enjoyment of indispensable outlets for its own productions to the weight, influence, and the future maritime strength of the Atlantic side of the Union, directed by an indissoluble community of interest, as one nation. Any other tenure by which the West can hold this essential advantage, whether derived from its own separate strength, or from an apostate and unnatural connexion with any foreign power, must be intrinsically precarious.

While then every part of our Country thus feels an immediate and particular interest in Union, all the parts combined cannot fail to find in the united mass of means and efforts, greater strength, greater resource, proportionably greater security from external danger, a less frequent interruption of their peace by foreign nations; and, what is of inestimable value! they must derive from union an exemption from those broils and wars between themselves, which so frequently afflict neighboring countries, not tied together by the same government; which their own rivalships alone would be sufficient to produce; but which opposite foreign alliances, attachments, and intrigues would stimulate and embitter. Hence likewise they will avoid the necessity of those overgrown military establishments, which under any form of government, are inauspicious to liberty, and which are to be regarded as particularly hostile to republican liberty: in this sense it is, that your Union, ought to be considered as a main prop of your liberty, and that the love of the one ought to endear to you the preservation of the other.

These considerations speak a persuasive language to every reflecting and virtuous mind—and exhibit the continuance of the Union as a primary object of patriotic desire. Is there a doubt, whether a common government can embrace so large a sphere? Let experience solve it. To listen to mere speculation in such a case were criminal. We are authorized to hope that a proper organization of the whole, with the auxiliary agency of governments for the respective subdivisions, will afford a happy issue to the experiment. 'Tis well worth a fair and full experiment. With such powerful and obvious motives to Union, affecting all parts of our country, while experience shall not have demonstrated its impracticability, there will always be reason to distrust the patriotism of those, who in any quarter may endeavor to weaken its bands.

In contemplating the causes which may disturb our Union, it occurs as matter of serious concern, that any ground should have been furnished for characterizing parties by geographical discriminations—Northern and Southern—Atlantic and Western; whence designing men may endeavor to excite a belief, that there is a real difference of local interests and views. One of the expedients of party to acquire influence, within particular districts, is to misrepresent the opinions and aims of other districts. You cannot shield yourselves too much against the jealousies and heartburnings which spring from these misrepresentations; they tend to render alien to each other those who ought to be bound together by fraternal affection. The inhabitants of our Western country have lately had a useful lesson on this head. They have seen, in the negotiation by the Executive, and in the unanimous ratification by the Senate, of the Treaty with Spain, and in the universal satisfaction at that event, throughout the United States, a decisive proof how unfounded were the suspicions propagated among them of a policy in the general Government and in the Atlantic States unfriendly to their interests in regard to the Mississippi. They have been witnesses to the formation of two treaties, that with Great Britain, and that with Spain, which secure to them every thing they could desire, in respect to our foreign relations, towards confirming their prosperity. Will it not be their wisdom to rely for the preservation of these advantages on the Union by which they were procured? Will they not henceforth be deaf to those advisers, if such there are, who would sever them from their brethren, and connect them with aliens?

To the efficacy and permanency of your Union, a Government for the whole is indispensable. No alliances however strict between the parts can be an adequate substitute. They must inevitably experience the infractions and interruptions which all alliances in all times have experienced. Sensible of this momentous truth, you have improved upon your first essay, by the adoption of a Constitution of government, better calculated than your former for an intimate Union, and for the efficacious management of your common concerns. This government, the offspring of our own choice uninfluenced and unawed, adopted upon full investigation and mature deliberation, completely free in its principles, in the distribution of its powers, uniting security with energy, and containing within itself a provision for its own amendment, has a just claim to your confidence and your support. Respect for its authority, compliance with its laws, acquiescence in its measures, are duties enjoined by the fundamental maxims of true liberty. The basis of our political systems is the right of the people to make and to alter their Constitutions of government. But the Constitution which at any time exists, 'till changed by an explicit and authentic act of the whole people, is sacredly obligatory upon all. The very idea of the power and the right of the people to establish government, presupposes the duty of every individual to obey the established government.

All obstructions to the execution of the laws, all combinations and associations, under whatever plausible character, with the real design to direct, control, counteract, or awe the regular deliberation and action of the constituted authorities, are destructive of this fundamental principle, and of fatal tendency. They serve to organize faction, to give it an artificial and extraordinary force—to put, in the place of the delegated will of the Nation, the will of a party; often a small but artful and enterprizing minority of the community; and, according to the alternate triumphs of different parties, to make the public administration the mirror of the ill-concerted and incongruous projects of faction, rather than the organ of consistent and wholesome plans digested by common councils, and modified by mutual interests. However combinations or associations of the above description may now and then answer popular ends, they are likely, in the course of time and things, to become potent engines, by which cunning, ambitious, and unprincipled men will be enabled to subvert the power of the people and to usurp for themselves the reins of government; destroying afterwards the very engines which have lifted them to unjust dominion.

Towards the preservation of your Government and the permanency of your present happy state, it is requisite, not only that you steadily discountenance irregular oppositions to its acknowledged authority, but also that you resist with care the spirit of innovation upon its principles, however specious the pretexts. One method of assault may be to effect, in the forms of the Constitution, alterations which will impair the energy of the system, and thus to undermine what cannot be directly overthrown. In all the changes to which you may be invited, remember that time and habit are at least as necessary to fix the true character of governments, as of other human institutions—that experience is the surest standard, by which to test the real tendency of the existing Constitution of a country—that facility in changes upon the credit of mere hypothesis and opinion exposes to perpetual change, from the endless variety of hypothesis and opinion: and remember, expecially, that for the efficient management of your common interests, in a country so extensive as ours, a government of as much vigour as is consistent with the perfect security of liberty is indispensable. Liberty itself will find in such a government, with powers properly distributed and adjusted, its surest guardian. It is indeed little else than a name, where the government is too feeble to withstand the enterprises of faction, to confine each member of the society within the limits prescribed by the laws, and to maintain all in the secure and tranquil enjoyment of the rights of person and property.

I have already intimated to you the danger of parties in the State, with particular reference to the founding of them on geographical discriminations. Let me now take a more comprehensive view, and warn you in the most solemn manner against the baneful effects of the spirit of party, generally.

This spirit, unfortunately, is inseparable from our nature, having its root in the strongest passions of the human mind. It exists under different shapes in all governments, more or less stifled, controlled, or repressed; but, in those of the popular form, it is seen it its greatest rankness, and is truly their worst enemy.

The alternate domination of one faction over another, sharpened by the spirit of revenge natural to party dissension, which in different ages and countries has perpetrated the most horrid enormities, is itself a frightful despotism. But this leads at length to a more formal and permanent despotism. The disorders and miseries, which result, gradually incline the minds of men to seek security and repose in the absolute power of an individual: and sooner or later the chief of some prevailing faction, more able or more fortunate than his competitors, turns this disposition to the purposes of his own elevation, on the ruins of public liberty.

Without looking forward to an extremity of this kind (which nevertheless ought not to be entirely out of sight), the common and continual mischiefs of the spirit of party are sufficient to make it the interest and duty of a wise people to discourage and restrain it.

It serves always to distract the public councils, and enfeeble the public administration. It agitates the community with ill-founded jealousies and false alarms, kindles the animosity of one part against another, foments occasionally riot and insurrection. It opens the doors to foreign influence and corruption, which find a facilitated access to the Government itself through the channels of party passions. Thus the policy and the will of one country, are subjected to the policy and will of another.

There is an opinion that parties in free countries are useful checks upon the administration of the Government, and serve to keep alive the spirit of liberty. This within certain limits is probably true—and in governments of a monarchical cast, patriotism may look with indulgence, if not with favour, upon the spirit of party. But in those of the popular character, in governments purely elective, it is a spirit not to be encouraged. From their natural tendency, it is certain there will always be enough of that spirit for every salutary purpose, and there being constant danger of excess, the effort ought to be, by force of public opinion, to mitigate and assuage it. A fire not to be quenched; it demands a uniform vigilance to prevent its bursting into a flame, lest, instead of warming, it should consume.

It is important, likewise, that the habits of thinking in a free country should inspire caution in those entrusted with its administration, to confine themselves within their respective constitutional spheres; avoiding in the exercise of the powers of one department to encroach upon another. The spirit of encroachment tends to consolidate the powers of all the departments in one, and thus to create, whatever the form of government, a real despotism. A just estimate of that love of power, and proneness to abuse it, which predominates in the human heart, is sufficient to satisfy us of the truth of this position. The necessity of reciprocal checks in the exercise of political power, by dividing and distributing it into different depositories, and constituting each the guardian of the public weal against invasions by the others, has been evinced by experiments ancient and modern; some of them in our country and under our own eyes. To preserve them must be as necessary as to institute them. If in the opinion of the people, the distribution or modification of the Constitutional powers be in any particular wrong, let it be corrected by an amendment in the way which the Constitution designates. But let there be no change by usurpation; for though this, in one instance, may be the instrument of good, it is the customary weapon by which free governments are destroyed. The precedent must always greatly overbalance in permanent evil any partial or transient benefit which the use can at any time yield.

Of all the dispositions and habits, which lead to political prosperity, religion and morality are indispensable supports. In vain would that man claim the tribute of patriotism, who should labour to subvert these great pillars of human happiness, these firmest props of the duties of men and citizens. The mere politician, equally with the pious man, ought to respect and to cherish them. A volume could not trace all their connexions with private and public felicity. Let it simply be asked where is the security for property, for reputation, for life, if the sense of religious obligation desert the oaths, which are the instruments of investigation in courts of justice? And let us with caution indulge the supposition, that morality can be maintained without religion. Whatever may be conceded to the influence of refined education on minds of peculiar structure—reason and experience both forbid us to expect, that national morality can prevail in exclusion of religious principle.

'Tis substantially true, that virtue or morality is a necessary spring of popular government. The rule indeed extends with more or less force to every species of free government. Who that is a sincere friend to it, can look with indifference upon attempts to shake the foundation of the fabric?

Promote, then, as an object of primary importance, institutions for the general diffusion of knowledge. In proportion as the structure of a government gives force to public opinion, it is essential that public opinion should be enlightened.

As a very important source of strength and security, cherish public credit. One method of preserving it is to use it as sparingly as possible—avoiding occasions of expense by cultivating peace, but remembering also that timely disbursements to prepare for danger frequently prevent much greater disbursements to repel it—avoiding likewise the accumulation of debt, not only by shunning occasions of expense, but by vigorous exertions in time of peace to discharge the debts which unavoidable wars may have occasioned, not ungenerously throwing upon posterity the burthen which we ourselves ought to bear. The execution of these maxims belongs to your Representatives, but it is necessary that public opinion should cooperate. To facilitate to them the performance of their duty, it is essential that you should practically bear in mind, that towards the payment of debts there must be revenue—that to have revenue there must be taxes—that no taxes can be devised which are not more or less inconvenient and unpleasant—that the intrinsic embarassment inseparable from the selection of the proper objects (which is always a choice of difficulties) ought to be a decisive motive for a candid construction of the conduct of the Government in making it, and for a spirit of acquiescence in the measures for obtaining revenue which the public exigencies may at any time dictate.

Observe good faith and justice towards all nations. Cultivate peace and harmony with all. Religion and morality enjoin this conduct; and can it be that good policy does not equally enjoin it? It will be worthy of a free, enlightened, and, at no distant period, a great nation, to give to mankind the magnanimous and too novel example of a people always guided by an exalted justice and benevolence. Who can doubt that in the course of time and things, the fruits of such a plan would richly repay any temporary advantages, which might be lost by a steady adherence to it? Can it be, that Providence has not connected the permanent felicity of a nation with its virtue? The experiment, at least, is recommended by every sentiment which ennobles human nature. Alas! is it rendered impossible by its vices?

In the execution of such a plan nothing is more essential than that permanent, inveterate antipathies against particular nations and passionate attachments for others should be excluded; and that in place of them just and amicable feelings towards all should be cultivated. The nation, which indulges towards another an habitual hatred or an habitual fondness, is in some degree a slave. It is a slave to its animosity or to its affection, either of which is sufficient to lead it astray from its duty and its interest. Antipathy in one nation against another disposes each more readily to offer insult and injury, to lay hold of slight causes of umbrage, and to be haughty and intractable, when accidental or trifling occasions of dispute occur. Hence frequent collisions, obstinate, envenomed and bloody contests. The nation promoted by ill-will and resentment sometimes impels to war the government, contrary to the best calculations of policy. The government sometimes participates in the national propensity, and adopts through passion what reason would reject; at other times, it makes the animosity of the nation subservient to projects of hostility instigated by pride, ambition, and other sinister and pernicious motives. The peace often, sometimes perhaps the liberty, of nations has been the victim.

So likewise a passionate attachment of one nation for another produces a variety of evils. Sympathy for the favourite nation, facilitating the illusion of an imaginary common interest in cases where no real common interest exists, and infusing into one the enmities of the other, betrays the former into a participation in the quarrels and wars of the latter, without adequate inducement or justification: it leads also to concessions to the favorite nation of privileges denied to others, which is apt doubly to injure the nation making the concessions; by unnecessarily parting with what ought to have been retained, and by exciting jealousy, ill-will, and a disposition to retaliate, in the parties from whom equal privileges are withheld; and it gives to ambitious, corrupted, or deluded citizens (who devote themselves to the favorite nation), facility to betray, or sacrifice the interests of their own country, without odium, sometimes even with popularity—gilding with the appearances of a virtuous sense of obligation, a commendable deference for public opinion, or a laudable zeal for public good, the base or foolish compliances of ambition, corruption or infatuation.

As avenues to foreign influence in innumerable ways, such attachments are particularly alarming to the truly enlightened and independent patriot. How many opportunities do they afford to tamper with domestic factions, to practice the arts of seduction, to mislead public opinion, to influence or awe the public councils! Such an attachment of a small or weak, towards a great and powerful nation, dooms the former to be the satellite of the latter.

Against the insidious wiles of foreign influence, I conjure you to believe me, follow-citizens, the jealousy of a free people ought to be constantly awake, since history and experience prove that foreign influence is one of the most baneful foes of republican government. But that jealousy to be useful must be impartial; else it becomes the instrument of the very influence to be avoided, instead of a defence against it. Excessive partiality for one foreign nation and excessive dislike of another, cause those whom they actuate to see danger only on one side, and serve to veil and even second the arts of influence on the other. Real patriots, who may resist the intrigues of the favourite, are liable to become suspected and odious; while its tools and dupes usurp the applause and confidence of the people, to surrender their interests.

The great rule of conduct for us, in regard to foreign nations, is, in extending our commercial relations, to have with them as little political connection as possible. So far as we have already formed engagements, let them be fulfilled with perfect good faith. Here let us stop.

Europe has a set of primary interests, which to us have none, or a very remote relation. Hence she must be engaged in frequent controversies, the causes of which are essentially foreign to our concerns. Hence therefore it must be unwise in us to implicate ourselves, by artificial ties in the ordinary vicissitudes of her politics, or the ordinary combinations and collisions of her friendships, or enmities.

Our detached and distant situation invites and enables us to pursue a different course. If we remain one people, under an efficient government, the period is not far off, when we may defy material injury from external annoyance; when we may take such an attitude as will cause the neutrality we may at any time resolve upon to be scrupulously respected. When belligerent nations, under the impossibility of making acquisitions upon us, will not lightly hazard the giving us provocation; when we may choose peace or war, as our interest guided by our justice shall counsel.

Why forego the advantages of so peculiar a situation? Why quit our own to stand upon foreign ground? Why, by interweaving our destiny with that of any part of Europe, entangle our peace and prosperity, in the toils of European ambition, rivalship, interest, humour, or caprice?

'Tis our true policy to steer clear of permanent alliances, with any portion of the foreign world—so far, I mean, as we are now at liberty to do it—for let me not be understood as capable of patronizing infidelity to existing engagements (I hold the maxim no less applicable to public than to private affairs, that honesty is always the best policy). I repeat it therefore let those engagements be observed in their genuine sense. But in my opinion it is unnecessary and would be unwise to extend them.

Taking care always to keep ourselves, by suitable establishments, on a respectably defensive posture, we may safely trust to temporary alliances for extraordinary emergencies.

Harmony, liberal intercourse with all nations, are recommended by policy, humanity, and interest. But even our commercial policy should hold an equal and impartial hand—neither seeking nor granting exclusive favours or preferences; consulting the natural course of things; diffusing and diversifying by gentle means the streams of commerce, but forcing nothing; establishing with powers so disposed—in order to give trade a stable course, to define the rights of our merchants, and to enable the Government to support them—conventional rules of intercourse, the best that present circumstances and mutual opinion will permit; but temporary, and liable to be from time to time abandoned or varied, as experience and circumstances shall dictate; constantly keeping in view, that 'tis folly in one nation to look for disinterested favours from another—that it must pay with a portion of its independence for whatever it may accept under that character—that by such acceptance, it may place itself in the condition of having given equivalents for nominal favours and yet of being reproached with ingratitude for not giving more. There can be no greater error than to expect, or calculate upon real favours from nation to nation. 'Tis an illusion which experience must cure, which a just pride ought to discard.

In offering to you, my countrymen, these counsels of an old and affectionate friend, I dare not hope they will make the strong and lasting impression, I could wish—that they will controul the usual current of the passions, or prevent our Nation from running the course which has hitherto marked the destiny of nations. But if I may even flatter myself, that they may be productive of some partial benefit; some occasional good; that they may now and then recur to moderate the fury of party spirit, to warn against the mischiefs of foreign intrigue, to guard against the impostures of pretended patriotism, this hope will be a full recompense for the solicitude for your welfare, by which they have been dictated.

How far in the discharge of my official duties, I have been guided by the principles which have been delineated, the public records and other evidences of my conduct must witness to you, and to the world. To myself, the assurance of my own conscience is, that I have at least believed myself to be guided by them.

In relation to the still subsisting war in Europe, my proclamation of the 22nd of April 1793 is the index to my plan. Sanctioned by your approving voice and by that of your Representatives in both Houses of Congress, the spirit of that measure has continually governed me—uninfluenced by any attempts to deter or divert me from it.

After deliberate examination with the aid of the best lights I could obtain, I was well satisfied that our country, under all the circumstances of the case, had a right to take, and was bound in duty and interest, to take a neutral position. Having taken it, I determined, as far as should depend upon me, to maintain it, with moderation, perseverance, and firmness.

The considerations which respect the right to hold this conduct, it is not necessary on this occasion to detail. I will only observe, that according to my understanding of the matter, that right, so far from being denied by any of the belligerent powers, has been virtually admitted by all.

The duty of holding a neutral conduct may be inferred, without any thing more, from the obligation which justice and humanity impose on every nation, in cases in which it is free to act, to maintain inviolate the relations of peace and amity towards other nations.

The inducements of interest for observing that conduct will best be referred to your own reflections and experience. With me, a predominant motive has been to endeavour to gain time to our country to settle and mature its yet recent institutions, and to progress without interruption to that degree of strength and consistency, which is necessary to give it, humanly speaking, the command of its own fortunes.

Though, in reviewing the incidents of my Administration, I am unconscious of intentional error—I am nevertheless too sensible of my defects not to think it probable that I may have committed many errors. Whatever they may be I fervently beseech the Almighty to avert or mitigate the evils to which they may tend. I shall also carry with me the hope that my country will never cease to view them with indulgence; and that after forty-five years of my life dedicated to its service, with an upright zeal, the faults of incompetent abilities will be consigned to oblivion, as myself must soon be to the mansions of rest.

Relying on its kindness in this as in other things, and actuated by that fervent love towards it, which is so natural to a man, who views in it the native soil of himself and his progenitors for several generations; I anticipate with pleasing expectation that retreat, in which I promise myself to realize, without alloy, the sweet enjoyment of partaking, in the midst of my fellow-citizens, the benign influence of good laws under a free government, the ever favorite object of my heart, and the happy reward, as I trust, of our mutual cares, labours, and dangers.

WASHINGTONIANA: EXTRACTS FROM WASHINGTON'S WRITINGS

This section, comprised of selected excerpts from hundreds of Washington's private letters and public speeches, draws on a lifetime of words written and spoken by Washington between 1754 and 1799. *Washingtoniana* covers his important political, philosophical, and theological writings and presents a complete and unique portrait of George Washington, written in his own words.

WASHINGTONIANA: EXTRACTS FROM WASHINGTON'S WRITINGS

1754

I heard the bullets whistle; and believe me, there is something charming in the sound.

I flatter myself, that, under a skillful Commander, or man of sense (which I most sincerely wish to serve under), with my own application and diligent study of my duty, I shall be able to conduct my steps without censure, and, in time, render myself worthy of the promotion that I shall be favored with now.

I have shown all the respect I could to them [prisoners of war] here, and have given them some necessary clothing, by which I have disfurnished myself; for, having brought no more than two or three shirts . . . , I was ill provided to supply them.

I have a constitution hardy enough to encounter and undergo the most severe trials; and, I flatter myself, resolution to face what any man dares, as shall be proved when it comes to the test.

The rank of office, to me, is much more important than the pay.

You [Colonel William Fitzhugh] make mention of my continuing in the service, and retaining my Colonel's commission. This idea has filled me with surprise; for, if you think me capable of holding a commission that has neither rank nor emolument annexed to it, you must entertain a very contemptible opinion of my weakness, and believe me to be more empty than the commission itself.

Nothing is more a stranger to my breast, or a sin that my soul more abhors, than that black and detestable one, of ingratitude.

1755

I beg, that you will be particularly careful, in seeing strict order observed among the soldiers, as that is the life of military discipline.

Do we not know, that every nation under the sun finds its account therein, and that, without it, no order or regularity can be observed? Why, then, should it be expected from us, who are all young and inexperienced, to govern and keep up a proper spirit of discipline, without laws, when the best and most experienced can scarcely do it with them? If we consult our interest, I am sure it loudly calls for them.

I am honored, Madam [Mary Washington], to be your most dutiful son.

If it is in my power to avoid going to Ohio again, I shall; but if the command is pressed upon me, by the general voice of the country, and offered upon such terms as cannot be objected against, it would reflect dishonor on me to refuse it; and that, I am sure, must or ought to give you greater uneasiness, than my going in an honorable command.

By the all-powerful dispensations of Providence, I have been protected, beyond all human probability, or expectation; for I had four bullets through my coat, and two horses shot under me, yet escaped unhurt, although death was leveling my companions on every side of me.

1756

The waste of provision they [the militia in the French and Indian War] make, is unaccountable; no method or order in being served, or purchasing at the best rates, but quite the reverse. Allowance for each man, as in the case of other soldiers, they look upon as the highest indignity, and would sooner starve, than carry a few days' provision on their backs, for conveniency. But upon their march, when breakfast is wanted, they knock down the first beef they meet with; and, after regaling themselves, march on till dinner, when they take the same method; and so for supper, to the great oppression of the people. Or if they chance to impress cattle for provision, the valuation is left to ignorant and interested neighbors, who have suffered by those practices, and, despairing of their pay, exact high prices, and thus the public is imposed upon at all events. I might add, I believe, that, for want of proper laws to govern the militia (I cannot ascribe it to any other cause), they are obstinate, self-willed, perverse, of little or no service to the people, and very burdensome to the country. Every individual has his own crude notions of things, and must undertake to direct. If his advice is neglected, he thinks himself slighted, abused, and injured; and, to redress his wrongs, will depart for his home. These are literally matters of fact, partly from persons of undoubted veracity, but chiefly from my own observations.

However absurd it may appear, it is nevertheless certain, that five hundred Indians have it more in their power to annoy the inhabitants, than ten times their number of regulars. Besides the advantageous way they have of fighting in the woods, their cunning and craft, their activity and patient sufferings, are not to be equalled. They prowl about, like wolves; and, like them, do their mischief by stealth. They depend upon their dexterity in hunting, and upon the cattle of the inhabitants, for provisions.

Unless we have Indians to oppose Indians, we may expect but small success.

A small number [of Indians], just to point out the wiles and tricks of the enemy, is better than none.

Great care should be observed, in choosing active marksmen. The manifest inferiority of inactive persons, unused to arms, in this kind of service (although equal in numbers), to men who have practised hunting, is inconceivable. The chance against them, is more than two to one.

Remember, that actions, and not the commission, make the officer. More is expected from him than the title. Do not forget, that there ought to be a time appropriated, to attain knowledge, as well as to indulge in pleasure. As we now have no opportunities to improve from example, let us read, for this desirable end.

The supplicating tears of the women, and moving petitions of the men, melt me into such deadly sorrow, that I solemnly declare, if I know my own mind, I could offer myself a willing sacrifice to the butchering enemy [the Indians], provided that would contribute to the people's ease.

This, I am certain of, and can call my conscience, and, what I suppose will be a still more demonstrative proof in the eyes of the world, my orders, to witness, how much I have, both by threats and persuasive means, endeavored to discountenance gaming, drinking, swearing, and irregularities of every other kind; while I have, on the other hand, practised every artifice, to inspire a laudable emulation, in the officers, for the service of their country, and to encourage the soldiers, in the unerring exercise of their duty.

I apprehend, it will be thought advisable, to keep a garrison always at Fort Loudoun; for which reason, I would beg to represent the number of tippling-houses in Winchester, as a great nuisance to the soldiers, who, by this means, in despite of the utmost care and vigilance, are, so long as their pay holds out, incessantly drunk, and unfit for service.

The want of a chaplain, I humbly conceive, reflects dishonor on the regiment, as all other officers are allowed. . . . The gentlemen of the corps are sensible of the want of a chaplain, and proposed to support one, at their private expense. But I think it would have a more graceful appearance, were he appointed as others are.

1757

As you [Governor Dinwiddie] were pleased to leave it to my discretion, to punish or pardon the criminals, I have resolved on the latter, since I find example of so little weight, and since those poor unhappy criminals have undergone no small pain of body and mind, in a dark prison, closely ironed.

1758

A trade with the Indians should be established, upon such terms, and transacted by men of such principles, as would at the same time redound to the reciprocal advantage of the Colony and the Indians, and effectually remove the bad impressions which the Indians have received, from the conduct of a set of villains, divested of all faith and honor; and give us such an early opportunity of establishing an interest with them, as would insure to us a large share of the fur-trade, not only of the Ohio Indians, but, in time, of the numerous nations possessing the back country westward. To prevent this advantageous commerce [between whites and Indians] from suffering in its infancy, by the sinister views of designing, selfish men, in the different provinces, I humbly conceive it advisable, that Commissioners from each of the colonies should be appointed, to regulate the mode of that trade, and fix it on such a basis, that all the attempts of one colony to undermine another, and thereby weaken and diminish the general system, might be frustrated.

Such is the nature of Indians, that nothing will prevent their going where they have any reason to expect presents; and their cravings are insatiable.

My men are very bare of regimental clothing, and I have no prospect of supply. So far from regretting this want, during the present campaign, if I were left to pursue my own inclinations, I would not only order the men to adopt the Indian dress, but cause the officers to do it also; and be the first to set the example myself. Nothing but the uncertainty of obtaining the general approbation, causes me to hesitate a moment, to leave my regimentals, and proceed, as light as an Indian in the woods. It is an unbecoming dress, I own, for an officer. But convenience, rather than show, I think, should be consulted. The reduction of bat-horses [baggage-horses] alone, would be sufficient to recommend it; for, nothing is more certain, than that less baggage would be required, and the public benefited in proportion.

It is evident, that soldiers, in that trim, are better able to carry their provisions, are fitter for the active service we must engage in, less liable to sink under the fatigues of a march; and we thus get rid of much baggage, which would lengthen our line of march. These, and not whim or caprice, were my reasons for ordering this [Indian] dress.

The last Assembly, in their Supply Bill, provided for a chaplain to our regiment. On this subject I had often, without any success, applied to Governor Dinwiddie. I now flatter myself that your Honor [the President of the Council] will be pleased to appoint a sober, serious man, for this duty. Common decency, sir, in a camp, calls for the services of a divine, which ought not to be dispensed with, although the world should be so uncharitable as to think us void of religion, and incapable of good instructions.

1759

I am now, I believe, fixed at this seat [Mount Vernon], with an agreeable partner [Martha Dandridge Custis] for life; and I hope to find more happiness in retirement, than I ever experienced amidst the wide and bustling world.

1765

The Stamp Act, imposed on the colonies by the Parliament of Great Britain, engrosses the conversation of the speculative part of the colonists, who look upon this unconstitutional method of taxation, as a direful attack upon their liberties, and loudly exclaim against the violation. What may be the result of this, and of some other (I think I may add ill-judged) measures, I will not undertake to determine; but this I may venture to affirm, that the advantage accruing to the mother-country will fall greatly short of the expectations of the ministry; for certain it is, that our whole substance already in a manner flows to Great Britain, and that whatsoever contributes to lessen our importations must be hurtful to our manufactures. The eyes of our people already begin to be opened; and they will perceive, that many luxuries, for which we lavish our substance in Great Britain, can well be dispensed with, while the neccessaries of life are mostly to be had within ourselves. This, consequently, will introduce frugality, and be a necessary incitement to industry. If Great Britain loads her manufactures with heavy taxes, will it not facilitate such results? They will not compel us, I think, to give our money for their exports, whether we will or not.

And I am certain, that none of their traders will part with them, without a valuable consideration. Where, then, is the utility of these restrictions?

As to the Stamp Act, regarded in a single view, one and the first bad consequence attending it, is, that our courts of judicature must inevitably be shut up; for it is impossible, or next to impossible, under our present circumstances, that the act of Parliament can be complied with, were we ever so willing, to enforce its execution. And, not to say (which alone would be sufficient) that we have not money to pay for the stamps, there are many other cogent reasons which prove, that it would be ineffectual. If a stop be put to our judicial proceedings, I fancy the merchants of Great Britain, trading to the colonies, will not be among the last to wish for a repeal of the act.

1766

The repeal of the Stamp Act, to whatever cause owing, ought much to be rejoiced at, for, had the Parliament of Great Britain resolved upon enforcing it, the consequences, I conceive, would have been more direful than is generally apprehended, both to the mother-country and her colonies. All, therefore, who were instrumental in procuring the repeal, are entitled to the thanks of every British subject, and have mine cordially.

1767

Those who were instrumental in procuring the repeal of the [Stamp A]ct, are, in my opinion, deservedly entitled to the thanks of the well-wishers to Britain and her colonies; and must reflect with pleasure, that, through their means, many scenes of confusion and distress have been prevented. Mine they accordingly have, and always shall have, for their opposition to any act of oppression; and that act could be looked upon in no other light, by every person who would view it in its proper colors.

1769

At a time, when our lordly masters in Great Britain will be satisfied with nothing less than the deprivation of American freedom, it seems highly necessary, that something should be done to avert the stroke, and maintain the liberty which we have derived from our ancestors. But the manner of doing it, to answer the purpose effectually, is the point in question. . . . That no man should scruple, or hesitate a moment, to use arms, in defence of so valuable a blessing, is clearly my opinion. . . . Arms should be the last resource, the dernier resort. . . . We have already, it is said, proved the inefficacy of addresses to the Throne, and remonstrances to Parliament. How far, then, their attention to our rights and privileges is to be awakened or alarmed, by starving their trade and manufactures, remains to be tried.

The Northern colonies are endeavoring to adopt this [non-importation] scheme. In my opinion, it is a good one, and must be attended with salutary effects, provided it can be carried pretty generally into execution. But to what extent it is practicable to do so, I will not take upon me to determine. That there will be a difficulty attending the execution of it every where, from clashing interests, and selfish, designing men, ever attentive to their own gains, and watchful of every turn that can assist their lucrative views, cannot be denied. In the tobacco colonies, where the trade is so diffused, and in a manner wholly conducted by factors for their principals at home, these difficulties are certainly enhanced, but, I think, not insurmountably increased, if the gentlemen, in their several counties, will be at some pains to explain matters to the people, and stimulate them to cordial agreements, to purchase none but certain enumerated articles, out of any of the stores, after a definite period, and neither import nor purchase any themselves. This, if it should not effectually withdraw the factors from their importations, would at least make them extremely cautious in doing it, as the prohibited goods could be vended to none but the non-associators, or those who would pay no regard to their association; both of whom ought to be stigmatized, and made the objects of public reproach. . . . The more I consider a scheme of this sort, the more ardently I wish success to it, because I think there are private as well as public advantages to result from it—the former certain, however precarious the latter may prove.

I have always thought, that, by virtue of the same power which assumes the right of taxation, the Parliament may attempt at least to restrain our manufacturers, especially those of a public nature, the same equity and justice prevailing in the one case as the other, it being no greater hardship to forbid my manufacturing, than it is to order me to buy goods loaded with duties, for the express purpose of raising a revenue. But as a measure of this sort would be an additional exertion of arbitrary power, we cannot be placed in a worse condition, I think, by putting it to the test. . . . That the colonies are considerably indebted to Great Britain, is a truth universally acknowledged. That many families are reduced, almost, if not quite, to penury, and want, by the low ebb of their fortunes, and that estates are daily selling for the discharge of debts, the public prints furnish too many melancholy proofs. That a [non-importation] scheme of this sort will contribute more effectually than any other that can be devised, to extricate the country from the distress it at present labors under, I most firmly believe, if it can be generally adopted.

I can see but one class of people, the merchants excepted, who will not, or ought not, to wish well to the [non-importation] scheme; namely, they who live genteelly and hospitably on clear estates. Such as these, were they not to consider the valuable object in view, and the good of others, might think it hard, to be curtailed in their living and enjoyments. As to the penurious man, he would thereby save his money and his credit, having the best plea for doing that, which before, perhaps, he had the most violent struggles to refrain from doing. The extravagant and expensive man has the same good plea, to retrench his expenses. He would be furnished with a pretext to live within bounds, and embrace it. Prudence dictated economy before, but his resolution was too weak to put it in practice. "How can I," says he, "who have lived in such and such a manner, change my method? I am ashamed to do it; and, besides, such an alteration in the system of my living, will create suspicions of the decay of my fortune; and such a thought the world must not harbor." He continues his course, till at last his estate comes to an end, a sale of it being the consequence of his perseverance in error. This, I am satisfied, is the way, that many, who have set out in the wrong track, have reasoned, till ruin has stared them in the face. And in respect to the needy man, he is only left in the same situation that he was found in; better, I may say, because, as he judges from comparison, his condition is amended, in proportion as it approaches nearer to those above him. I think the scheme a good one.

Having once or twice heard you speak highly of the New Jersey College, as if you had a desire of sending your son William there (who, I am told, is a youth fond of study and instruction, and disposed to a studious life, in following which he may not only promote his own happiness, but the future welfare of others), I should be glad, if you have no other objection to it than the expense, if you would send him to that college, as soon as convenient, and depend on me for twenty-five pounds a year for his support, so long as it may be necessary for the completion of his education. If I live to see the accomplishment of this term, the sum here stipulated shall be annually paid. And if I die in the mean time, this letter shall be obligatory upon my heirs or executors to do it according to the true intent and meaning hereof. No other return is expected or wished, for this offer, than that you will

accept it with the same freedom and good will with which
it is made, and that you may not even consider it in the light
of an obligation, or mention it as such; for, be assured, that
from me it will never be known.

1771

We do not wish to be the only people, who may taste the
sweets of an equal and good government. We look, with an
anxious eye, to the time, when happiness and tranquillity
shall prevail, and when all Europe shall be freed from com-
motions, tumults, and alarms.

1773

His [John Parke Custis'] youth, inexperience, and unripened
education are, and will be, insuperable obstacles, in my opinion, to the completion of the marriage. As his guardian, I
conceive it my indispensable duty, to endeavor to carry him
through a regular course of education (many branches of
which, I am sorry to add, he is totally deficient in), and to
guard his youth to a more advanced age, before an event, on
which his own peace and the happiness of another are to depend, takes place. Not that I have any doubt of the warmth
of his affections, nor, I hope I may add, any fears of a change
in them. But, at present, I do not conceive that he is capable
of bestowing that attention to the important consequences of
the married state, which is necessary to be given by those
who are about to enter into it, and, of course, I am unwilling
he should do it, till he is. If the affection which they have
avowed for each other, is fixed upon a solid basis, it will
receive no diminution in the course of two or three years, in
which time he may prosecute his studies, and thereby render
himself more deserving of the lady, and useful to society. If,
unfortunately, as they are both young, there should be an
abatement of affection, on either side, or both, it had better
precede, than follow, marriage. To postpone, is all I have in
view; for I shall recommend to the young gentleman, with

the warmth that becomes a man of honor (notwithstanding
he did not vouchsafe to consult either his mother or me, on
the occasion), to consider himself as much engaged to your
[Benedict Calvert's] daughter, as if the indissoluble knot
were tied; and, as the surest means of effecting this, to apply
himself closely to his studies (and in this advice, I flatter
myself, you will join me), by which he will, in a great measure, avoid those flirtations with other young ladies, that
may, by dividing the attention, contribute not a little to divide the affection.

1774

The voice of mankind is with me.

None of [the American Colonies] will ever submit to the loss
of those valuable rights and privileges, which are essential to
the happiness of every free State, without which, life, liberty,
and property are rendered totally insecure.

I would heartily join in an humble and dutiful petition to
the throne [protesting taxation], provided there was the most
distant hope of success. But have we not tried this, already?
Have we not addressed the Lords, and remonstrated to the
Commons? And to what end? Did they deign to look at
our petitions?

Does it not appear, as clear as the sun in meridian brightness,
that there is a regular, systematic plan formed, to fix the
right and practice of taxation upon us? Does not the uniform
conduct of Parliament, for some years past, confirm this? Do
not all the debates, especially those just brought to us, in the
House of Commons, on the side of government, expressly
declare, that America must be taxed in aid of British funds,
and that she has no longer resources within herself? Is there
any thing to be expected from petitioning, after this? Is not
the attack upon the liberty and property of the people of

Boston, before restitution of the loss to the India Company was demanded, a plain and self-evident proof of what they are aiming at? Do not the subsequent bills (now, I dare say, acts), for depriving Massachusetts Bay of its charter, and for transporting offenders into other colonies or to Great Britain, for trial, where it is impossible, from the nature of the thing, that justice can be obtained, convince us, that the Administration is determined to stick at nothing, to carry its point? Ought we not, then, to put our virtue and fortitude to the severest test? I think it folly, to attempt more than we can execute, as that will not only bring disgrace upon us, but weaken our cause; yet I think we may do more than is generally believed, in respect to the non-importation scheme. As to the withholding our remittances, that is another point, in which I own I have my doubts on several accounts, but principally on that of justice; for I think, whilst we are accusing others of injustice, we should be just, ourselves; and how this can be, whilst we owe a considerable debt, and refuse payment of it, to Great Britain, is to me inconceivable. Nothing but the last extremity, I think, can justify it. Whether this is now come, is the question.

What is it we are contending against? Is it against paying the duty of three pence per pound on tea, because burdensome? No; it is the right only, that we have all along disputed.

If, then, as the fact really is, it is against the right of taxation that we now do, and, as I before said, all along have contended, why should they suppose an exertion of this power would be less obnoxious now than formerly? And what reason have we to believe that they would make a second attempt, whilst the same sentiments fill the breast of every American, if they did not intend to enforce it, if possible?

I think, the Parliament of Great Britain have no more right to put their hands into my pocket, without my consent, than I have to put my hands into yours. This being already urged to them, in a firm but decent manner, by all the colonies, what reason is there to expect anything from their justice?

I should much distrust my own judgment, upon the occasion, if my nature did not recoil at the thought of submitting to [taxation] measures which I think subversive of every thing that I ought to hold dear and valuable, and did I not find, at the same time, that the voice of mankind is with me.

An innate spirit of freedom first told me, that the [taxation] measures which the Administration have, for some time, been, and now are, most violently pursuing, are opposed to every principle of natural justice; whilst much abler heads than my own have fully convinced me, that they are not only repugnant to natural right, but subversive of the laws and constitution of Great Britain itself, in the establishment of which some of the best blood in the kingdom has been spilt.

I believe, or at least I hope, that there is public virtue enough left among us, to deny ourselves every thing but the bare necessaries of life, to accomplish our end.

1775

Unhappy it is, to reflect, that a brother's sword has been sheathed in a brother's breast, and that the once happy and peaceful plains of America are either to be drenched with blood, or inhabited by slaves. Sad alternative! But can a virtuous man hesitate in his choice?

Be strict in your discipline. Require nothing unreasonable of your officers and men; but see, that whatever is required be punctually complied with. Reward and punish every man according to his merit, without partiality or prejudice. Hear his complaints. If they are well-founded, redress them; if otherwise, discourage them, in order to prevent frivolous ones. . . . Discourage vice, in every shape. Impress upon the mind of every man, from the first to the lowest, the importance of the cause, and what it is he is contending for.

Be easy and condescending in your deportment to your officers; but not too familiar, lest you subject yourself to a want of that respect, which is necessary to support a proper command.

The virtue, spirit, and union in the provinces, leave them nothing to fear, but the want of ammunition.

I cannot conceive [of a gift] more honorable, than that which flows from the uncorrupted choice of a brave and free people—the purest source and original fountain of all power.

Under God's providence, those who influence the counsels of America, and all other inhabitants of the United Colonies, at the hazard of their lives, are determined to hand down to posterity those just and invaluable privileges, which they received from their ancestors.

Perseverance and spirit have done wonders in all ages.

When we assumed the soldier, we did not lay aside the citizen. We shall most sincerely rejoice, with you, in that happy hour, when the establishment of American liberty, upon the most firm and solid foundations, shall enable us to return to our private stations, in the bosom of a free, peaceful, and happy country.

It has been represented to me, that the free Negroes who have served in this army, are very much dissatisfied at being discarded. As it is to be apprehended, that they may seek employ in the ministerial army, I have presumed to depart from this resolution respecting them, and have given license for their being enlisted.

The Continental Congress recommends my procuring, from the colonies of Rhode Island and Connecticut, a quantity of tow-cloth, for the purpose of making Indian or hunting-shirts for the men, many of whom are destitute of clothing. It is designed as a species of uniform, both cheap and convenient.

If Lord Chatham's son should be in Canada, and in any way should fall into your [Colonel Benedict Arnold's] power, you are enjoined to treat him with all possible deference and respect. You cannot err in paying too much honor to the son of so illustrious a character, and so true a friend to America. Any other prisoners who may fall into your hands, you may treat with as much humanity and kindness, as may be consistent with your own safety and the public interest.

Be very particular in restraining, not only your own troops, but the Indians, from all acts of cruelty and insult, which will disgrace the American arms, and irritate our fellow-subjects against us.

[Major] Andre has met his fate; and with that fortitude which was to be expected from an accomplished man and gallant officer.

The cause of virtue and liberty is confined to no continent or climate. It comprehends, within its capacious limits, the wise and good, however dispersed and separated in space and distance.

As the Congress desire it, I will enter upon the momentous

duty [of Commander-in-chief], and exert every power I possess, in their service, and for the support of the glorious cause.

I shall rely, confidently, on that Providence which has hitherto preserved and been bountiful to me.

As it has been a kind of destiny that has thrown me upon this service, I shall hope that my undertaking it is designed to answer some good purpose.

In exchanging the enjoyments of domestic life for the duties of my present honorable and arduous station [Commander-in-chief], I only emulate the virtue and public spirit of the whole province of Massachusetts Bay, which, with a firmness and patriotism without example in modern history, has sacrificed all the comforts of social and political life, in support of the rights of mankind, and the welfare of our common country. My highest ambition is, to be the happy instrument of vindicating those rights, and to see this devoted province again restored to peace, liberty, and safety.

Connecticut wants no Massachusetts man in her Corps. Massachusetts thinks there is no necessity for a Rhode Islander to be introduced amongst them; and New Hampshire says, it is very hard that her valuable and experienced officers (who are willing to serve), should be discarded, because her own regiments under the new establishment cannot provide for them.

It is my full intention, to devote my life and fortune, in the cause we are engaged in, if needful.

You may believe me, my dear Patsy [his name for Martha], when I assure you, in the most solemn manner, that, so far from seeking this appointment [Commander-in-chief], I have used every endeavor in my power to avoid it, not only from my unwillingness to part with you and the family, but from a consciousness of its being a trust too great for my capacity; and that I should enjoy more real happiness in one month with you at home, than I have the most distant prospect of finding abroad, if my stay were to be seven times seven years.

I shall rely, confidently, on that Providence, which has heretofore preserved and been bountiful to me, not doubting but that I shall return safe to you in the fall. I shall feel no pain, from the toil or the danger of the campaign. My unhappiness will flow from the uneasiness I know you [Martha] will feel from being left alone.

I shall hope, that my friends will visit, and endeavor to keep up the spirits of my wife, as much as they can; for my departure will, I know, be a cutting stroke upon her.

As life is always uncertain, and common prudence dictates to every man the necessity of settling his temporal concerns, whilst it is in his power, and whilst the mind is calm and undisturbed, I have, since I came to this place [Philadelphia] (for I had not time to do it before I left home), got Colonel Pendleton to draft a will for me by the directions I gave him; which will I now inclose. The provision made for you [Martha] in case of my death, will, I hope, be agreeable.

I can never think of promoting my convenience at the expense of a friend's interest and inclination.

The account which you [General Joseph Reed] have given of the sentiments of the people respecting my conduct, is extremely flattering. Pray God I may continue to deserve them, in the perplexed and intricate situation I stand in.

I have studiously avoided, in all letters intended for the public eye (I mean for that of Congress), every expression that could give pain or uneasiness. I shall observe the same rule, with respect to private letters, further than appears absolutely necessary for the elucidation of facts.

There is no restraining men's tongues or pens, when charged with a little vanity.

I cannot charge myself with incivility, or, what in my opinion is tantamount, ceremonious civility.

The General most earnestly requires and expects a due observance of those articles of war, established for the government of the army, which forbid profane cursing, swearing, and drunkenness.

As the contempt of the religion of a country, by ridiculing any of its ceremonies, or affronting its ministers or votaries, has ever been deeply resented, you [Benedict Arnold] are to be particularly careful, to restrain every officer and soldier from such imprudence and folly, and to punish every instance of it. On the other hand, as far as lies in your power, you are to protect and support the free exercise of the religion of the country, and the undisturbed enjoyment of the rights of conscience in religious matters, with your utmost influence and authority.

Avoid all disrespect of the religion of the country and its ceremonies. Prudence, policy, and a true Christian spirit, will lead us to look with compassion upon their errors, without insulting them [the Canadians]. While we are contending for our own liberty, we should be very cautious, not to violate the rights of conscience in others, ever considering, that God alone is the judge of the hearts of men, and to Him only, in this case, they are answerable.

Having heard that it is doubtful, whether the Reverend Mr. Leonard, from your colony, will have it in his power to continue as chaplain, I cannot but express some concern, as I think his departure will be a loss. His general conduct has been exemplary and praiseworthy; in discharging the duties of his office, active and industrious. He has discovered himself to be a warm and steady friend to his country, and taken great pains to animate the soldiers, and impress them with a knowledge of the important rights they are contending for. Upon the late desertion of the troops, he gave a sensible and judicious discourse, holding forth the necessity of courage and bravery, and, at the same time, of obedience and subordination to those in command. In justice to the merits of this gentleman, I thought it only right, to give you [Governor Trumbull] this testimonial of my opinion of him, and to mention him to you, as a person worthy of your esteem and that of the public.

The Reverend Mr. [Samuel] Kirkland, having been introduced to the honorable Congress, can need no particular recommendation from me. But as he now wishes to have the affairs of his mission and public employ put upon some suitable footing, I cannot but intimate my sense of the importance of his station, and the great advantages which may result to the United Colonies, from his situation being made respectable. All accounts agree, that much of the favorable disposition shown by the Indians, may be ascribed to his labor and influence. He has accompanied a chief of the Oneidas to this camp, which I have endeavored to make agreeable to him, both by civility, and some small presents. Mr. Kirkland also being in some necessity for money, to bear his traveling expenses, I have supplied him with thirty-two pounds lawful money.

I have long had it on my mind, to mention to Congress, that frequent applications have been made to me, respecting the chaplains' pay, which is too small to encourage men of abilities. Some of them, who have left their flocks, are obliged to pay the parson acting for them more than they receive. I need not point out the great utility of gentlemen, whose lives and conversation are unexceptionable, being employed for that service in this army. There are two ways of making it worth the attention of such. One is, an advancement of their pay; the other, that one chaplain be appointed to two regiments. This last, I think, may be done without inconvenience. I beg leave to recommend this matter to Congress, whose sentiments hereon I shall impatiently expect.

The General requires and expects of all officers and soldiers, not engaged on actual duty, a punctual attendance on divine service, to implore the blessings of Heaven upon the means used for our safety and defence.

Let the hospitality of the house, with respect to the poor, be kept up. Let no one go hungry away. If any of this kind of people should be in want of corn, supply their necessities, provided it does not encourage them in idleness. And I have no objection to your giving my money in charity, to the amount of forty or fifty pounds a year, when you think it well bestowed. What I mean by having no objection is, that it is my desire it should be done. You must consider, that neither myself nor my wife is now in the way to do these good offices. In all other respects, I recommend it to you, and have no doubt of your observing the greatest economy and frugality, as I suppose you know that I do not get a farthing for my services here, more than my expenses. It becomes necessary, therefore, for me to be saving at home.

Every exertion of my colleagues and myself will be extended, to the re-establishment of peace and harmony between the mother-country and the colonies.

1776

I am glad to hear, that the vessels for the Lakes are going on with such industry. Maintaining the superiority over the water, is certainly of infinite importance. I trust, neither courage nor activity will be wanting in those to whom the business is committed.

The hour is fast approaching, on which the honor and success of the army, and the safety of our bleeding country, will depend. . . . Remember, officers and soldiers, that you are freemen, fighting for the blessings of liberty; that slavery will be your portion and that of your posterity, if you do not acquit yourselves like men. Remember, how your courage and spirit have been despised and traduced by your cruel invaders; though they have found, by dear experience, at Boston, Charlestown, and other places, what a few brave men, contending in their own land and in the best of causes, can do against hirelings and mercenaries. . . . Be cool, but determined. Do not fire, at a distance; but wait for orders from your officers.

It is the General's express orders, that, if any man attempt to skulk, lie down, or retreat without orders, he be instantly shot down, as an example. He hopes, no such will be found in this army; but, on the contrary, that every one, for himself resolving to conquer or die, and trusting in the smiles of Heaven upon so just a cause, will behave with bravery and resolution. Those who are distinguished for their gallantry and good conduct, may depend upon being honorably noticed and suitably rewarded; and if this army will but emulate and imitate their brave countrymen in other parts of America, he has no doubt they will, by a glorious victory, save their country, and acquire to themselves immortal honor.

With hope and confidence, the General most earnestly exhorts every officer and soldier, to pay the utmost attention to his arms and health; to have the former in the best order for action, and, by cleanliness and care, to preserve the latter; to be exact in discipline, obedient to superiors, and vigilant on duty. With such preparation, and a suitable spirit, there can be no doubt but, by the blessing of Heaven, we shall repel our cruel invaders, preserve our country, and gain the greatest honor.

The General hopes, that every man's mind and arms will be prepared for action, and, when called to it, show our enemies and the whole world, that freemen, contending on their own land, are superior to any mercenaries on earth.

The General calls upon officers and men, to act up to the noble cause in which they are engaged, and to support the honor and liberties of their country.

Men who are not employed as mere hirelings, but have stepped forth in defence of every thing that is dear and valuable, not only to themselves but to posterity, should take uncommon pains to conduct themselves with the greatest propriety and good order, as their honor and reputation call loudly upon them to do it.

Men who are familiarized to danger, meet it without shrinking; whereas troops unused to service, often apprehend danger where no danger is.

Three things prompt men to a regular discharge of their duty, in time of action: natural bravery, hope of reward, and fear of punishment.

Natural bravery and hope of reward are common to the untutored and the disciplined soldier; but fear of punishment most obviously distinguishes the one from the other.

A coward, when taught to believe, that, if he breaks his ranks and abandons his colors, he will be punished with death by his own party, will take his chance against the enemy; but a man who thinks little of the one, and is fearful of the other, acts from present feelings, regardless of consequences.

Men just dragged from the tender scenes of domestic life, unaccustomed to the din of arms, totally unacquainted with every kind of military skill (which is followed by want of confidence in themselves, when opposed to troops regularly trained, disciplined, and appointed, superior in knowledge, and superior in arms), are timid, and ready to fly from their own shadows.

The usual time for exploits of this kind is a little before day; for which reason a vigilant officer is then more on the watch. I therefore recommend a midnight hour. A dark night, and even a rainy one, if you can find the way, will contribute to your success.

One circumstance in this important business ought to be cautiously guarded against; and that is, the soldiers and officers being too nearly on a level. Discipline and subordination add life and vigor to military movements. One person commanded yields but a reluctant obedience, to those who, he conceives, are undeservedly made his superiors. The degrees of rank are frequently transferred from civil life into the departments of the army. The true criterion to judge by, when past services do not enter into the competition, is, to consider whether the candidate for office has a just pretension to the character of a gentleman, a proper sense of honor, and some reputation to lose.

I have labored, ever since I have been in the service, to discourage all kinds of local attachments, and distinctions of country, denominating the whole by the greater name of "American"; but I have found it impossible to overcome prejudice. And under the new establishment, I conceive it best to stir up an emulation; in order to do which, would it not be better, for each State to furnish, though not to appoint, their own brigadiers?

I am sensible, a retreating army is encircled with difficulties; that declining an engagement subjects a general to reproach; and that the common cause may be affected, by the discouragement it may throw over the minds of many. Nor am I insensible of the contrary effects, if a brilliant stroke could be made, with any probability of success, especially after our loss on Long Island. But when the fate of America may be at stake on the issue, when the wisdom of cooler moments and experienced men have decided, that we should protract the war if possible, I cannot think it safe or wise to adopt a different system, when the season for action draws so near to a close.

On our side, the war should be defensive. It has ever been called a war of posts. We should, on all occasions, avoid a general action, and not put any thing to the risk, unless compelled by a necessity into which we ought never to be drawn.

Enjoin this upon the officers, and let them inculcate and press home upon the soldiery, the necessity of order and harmony among those who are embarked in one common cause, and mutually contending for all that freemen hold dear. I am persuaded, if the officers will but exert themselves, that these animosities and disorders will, in a great measure, subside; and nothing being more essential to the service, than that they should, I hope nothing on their part will be wanting, to effect it.

The General most earnestly entreats the officers and soldiers, to consider the consequences; that they can no way assist our enemies more effectually, than by making divisions among themselves; that the honor and success of the army, and the safety of our bleeding country, depend upon harmony and good agreement with each other; that the Provinces are all united to oppose the common enemy; and all distinctions sunk in the name of *an American*. To make this name honorable, and to preserve the liberty of our country, ought to be our only emulation; and he will be the best soldier and the best patriot, who contributes most to this glorious work, whatever his station, or from whatever part of the continent he may come. Let all distinctions of nations, countries, and provinces, therefore, be lost, in the generous contest, who shall behave with the most courage against the enemy, and the most kindness and good humor to each other. If there be any officers or soldiers so lost to virtue and a love of their country, as to continue in such practices, after this order, the General assures them, and is authorized by Congress to declare to the whole army, that such persons shall be severely punished, and dismissed from the service with disgrace.

The burning of houses, where the apparent good of the service is not promoted by it, and the pillaging of them, at all times and upon all occasions, are to be discountenanced, and punished with the utmost severity. It is to be hoped, that men who have property of their own, and a regard for the rights of others, will shudder at the thought of rendering any man's situation, to whose protection he has come, more insufferable than his open and avowed enemy would make it; when, by duty and every rule of humanity, they ought to aid, and not oppress, the distressed, in their habitations. The distinction between a well-regulated army and a mob, is the good order and discipline of the former, and the licentious and disorderly behavior of the latter.

The General does not admit of any pretence for plundering; whether it be Tory property, taken beyond the lines, or not, it is equally a breach of orders, and to be punished, in the officer who gives [the] order, or the soldier.

They [the Army] were, at first, a band of undisciplined husbandmen; but it is, under God, to their bravery, and attention to their duty, that I am indebted, for that success, which has procured me the only reward I wish to receive, the affection and esteem of my countrymen.

I am persuaded, and as fully convinced as I am of any one fact that has happened, that our liberties must of necessity be hazarded, if not entirely lost, if their defence is left to any but a permanent standing Army: I mean, one to exist during the war.

It becomes evident to me, that, as this contest is not likely to be the work of a day, as the war must be carried on systematically (and to do it you must have good officers), there are no other possible means to obtain them, but by establishing an army upon a permanent footing, and, giving the officers good pay. This will induce gentlemen, and men of character, to engage; and, till the bulk of the officers is composed of such persons as are actuated by principles of honor and a spirit of enterprise, you have little to expect from them. They ought to have such allowances, as will enable them to live like, and support the character of, gentlemen, and not be driven, by a scanty pittance, to the low and dirty arts which many of them practise, to filch from the public more than the difference of pay would amount to, upon an ample allowance. Besides, something is due to the man who puts his life in your hands, hazards his health, and forsakes the sweets of domestic enjoyment. Why a Captain, in the Continental Service, should receive no more than five shillings currency per day, for performing the same duties that an officer of the same rank in the British service receives ten shillings sterling for, I never could conceive; especially when the latter is provided with every necessary he requires, upon the best terms, and the former can scarce procure them, at any rate. There is nothing that gives a man consequence, and renders him fit to command, like a support that renders him independent of every body but the State he serves.

In my opinion, it is neither consistent with the rules of war, nor politic [to enlist prisoners of war]. Nor can I think, that, because our enemies have committed an unjustifiable action, by enticing, and, in some instances, intimidating, our men into their service, we ought to follow their example.

It is not my wish, that severity should be exercised, toward any whom the fortune of war has thrown, or shall throw, into our hands [as prisoners of war]. On the contrary, it is my desire, that the utmost humanity should be shown them. I am convinced, that the latter has been the prevailing line of conduct to prisoners. There have been instances, in which some have met with less indulgence than could be wished, owing to refractory conduct and a disregard of parole. If there are other instances, in which a strict regard to propriety has not been observed, they have not come to my knowledge.

When I consider, that the city of New York will, in all human probability, very soon be the scene of a bloody conflict; I cannot but view the great numbers of women, children, and infirm persons, remaining in it, with the most melancholy concern. It would relieve me from great anxiety, if your honorable body [the New York Convention] would immediately deliberate upon it, and form and execute some plan, for their removal and relief; in which I will co-operate and assist, to the utmost of my power.

The case of our sick is worthy of much consideration. Their number, by the returns, forms at least one fourth of the army. Policy and humanity require, that they should be made as comfortable as possible.

When the councils of the British nation had formed a plan for enslaving America, and depriving her sons of their most sacred and invaluable privileges, against the clearest remonstrances of the Constitution, of justice, and of truth, and, to execute their schemes, had appealed to the sword, I esteemed it my duty to take a part in the contest, and more especially on account of my being called thereto by the unsolicited suffrages of the representatives of a free people; wishing for no other reward, than that arising from a conscientious discharge of the important trust, and that my services might contribute to the establishment of freedom and peace, upon a permanent foundation, and merit the applause of my countrymen, and every virtuous citizen.

With respect to myself, I have never entertained an idea of an accommodation, since I heard of the measures which were adopted in consequence of the Bunker's Hill fight. The King's speech has confirmed the sentiments I entertained upon the news of that affair; and if every man was of my mind, the ministers of Great Britain should know in a few words, upon what issue the cause should be put. I would not be deceived by artful declarations or specious pretences; nor would I be amused by unmeaning propositions; but in open, undisguised, and manly terms, proclaim our wrongs and our resolutions to be redressed. I would tell them, that we had borne much; that we had long and ardently sought for reconciliation upon honorable terms; that it had been denied us; that all our attempts after peace had proved abortive, and had been grossly misrepresented; that we had done every thing that could be expected from the best of subjects; that the spirit of freedom beat too high in us to submit to slavery; and that, if nothing else would satisfy a tyrant and his diabolical ministry, we were determined to shake off all connections with a State so unjust and unnatural. This I would tell them, not under covert, but in words as clear as the sun in his meridian brightness.

While I have the honor to remain in the service of the United States, I shall obey, to the utmost of my power and to the best of my abilities, all orders of Congress, with a scrupulous exactness.

I have ever thought, and am still of opinion, that no terms of accommodation will be offered by the British ministry, but such as cannot be accepted by America. We have nothing to depend upon, but the protection of a kind Providence, and unanimity among ourselves.

Nothing but *disunion* can hurt our cause. This will ruin it, if great prudence, temper, and moderation are not mixed in our counsels, and made the governing principles of the contending parties.

To be in any degree instrumental, in procuring to my American brethren a restitution of their just rights and privileges, will constitute my chief happiness.

The hints you [General Joseph Reed] have communicated from time to time, not only deserve, but do most sincerely and cordially meet with my thanks. You cannot render a more acceptable service, nor, in my estimation, give a more convincing proof of your friendship, than by a free, open, and undisguised account of every matter relative to myself or conduct. I can bear to hear of imputed or real errors. The man who wishes to stand well in the opinion of others, must do this, because he is thereby enabled to correct his faults, or remove prejudices which are imbibed against him. For this reason, I shall thank you for giving me the opinions of the world, upon such points as you know me to be interested in. As I have but one capital object in view, I could wish to make my conduct coincide with the wishes of mankind, as far as I can consistently. I mean, without departing from that great line of duty, which, though hid under a cloud for some time, from a peculiarity of circumstances, may nevertheless bear a scrutiny.

Nothing would give me more real satisfaction, than to know the sentiments which are entertained of me by the public, whether they be favorable or otherwise. . . . The man who wishes to steer clear of shelves and rocks, must know where they lie. . . . I know (but to declare it, unless to a friend, may be an argument of vanity), the integrity of my own heart. I know the unhappy predicament I stand in. I know, that much is expected of me. I know, that without men, without arms, without any thing fit for the accommodation of a soldier, little is to be done; and (which is mortifying), I know, that I cannot stand justified to the world, without exposing my own weakness, and injuring the cause by declaring my wants, which I am determined not to do, further than unavoidable necessity brings every man acquainted with them. If, under these circumstances, I am able to keep above water, as it were, in the esteem of mankind, I shall feel myself happy. But if, from the unknown peculiarity of my circumstances, I suffer in the opinion of the world, I shall not think you [General Joseph Reed] take the freedom of a friend, if you conceal the reflections that may be cast upon my conduct. My own situation feels so irksome to me at times, that if I did not consult the public good more than my own tranquillity, I should, long ere this, have put every thing to the cast of a die.

Gaming, of every kind, is expressly forbidden, as being the foundation of evil, and the cause of many a brave and gallant officer's ruin. Games of exercise, for amusement, may not only be permitted, but encouraged.

I shall always be happy to manifest my disinclination to any undue severities, towards those whom the fortunes of war may chance to throw into my hands.

To trust altogether in the justice of our cause, without our own utmost exertions, would be tempting Providence.

Liberty, honor, and safety, are all at stake; and, I trust, Providence will smile upon our efforts, and establish us, once more, the inhabitants of a free and happy country.

The honor and safety of our bleeding country, and every other motive that can influence the brave and heroic patriot, call loudly upon us, to acquit ourselves with resolution. In short, we must now determine, to be enslaved or free. If we make freedom our choice, we must obtain it, by the blessing of Heaven on our united and vigorous efforts.

The General hopes and trusts, that every officer and man will endeavor to live and act, as becomes *a Christian soldier*, defending the dearest rights and liberties of his country.

The honorable Continental Congress having been pleased to allow a chaplain to each regiment, with the pay of thirty-three dollars and one-third per month, the Colonels or commanding officers of each regiment are directed to procure chaplains accordingly; persons of good characters and exemplary lives; and to see, that all inferior officers and soldiers pay them a suitable respect. The blessing and protection of Heaven are, at all times, necessary; but, especially so, in times of public distress and danger.

The Continental Congress having ordered Friday, the 17th instant [May, 1776], to be observed as a day of fasting, humiliation, and prayer, humbly to supplicate the mercy of Almighty God, that it would please him to pardon our manifold sins and transgressions, and to prosper the arms of the United Colonies, and finally establish the peace and freedom of America, upon a solid and lasting foundation; the General commands all officers and soldiers, to pay strict obedience to the orders of the Continental Congress, that, by their unfeigned and pious observance of their religious duties, they may incline the Lord and Giver of Victory, to prosper our arms.

That the troops may have an opportunity of attending public worship, as well as to take some rest after the great fatigue they have gone through, the General, in future, excuses them from fatigue duty, on Sundays, except at the shipyards, or on special occasions, until further orders.

When the order issued, for embarking the troops in Boston, no electric shock, no sudden flash of lightning, in a word, not even the last trump, could have struck them [the Royalists] with greater consternation. They were at their wit's end; and, conscious of their black ingratitude, chose to commit themselves to the mercy of the winds and waves, in a tempestuous season, rather than meet their offended countrymen; and with this declaration I am told they have done it—that if they could have thought, that the most abject submission would have procured peace for them, they would have humbled themselves in the dust, and kissed the rod that should be held out for chastisement. Unhappy wretches! Deluded mortals! Would it not be good to grant a generous amnesty, and conquer these people, by a *generous forgiveness?*

1777

Several of our officers have broken their paroles, and stolen away. This practice, ignominious to themselves, dishonorable to the service, and injurious to the officers of sentiment and delicacy, who remain behind to experience the rigors of resentment and distrust on their account, cannot be tolerated, whatever be the pretence.

I confess, I have felt myself greatly embarrassed, with respect to a vigorous exercise of military power. An ill-placed humanity, perhaps, and a reluctance to give distress, may have restrained me too far; but these were not all. I have been well aware of the present jealousy of military power; and that this has been considered as an evil much to be apprehended, even by the best and most sensible among us. Under this idea, I have been cautious, and wished to avoid, as much as possible, any act that might increase it.

The people at large are governed much by custom. To acts of legislation or civil authority they have ever been taught to yield a willing obedience, without reasoning about their propriety; on those of military power, whether immediate, or derived originally from another source, they have ever looked with a jealous and suspicious eye.

It is our business to give protection and support to the poor distressed inhabitants, not to multiply and increase their calamities.

Our troops being already formed and fully officered, and the number of foreign gentlemen, already commissioned, and continually arriving with fresh applications, throw such obstacles in the way of any future appointments, that every new arrival is only a new source of embarrassment to Congress and myself, and of disappointment and chagrin to the gentlemen who come over. Had there been only a few to provide for, we might have found employment for them, in a way advantageous to the service, and honorable to themselves. But, as they have come over in such crowds, we either must not employ them, or we must do it at the expense of one half of the officers of the army, which would be attended with the most ruinous effects, and could not fail to occasion a general discontent. It is impossible, for these gentlemen to raise men for themselves. And it would be equally impolitic and unjust, to displace others, who have been at all the trouble and at considerable expense in raising corps, in order to give them the command. Even when vacancies happen, there are always those who have a right of succession by seniority, and who are as tenacious of this right as of the places they actually hold; and in this they are justified by the common principles and practice of all armies, and by resolutions of Congress. Were these vacancies to be filled by the foreign officers, it would not only cause the resignation of those who expect to succeed to them, but it would serve to disgust others, both through friendship to them, and from an apprehension of their being liable to the same inconvenience themselves. This, by rendering the hope of preferment precarious, would remove one of the principal springs of emulation, absolutely necessary to be upheld in the army.

To place them [foreign officers] at the head of companies, over officers that have been at great trouble, pains, and expense, in raising men, would be both unmilitary and unjust. It will be well, in all cases of foreign and indeed other applications, that the consequences which granting them will involve, should be maturely weighed, and taken in every point of view.

I want to form a company for my Guard. In doing this, I wish to be extremely cautious, because it is more than probable, that, in the course of the campaign, my baggage, papers, and other matters of great public import, may be committed to the sole care of these men. This being premised, in order to impress you with proper attention in the choice, I have to request, that you will immediately furnish me with four men of your regiment; and, as it is my further wish, that this company should look well and be nearly of a size, I desire that none of the men may exceed in stature five feet ten inches, nor fall short of five feet nine inches; sober, young, active, and well made. When I recommend care in your choice, I would be understood to mean, men of good character in the regiment, that possess the pride of appearing clean and soldier-like. I am satisfied, that there can be no absolute security for the fidelity of this class of people, but yet I think it most likely to be found, in those who have family connections in the country. You will therefore send me none but natives, and men of some property, if you have them. I must insist, that, in making this choice, you give no intimation of my preference of natives, as I do not want to create any invidious distinction between them and the foreigners.

I advised the Council of Safety, to separate the Hessian prisoners from their officers, and canton them in the German counties. If proper pains are taken, to convince them, how preferable the situation of their countrymen, the inhabitants of those counties, is to theirs, I think they may be sent back in the spring, so fraught with a love of liberty and property too, that they may create a disgust to the service, among the remainder of the foreign troops, and widen that breach which is already opened between them and the British. One thing

I must remark in favor of the Hessians; and that is, that our people who have been prisoners, generally agree, that they received much kinder treatment from them, than from the British officers and soldiers.

Unnecessary severity, and every species of insult [toward prisoners of war], I despise; and, I trust, none will ever have just reason to censure me, in this respect.

It occurs to me, that if you [Colonel Daniel Morgan] were to dress a company or two of true woodsmen, in Indian style, and let them make the attack, with screaming and yelling, as the Indians do, it would have very good consequences.

Trifling punctilios [of honor] should have no influence upon a man's conduct, in such a case and at such a time as this. . . . If smaller matters do not yield to greater; if trifles light as air, in comparison with what we are contending for, can withdraw or withhold gentlemen from service, when our all is at stake, and a single cast of a die may turn the tables; what are we to expect? It is not a common contest we are engaged in. Every thing valuable to us depends upon the success of it; and the success, upon a steady and vigorous exertion.

We should never despair. Our situation has before been un-promising, and has changed for the better; so, I trust, it will again. If new difficulties arise, we must only put forth new exertions, and proportion our efforts to the exigency of the times.

It is a happy circumstance, that such an animation prevails among the people. I would wish to let it operate and draw as many as possible together, which will be a great discour-agement to the enemy, by showing that the popular spirit is at such a height; and at the same time it will inspire the people themselves with confidence in their own strength, by discovering to every individual the zeal and spirit of his neighbors. But after they have been collected a few days, I would have the greater part of them dismissed, as not being immediately wanted, desiring them to hold themselves in readiness for any sudden call, and concerting signals with them, at the appearance of which they are to fly to arms.

Lenity will operate with greater force, in some instances, than rigor. It is, therefore, my first wish, to have my whole conduct distinguished by it.

In behalf of the United States, by virtue of the powers committed to me by Congress, I grant full liberty to all such as prefer the interest and protection of Great Britain [the Tories], to the freedom and happiness of their country, forthwith to withdraw themselves and families within the enemy's lines.

With respect to the Tory, who was executed by your [Brigadier-General Deborre's] order; though his crime was heinous enough to deserve the fate he met with, and though I am convinced you acted in the affair with good intention, yet I cannot but wish it had not happened. In the first place, it was a matter that did not come within the jurisdiction of martial law; and, therefore, the whole proceeding was irregular and illegal, and will have a tendency to excite discontent, jealousy, and murmurs, among the people. In the second place, if the trial could properly have been made by a Court-Martial, as the Division you command is only a detachment from the army, and you cannot have been considered as in a separate department, there is none of our articles of war, that will justify your inflicting capital punishment, even on a soldier, much less on a citizen. I mention these things, for your future government; as what is past cannot be recalled. The temper of the Americans, and the principles on which the present contest turns, will not countenance proceedings of this nature.

Retaliation is certainly just, and sometimes necessary, even where attended with the severest penalties. But, when the evils which may and must result from it, exceed those intended to be redressed, prudence and policy require, that it should be avoided.

I flatter myself, that a superintending Providence is ordering every thing for the best, and that, in due time, all will end well. That it may be so, and soon, is my most fervent wish.

I most devoutly congratulate my country, and every well-wisher to the cause, on this signal stroke of Providence [General Burgoyne's defeat].

Should Providence be pleased to crown our arms, in the course of this campaign, with one more fortunate stroke, I think we shall have no great cause for anxiety, respecting the future designs of Britain. I trust all will be well, in His good time.

Harassed as we are by unrelenting persecution, obliged by every tie to repel violence by force, urged by self-preservation to exert the strength which Providence has given us to defend our natural rights against the aggressor, we appeal to the hearts of all mankind for the justice of our cause. Its event we leave to Him who speaks the fate of nations, in humble confidence that, as His omniscient eye taketh note even of the sparrow that falleth to the ground, so He will not withdraw His countenance from a people who humbly *array themselves under his banner*, in defence of the noblest principles with which He has adorned humanity.

As a chaplain is allowed to each regiment, see that the men regularly attend divine worship.

The situation of the army frequently not admitting of the regular performance of divine service on Sundays, the chaplains of the army are forthwith to meet together, and agree on some method of performing it at other times, which method they will make known to the Commander-in-chief.

Tomorrow [December 18, 1777] being the day set apart by the honorable Congress for public thanksgiving and praise; and duty calling us devoutly to express our grateful acknowledgments to God, for the manifold blessings He has granted us, the General directs, that the army remain in its present quarters, and that the chaplains perform divine service with their several corps and brigades; and earnestly exhorts all officers and soldiers, whose absence is not indispensably necessary, to attend with reverence the solemnities of the day.

I am extremely sorry for the death of Mrs. Putnam, and sympathize with you [General Putnam] on the occasion. Remembering, that all must die, and that she had lived to an honorable age, I hope you will bear the misfortune, with that fortitude and complacency of mind, that become a man and a Christian.

1778

It appears as clear to me as ever the sun did in its meridian brightness, that America never stood in more eminent need of the wise, patriotic, and spirited exertions of her sons, than at this period. And if it is not a sufficient cause for general lamentation, my misconception of the matter impresses it too strongly upon me, that the States, separately, are too much engaged in their local concerns, and have too many of their ablest men withdrawn from the General Council, for the good of the common weal.

I think, our political system may be compared to the mechanism of a clock, and we should derive a lesson from it; for it answers no good purpose to keep the smaller wheels in order, if the greater one, which is the support and prime mover of the whole, is neglected.

As there can be no harm in a pious wish for the good of one's country, I shall offer it as mine, that each State would not only choose, but absolutely compel, their ablest men to attend Congress, and that they would instruct them to go into a thorough investigation of the causes, that have produced so many disagreeable effects, in the army and country; in a word, that public abuses should be corrected.

It is devoutly to be wished, that faction was at an end; and that those to whom every thing dear and valuable is intrusted, would lay aside party views, and return to first principles. Happy, happy, thrice happy country, if such were the government of it! But, alas, we are not to expect, that the path is to be strowed with flowers. That Great Good Being who rules the universe, has disposed matters otherwise, and for wise purposes, I am persuaded.

I am under more apprehensions on account of our own dissensions, than of the efforts of the enemy.

I should suppose, no individual State can, or ought to, deprive an officer of rank derived from the States at large; and that it will not be improper for Congress to prohibit the exercise of such a power. The principle and practice are what I cannot reconcile to my ideas of propriety.

In a free and republican government, you cannot restrain the voice of the multitude. Every man will speak as he thinks, or, more properly, without thinking, and consequently will judge of effects without attending to their causes.

Great Britain understood herself perfectly well, in this dispute, but did not comprehend America. She meant (and this was) clearly and explicitly declared, to drive America into rebellion, that her own purposes might be more fully answered by it. But take this along with it, that this plan originated in a firm belief, founded on misinformation, that no effectual opposition would or could be made. They little dreamt of what has happened, and are disappointed in their views. Does not every act of administration, from the Tea Act to the present session of Parliament, declare this, in plain and self-evident characters? Had the Commissioners any powers to treat with America? If they meant peace, would Lord Howe have been detained in England five months after passing the act? Would the powers of these Commissioners have been confined to mere acts of grace, upon condition of absolute submission? No! surely no! They meant to drive us into what they termed rebellion, that they might be furnished with a pretext to disarm, and then strip us of the rights and privileges of Englishmen and citizens. If they were actuated by the principles of justice, why did they refuse, indignantly, to accede to the terms which were humbly supplicated before hostilities commenced, and this country was deluged in blood; and now make their principal officers, and even the Commissioners themselves, say, that these terms are just and reasonable; nay, that more will be granted than we have yet asked, if we will relinquish our claim to independency? What name does such conduct as this deserve? And what punishment is there in store for the men who have distressed millions, involved thousands in ruin, and plunged numberless families in inextricable woe? Could that which is just and reasonable now, have been unjust four years ago? They must either be wantonly wicked and cruel, or (which is only another mode of describing the same thing), under false colors are now endeavoring to deceive the great body of the people, by industriously propagating a belief, that Great Britain is willing to offer *any* terms, and that we will accept *none*; thereby hoping to poison and disaffect the minds of those who wish for peace, and to create feuds and dissensions among ourselves. In a word, having less dependence now in their arms than their arts, they are practising such low and dirty tricks, that men of sentiment and honor must blush at their fall. Among other maneuvers in this way, they are forging letters, and publishing them as intercepted ones of mine, to prove that I am an enemy to the present measures, and have been led into them, step by step, still hoping that Congress would recede from their claims.

To discerning men, nothing can be more evident, than that a peace, on the principles of dependence, however limited, after what has happened, would be, to the last degree, dishonorable and ruinous.

It really seems to me, from a comprehensive view of things, that a period is fast approaching, big with events of the most interesting importance; when the counsels we pursue, and the part we act, may lead decisively to liberty or to slavery. Under this idea, I cannot but regret that inactivity, that inattention, that want of something, which unhappily I have but too often experienced in our public affairs. I wish, that our representation in Congress was full from every State, and that it was formed on the first abilities among us. Whether we continue to prosecute the war, or proceed to negotiate, the wisdom of America in council cannot be too great. Our situation will be truly delicate. To enter into a negotiation too hastily, or to reject it altogether, may be attended with consequences equally fatal. The wishes of the people, seldom founded on deep disquisitions, or resulting from other reasonings than their present feelings, may not entirely accord with our true policy and interest. If they do not, to observe a proper line of conduct for promoting the one, and avoiding offence to the other, will be a work of great difficulty.

Nothing short of independence, it appears to me, can possibly do. A peace on other terms would, if I may be allowed the expression, be a peace of war. The injuries we have received from the British nation were so unprovoked, and have been so great and so many, that they can never be forgotten. Besides the feuds, the jealousies, the animosities, that would ever attend a union with them; besides the importance, the advantages, which we should derive from an unrestricted commerce; our fidelity as a people, our gratitude, our character as men, are opposed to a coalition with them as subjects, but in case of the last extremity. Were we easily to accede to terms of dependence, no nation, upon future occasions, let the oppressions of Britain be ever so flagrant and unjust, would interpose for our relief; or, at most, they would do it with a cautious reluctance, and upon conditions, most probably, that would be hard, if not dishonorable to us. France, by her supplies, has saved us from the yoke, thus far; and a wise and virtuous perseverance would, and I trust will, free us entirely.

I do not like to add to the number of our national obligations. I would wish, as much as possible, to avoid giving a foreign power new claims of merit for services performed to the United States, and would ask no assistance that is not indispensable.

If the Spaniards . . . would unite their fleet to that of France, together they would soon humble the pride of haughty Britain, and no longer suffer her to reign sovereign of the seas, and claim the privilege of giving laws to the main.

The opening is now fair; and God grant, that they [the British] may embrace the opportunity of bidding an eternal adieu to our (once quit of them) happy land. If the Spaniards would but join their fleets to those of France, and commence hostilities, my doubts would subside; without it, I fear the British navy has it too much in its power to counteract the schemes of France.

I very much fear, that we, taking it for granted, that we have nothing more to do, because France has acknowledged our independency, and formed an alliance with us, shall relapse into a state of supineness and false security.

I think it more than probable, from the situation of affairs in Europe, that the enemy will receive no considerable, if any, reinforcements. But suppose they should not, their remaining force, if well directed, is far from being contemptible. In the desperate state of British affairs, it is worth a desperate attempt to extricate themselves; and a blow at our main army, if successful, would have a wonderful effect upon the minds of a number of people, still wishing to embrace the present terms, or indeed any terms offered by Great Britain.

I am well aware, that appearances ought to be upheld, and that we should avoid, as much as possible, recognizing, by any public act, the depreciation of our currency. But, I conceive, this end would be answered, as far as might be necessary, by stipulating, that all money payments should be made in gold and silver, being the common medium of commerce among nations, at the rate of four shillings and sixpence for a Spanish milled dollar; by fixing the price of rations on an equitable scale relatively to our respective circumstances; and by providing for the payment of what we owe, by sending in provision and selling it at their market.

It is our interest and truest policy, as far as it may be practicable, on all occasions, to give a currency and value to that which is to be the medium of our internal commerce, and the support of the war.

Can we carry on the war much longer? Certainly not, unless some measures can be devised and speedily executed, to restore the credit of our currency, restrain extortion, and punish forestallers. Unless these can be effected, what funds can stand the present expenses of the army? And what officers can bear the weight of prices that every necessary article has got to? A rat, in the shape of a horse, is not to be bought at this time, for less than two hundred pounds; nor a saddle, under thirty or forty; boots, twenty; and shoes and other articles, in like proportion. How is it possible, therefore, for officers to stand this, without an increase of pay? And how is it possible to advance their pay, when flour is selling, at different places, from five to fifteen pounds per hundred weight, hay from ten to thirty pounds per ton, and beef and other essentials, in this proportion? To make and extort money, in every shape that can be devised, and at the same time to decry its value, seems to have become a mere business, and an epidemical disease, calling for the interposition of every good man and body of men.

It is much to be lamented, that each State, long ere this, has not hunted them [currency speculators] down, as pests to society, and the greatest enemies we have to the happiness of America. I would to God, that some one of the most atrocious in each State, was hung upon a gallows, five times as high as the one prepared by Haman. No punishment, in my opinion, is too great for the man who can build his greatness upon his country's ruin.

If any officers leave their posts before they are regularly drawn off and relieved, or shall, directly or indirectly, cause any soldier to do the like, they shall be punished, as far as martial law will extend, without fear or mitigation.

A refusal to obey the commands of a superior officer, especially where the duty required was evidently calculated for the good of the service, cannot be justified, without involving consequences subversive of all military discipline. A precedent, manifestly too dangerous, would be established, of dispensing with orders, and subordination would be at an end, if men's ideas were not rectified in a case of this kind, and such notice taken, as has been, on my part.

The custom, which many officers have, of speaking freely of things, and reprobating measures, which, upon investigation, may be found to be unavoidable, is never productive of good, but often of very mischievous consequences.

I am well convinced, that the enemy, long ere this, are perfectly well satisfied, that the possession of our towns, while we have an army in the field, will avail them little. It involves us in difficulty, but does not by any means ensure conquest to them. They well know, that it is our arms, not defenceless towns, which they have to subdue, before they can arrive at the haven of their wishes; and that, till this is accomplished, the superstructure they have been endeavoring to raise, will, "like the baseless fabric of a vision," fall to nothing.

The Army and the country have a mutual dependence upon each other; and it is of the last importance, that their several duties should be so regulated and enforced, as to produce, not only the greatest harmony and good understanding, but the truest happiness and comfort to each.

It will never answer, to procure supplies of clothing or provisions, by coercive measures. Such procedures may give a momentary relief; but, if repeated, will prove of the most pernicious consequence.

No order of men in the Thirteen States have paid a more sacred regard to the proceedings of Congress, than *the Army*. Without arrogance, or the smallest deviation from truth, it may be said, that no history, now extant, can furnish an instance of an army's suffering such uncommon hardships as ours has done, and bearing them with the same patience and fortitude. To see men, without clothes to cover their nakedness, without blankets to lie on, without shoes (for the want of which their marches might be traced by the blood of their feet), and almost as often without provisions as with them, marching through the frost and snow, and at Christmas taking up their winter-quarters, within a day's march of the enemy; without a house or hut to cover them, till they could be built; and submitting, without a murmur; is a proof of patience and obedience, which, in my opinion, can scarce be paralleled.

The commonly received opinion, under proper limitations is certainly true, that standing armies are dangerous to the State. The prejudices, in other countries, have only gone to them in time of peace; and these, from their not having, in general cases, any of the ties, the concerns, or interests, of citizens, or any other dependence than what flowed from their military employ; in short, from their being mercenary hirelings. It is our policy, to be prejudiced against them, in time of war; though they are citizens, having all the ties and interests of citizens, and, in most cases, property totally unconnected with the military line. If we would pursue a right system of policy, in my opinion, there should be none of these distinctions. We should all, Congress and Army, be considered as one people, embarked in one cause, in one interest; acting on the same principle, and to the same end.

I have declared, and I now repeat it, that I never will receive the smallest benefit from the half-pay establishment. But, as a man who fights under the weight of a proscription, and as a citizen who wishes to see the liberty of his country established upon a permanent foundation, and whose property depends upon the success of our arms, I am deeply interested. Upon the single ground of economy and public saving, I will maintain the utility of it; for I have not the least doubt, that, until officers consider their commissions in an honorable and interested point of view, and are afraid to endanger them by negligence and inattention, no order, regularity, or care, either of the men or public property, will prevail. To prove this, I need only refer to the general courts-martial, which are constantly sitting for the trial of them, and the number who have been cashiered within the last three months, for misconduct of different kinds.

The difference between our service and that of the enemy, is very striking. With us, from the peculiar, unhappy situation of things, the officer, a few instances excepted, must break in upon his private fortune, for present support, without a prospect of future relief. With them, even companies are esteemed so honorable and so valuable, that they have sold for, of late, from fifteen to twenty-two hundred pounds sterling. And I am credibly informed, that four thousand guineas have been given for a troop of dragoons.

We must take the passions of men, as nature has given them, and those principles, as a guide, which are generally the rule of action. I do not mean to exclude, altogether, the idea of patriotism. I know it exists. And I know it has done much, in the present contest. But I will venture to assert, that a great and lasting war can never be supported, on this principle. It must be aided, by a prospect of interest, or some reward. For the time, it may, of itself, push men to action, to bear much, to encounter difficulties; but it will not endure, unassisted by interest.

The lavish manner in which rank has hitherto been bestowed on these [foreign] gentlemen, will certainly be productive of one or the other of these two evils; either to make it despicable in the eyes of Europe, or become the means of pouring them in upon us like a torrent, and adding to our present burden. But it is neither the expense nor trouble of them that I most dread. There is an evil, more extensive in its nature, and fatal in its consequences, to be apprehended; and that is, the driving of all our own officers out of the service, and throwing not only our army, but our military councils, entirely into the hands of foreigners.

The officers on whom you most depend for the defence of this cause, distinguished by length of service, their connections, property, and, in behalf of many, I may add, military merit, will not submit, much if any longer, to the unnatural promotion of men over them, who have nothing more than a little plausibility, unbounded pride and ambition, and a perseverance in application not to be resisted but by uncommon firmness, to support their pretensions; men, who, in the first instance, tell you they wish for nothing more than the honor of serving in so glorious a cause as volunteers, the next day solicit rank without pay, the day following want money advanced to them, and in the course of a week want further promotion, and are not satisfied with any thing you can do for them. When I speak of officers not submitting to these appointments, let me be understood to mean, that they have no more doubt of their right to resign, when they think themselves aggrieved, than they have of a power in Congress to appoint. Both being granted, then, the expediency and the policy of the measure remain to be considered; and whether it is consistent with justice and prudence, to promote these military fortune-hunters, at the hazard of the army.

They [foreign officers] may be divided into three classes; namely, 1. Mere adventurers, without recommendation, or recommended by persons who do not know how else to dispose of or provide for them; 2. Men of great ambition, who would sacrifice every thing to promote their own personal glory; or, 3. Mere spies, who are sent here to obtain a thorough knowledge of our situation and circumstances, in the execution of which, I am persuaded, some of them are faithful emissaries, as I do not believe a single matter escapes unnoticed, or unadvised at a foreign court.

The ambition of these men [foreign officers] . . . is unbounded. And the singular instances of rank which have been conferred upon them, in but too many cases, have occasioned great dissatisfaction and general complaint. The feelings of our own officers have been hurt by it, and their ardor and love for the service greatly damped. Should a like proceeding still be practised, it is not easy to say what extensive murmurings and consequences may ensue. I will still further add, that we have already a full proportion of foreign officers in our general councils; and, should their number be increased, it may happen, upon many occasions, that their voices may equal, if not exceed, the rest.

I trust you think me so much of a citizen of the world, as to believe I am not easily warped or led away, by attachments merely local or American. Yet I confess I am not entirely without them; nor does it appear to me, that they are unwarrantable, if confined within proper limits. Fewer promotions, in the foreign line, would have been productive of more harmony, and made our warfare more agreeable to all parties. The frequency of them is a source of jealousy, and of disunion. We have many, very many deserving officers, who are not opposed to merit wheresoever it is found, nor insensible to the advantages derived from a long service in an experienced army, nor to the principles of policy. Where any of these principles mark the way to rank, I am persuaded, they yield a becoming and willing acquiescence; but where they are not the basis, they feel severely.

It gives me inexpressible concern, to have repeated information from the best authority, that the Committees of the different towns and districts, in your State [Massachusetts], hire deserters from [the British A]rmy, and employ them as substitutes, to excuse the personal service of the inhabitants. I need not enlarge upon the danger of substituting, as soldiers, men who have given a glaring proof of a treacherous disposition, and who are bound to us by no motives of attachment, instead of citizens, in whom the ties of country, kindred, and sometimes property, are so many securities for their fidelity. The evils with which this measure is pregnant, are obvious; and of such a serious nature as make it necessary, not only to stop the further progress of it, but likewise to apply a retrospective remedy, and, if possible, to annul it, so far as it has been carried into effect.

I never gave any encouragement to enlisting deserters. I have ever found them of the greatest injury to the service, by debauching our men; and I had therefore given positive orders, to all recruiting officers, not to enlist them upon any terms. The Congress have since made an express resolve against it; and also against enlisting prisoners.

Your [General Burgoyne's] indulgent opinion of my character, and the polite terms in which you are pleased to express it, are peculiarly flattering. I take pleasure in the opportunity you have afforded me, of assuring you, that, far from suffering the views of national opposition to be embittered and debased by personal animosity, I am ever ready to do justice to the merit of the man and soldier, and to esteem where esteem is due, however the idea of a public enemy may interpose. You will not think it the language of unmeaning ceremony, if I add, that sentiments of personal respect, in the present instance, are reciprocal. Viewing you in the light of an officer, contending against what I conceive to be the rights of my country, the reverses of fortune you experienced in the field cannot be unacceptable to me; but, abstracted from considerations of national advantage, I can sincerely sympathize with your feelings as a soldier, the unavoidable difficulties of whose situation forbade his success; and as a man, whose lot combines the calamity of ill health, the anxieties of captivity, and the painful sensibility for reputation exposed, where he most values it, to assaults of malice and detraction.

The conduct of Lieutenant-Colonel Brooks, in detaining John Miller [a deserter], requires neither palliation nor excuse. I justify and approve it. There is nothing so sacred, in the character of the King's trumpeter, even when sanctified by a flag, as to alter the nature of things, or to consecrate infidelity and guilt. He was a deserter from the army under my command; and whatever you [General Howe] have been pleased to assert to the contrary, it is the practice of war and nations, to seize and punish deserters, wherever they may be found. His appearing in the character he did, was an aggravation of his offence, inasmuch as it added insolence to infamy. My scrupulous regard to the privileges of flags, and a desire to avoid every thing that partiality itself might affect to consider as a violation of them, induced me to send orders for the release of the trumpeter, before the receipt of your letter; the improper and peremptory terms of which, had it not been too late, would have strongly operated to produce a less compromising conduct. I intended, at the same time, to assure you, and I wish it to be remembered, that my indulgence, in this instance, is not to be drawn into precedent; and that, should any deserters from the American army hereafter have the daring folly to approach our lines, in a similar manner, they will fall victims to their rashness and presumption.

Were an opinion once to be established (and the enemy and their emissaries know very well how to inculcate it, if they are furnished with a plausible pretext), that we designedly avoided an exchange [of prisoners of war], it would be a cause of dissatisfaction and disgust, to the country and to the army, of resentment and desperation to our officers and soldiers. To say nothing of the importance of not hazarding our national character but upon the most solid grounds, especially in our embryo state, from the influence it may have on our affairs abroad, it may not be a little dangerous to beget in the minds of our countrymen a suspicion, that we do not pay the strictest observance to the maxims of honor and good faith.

Imputations of this nature would have a tendency to unnerve our operations, by diminishing that respect and confidence, which are essential to be placed in those who are at the head of affairs, either in the civil or military line. This, added to the prospect of hopeless captivity, would be a great discouragement to the service. The ill consequences of both would be immense, by increasing the causes of discontent in the army, which are already too numerous, and many of which are, in a great measure, unavoidable; by fortifying that unwillingness, which already appears too great, toward entering into the service, and of course impeding the progress both of drafting and recruiting; by dejecting the courage of the soldiery, from an apprehension of the horrors of captivity; and finally, by reducing those, whose lot it is to drink the bitter cup, to a despair, which can only find relief, by renouncing their attachment, and engaging with their captors. The effects have already been experienced in part, from the obstacles that have lain in the way of [prisoner of war] exchanges. But if these obstacles were once to seem the result of system, they would become ten-fold. Nothing has operated more disagreeably upon the minds of the militia, than the fear of captivity, on the footing on which it has hitherto stood. What would be their reasonings, if it should be thought to stand upon a worse?

I am convinced, that more mischief has been done by the British officers who have been prisoners, than by any other set of people. During their captivity, they have made connections in the country, they have confirmed the disaffected, converted many ignorant people, and frightened the lukewarm and timid, by their stories of the power of Britain. I hope a general exchange is not far off, by which means we shall get rid of all that sort of people; and I am convinced, that we had better, in future, send all officers in upon parole, than keep them among us.

By a resolve of Congress, I am empowered to employ a body of four hundred Indians, if they can be procured upon proper terms. Divesting them of the savage customs exercised in their wars against each other, I think they may be made of excellent use, as scouts and light troops, mixed with our own parties. I propose to raise about one half the number, among the southern, and the remainder, among the northern, Indians. The Oneidas have manifested the strongest attachment to us, throughout this dispute, and therefore, I suppose, if any can be procured, they will be most numerous. Their missionary, Mr. Kirkland, seemed to have an uncommon ascendency over that tribe; and I should therefore be glad to see him accompany them.

The Emancipation of Canada, is an object which Congress have much at heart.

It [the liberation of Canada] is a measure much to be wished; and, I believe, would not be displeasing to the body of the people.

While Carleton [the Royal Governor of Quebec] remains among them, with three or four thousand troops, they dare not avow their sentiments, if really they are favorable, without a strong support.

If that country [Canada] is not with us; from its proximity to the Eastern States, its intercourse and connection with the numerous tribes of western Indians, its communication with them by water, and other local advantages, it will be at least a troublesome, if not a dangerous, neighbor to us; and ought, at all events, to be in the same interest and politics as the other States.

The question of the Canadian expedition, in the form in which it now stands, appears to me one of the most interesting that has hitherto agitated our national deliberations.

I have one objection to it [the expedition to Canada], which is, in my estimation, insurmountable, and alarms all my feelings for the true and permanent interests of my country. This is, the introduction of a large body of French troops into Canada, and putting them in possession of the capital of that province, attached to them by all the ties of blood, habits, manners, religion, and former connection of government. I fear, this would be too great a temptation to be resisted, by any power actuated by the common maxims of national policy.

Let us realize, for a moment, the striking advantages France would derive from the possession of Canada; the acquisition of an extensive territory, abounding in supplies, for the use of her islands; the opening a vast source of the most beneficial commerce with the Indian nations, which she might then monopolize; the having ports of her own, on this continent, independent of the precarious good-will of an ally; the engrossing of the whole trade of Newfoundland, whenever she pleased, the finest nursery of seamen in the world; the security afforded to her islands; and, finally, the facility of [owning] and controlling these States, the natural and most formidable rival of every maritime power in Europe. Canada would be a solid acquisition to France, on all these accounts, and because of the numerous inhabitants, subjects to her by inclination, who would aid in preserving it under her power, against the attempts of every other.

France, acknowledged, for some time past, the most powerful monarchy in Europe, by land; able now to dispute the empire of the sea with Great Britain, and, if joined by Spain, I may say, certainly superior; possessed of New Orleans on our right, Canada on our left; and seconded by the numerous tribes of Indians in our rear, from one extremity to the other, a people so generally friendly to her, and whom she knows so well how to conciliate, would, it is much to be apprehended, have it in her power, to give law to these States.

Suppose, that, when the five thousand French troops (and, under the idea of that number, twice as many might be introduced), had entered the city of Quebec, they should declare an intention to hold Canada, as a pledge and surety for the debts due to France from the United States, or, under other specious pretences, hold the place till they can find a bone of contention, and, in the mean while, should excite the Canadians to engage in supporting their pretences and claims, what should we be able to say, with only four or five thousand men to carry on the dispute? It may be supposed, that France would not choose to renounce our friendship, by a step of this kind, as the consequence would be reunion with

England, on some terms or other, and the loss of what she had acquired in so violent and unjustifiable a manner, with all the advantages of an alliance with us. This, in my opinion, is too slender a security against the measure, to be relied on.

If France and Spain should unite, and obtain a decided superiority by sea, a reunion with England would avail us very little, and might be set at defiance. . . . France, with a numerous army at command, might throw in what number of land forces she thought proper, to support her pretensions. And England, without men, without money, and inferior on her favorite element, could give no effectual aid to oppose them. Resentment, reproaches, and submission, seem to be all that would be left to us.

Men are very apt to run into extremes. Hatred to England may carry some into an excess of confidence in France, especially when motives of gratitude are thrown into the scale. Men of this description, would be unwilling to suppose France capable of acting an ungenerous part.

I am heartily disposed to entertain the most favorable sentiments of our new ally, and to cherish them in others, to a reasonable degree. But it is a maxim, founded on the universal experience of mankind, that no nation is to be trusted, further than it is bound by its interest; and no prudent statesman or politician will venture to depart from it. In our circumstances, we ought to be particularly cautious; for we have not yet attained sufficient vigor and maturity, to recover from the shock of any false step into which we may unwarily fall.

Nothing can give me more pleasure, than to patronize the essays of genius, and a laudable cultivation of the arts and sciences, which had begun to flourish in so eminent a degree, before the hand of oppression was stretched over our devoted country. I shall esteem myself happy, if a poem which has employed the labor of years, will derive any advantage, or bear more weight in the world, by making its appearance under a dedication to me.

The friendship which I ever professed and felt for you [the Reverend Bryan Fairfax, who later became the eighth and last Lord Fairfax], met with no diminution, from the difference of our political sentiments. I know the rectitude of my own intentions; and, believing in the sincerity of yours, lamented, though I did not condemn your renunciation of the creed I had adopted. Nor do I think any person or power ought to do it, whilst your conduct is not opposed to the general interest of the people, and the measures they are pursuing. Our actions, depending upon ourselves, may be controlled, while the powers of thinking, originating in higher causes, cannot always be moulded to our wishes.

There is nothing I have more at heart, than to discharge the great duties incumbent on me, with the strictest attention to the ease and convenience of the people.

The soldiers have two or three times been, days together, without provisions; and once, six days without any thing of the meat kind. Could the poor horses tell their tale, it would be in a strain still more lamentable, as numbers have actually died from pure want.

The generous spirit of chivalry, exploded by the rest of the world, finds a refuge, my dear friend [Lafayette, planning to challenge Lord Carlisle to a duel], in the sensibility of your nation only. But it is in vain to cherish it, unless you can find antagonists to support it; and, however well adapted it might have been to the times in which it existed, in our days, it is to be feared, that your opponent, sheltering himself behind modern opinions, and under his present public character of Commissioner, would turn a virtue of such ancient date into ridicule. Besides, supposing his Lordship accepted your terms, experience has proved, that chance is often as much concerned, in deciding these matters, as bravery; and always more than the justice of the cause. I would not, therefore, have your life, by the remotest possibility, exposed, when it may be reserved for so many greater occasions. His Excellency, the Admiral [Count D'Estaing], I flatter myself, will be in sentiment with me; and, as soon as he can spare you, will send you to head-quarters, where I anticipate the pleasure of seeing you.

The coincidence between your Excellency's [Count D'Estaing's] sentiments, respecting the Marquis de Lafayette's challenge, communicated in the letter with which you honored me on the 20th [October, 1778], and those which I expressed to him, on the same subject, is peculiarly flattering to me. I am happy to find, that my disapprobation of this measure was founded on the same arguments, which, in your Excellency's hands, acquire new force and persuasion. . . . I omitted neither serious reasoning nor pleasantry, to divert him from a scheme in which he could be so easily foiled, without having any credit given to him, by his antagonist, for his generosity and sensibility. He intimated, that your Excellency did not discountenance it, and that he had pledged himself, to the principal officers of the French squadron, to carry it into execution. . . . The charms of vindicating the honor of his country were irresistible. But, besides, he had, in a manner, committed himself, and could not decently retract. I continued to lay my friendly commands upon him, to renounce his project; but I was well assured, that, if he determined to persevere in it, neither authority nor vigilance would be of any avail, to prevent his message to Lord Carlisle. . . . Though his ardor overreached my advice and influence, I console myself with the reflection, that his Lordship will not accept the challenge; and that, while our friend gains all the applause which is due to him, for wishing to become the champion of his country, he will be secure from the possibility of such dangers as my fears would otherwise create for him, by those powerful barriers which shelter his Lordship, and which, I am persuaded, he will not, in the present instance, violate.

It is our duty, to make the best of our misfortunes, and not suffer passion to interfere with our interest and the public good.

To stand well in the good opinion of my countrymen, constitutes my chief happiness, and will be my best support under the perplexities and difficulties of my present station.

No expression of personal politeness to me, can be acceptable, accompanied by reflections on the representatives of a free people, under whose authority I have the honor to act. The delicacy I have observed, in refraining from every thing offensive in this way, entitled me to expect a similar treatment from you. I have not indulged myself in invectives against the present rulers of Great Britain, in the course of our correspondence; nor will I, even now, avail myself of so fruitful a theme.

As peace and retirement are my ultimate aim, and the most pleasing and flattering wish of my soul, every thing advancive of this end contributes to my satisfaction, however difficult and inconvenient in the attainment, and will reconcile any place and all circumstances to my feelings, whilst I remain in service.

I feel every thing that hurts the sensibility of a gentleman.

Ingratitude, I hope, will never constitute a part of my character, nor find a place in my bosom.

The thinking part of mankind do not form their judgment from events; and their equity will ever attach equal glory, to those actions which deserve success, and those which have been crowned with it. It is in the trying circumstances to which your Excellency [Count D'Estaing] has been exposed, that the virtues of a great mind are displayed in their brightest lustre, and that a General's character is better known, than in the moment of victory. It was yours, by every title that can give it; and the adverse element which robbed you of your prize, can never deprive you of the glory due to you. Though your success has not been equal to your expectations, yet you have the satisfaction of reflecting, that you have rendered essential services to the common cause.

It is a severe tax, which all must pay, who are called to eminent stations of trust, not only to be held up, as conspicuous marks to the enmity of the public adversaries of their country, but to the malice of secret traitors, and the envious intrigues of false friends and factions.

Among individuals, the most certain way to make a man your enemy, is to tell him you esteem him such. So, with public bodies.

It is the nature of man, to be displeased with every thing that disappoints a favorite hope or flattering project; and it is the folly of too many of them, to condemn without investigating circumstances.

Why should I expect to be exempt from censure, the unfailing lot of an elevated station? Merit and talents, which I cannot pretend to rival, have ever been subject to it.

Americans have the feelings of sympathy, as well as other men. A series of injuries may exhaust their patience; and it is natural, that the sufferings of their friends in captivity should, at length, irritate them into resentment, and to acts of retaliation.

The determinations of Providence are always wise, often inscrutable; and, though its decrees appear to bear hard upon us at times, they are nevertheless meant for gracious purposes.

Providence has heretofore taken us up, when all other means and hope seemed to be departing from us. In this I will confide.

General Lee, having command of the van of the army, consisting of full five thousand chosen men, was ordered to begin the attack next morning, so soon as the enemy began to march; to be supported by me; but, strange to tell! when he came up with the enemy, a retreat commenced; whether by his order, or from other causes, is now a subject of inquiry, and consequently improper to be descanted upon, as he is in arrest, and a court-martial is sitting for his trial. A retreat, however, was the fact, be the causes what they may; and the disorder arising from it would have proved fatal to the army, had not that bountiful Providence, which has never failed us in the hour of distress, enabled me to form a regiment or two (of those that were retreating), in the face of the enemy, and under their fire; by which means, a stand was made long enough (the place through which the enemy were pursuing being narrow), to form the troops, that were advancing, upon an advantageous piece of ground, in the rear. Here our affairs took a favorable turn.

It having pleased the Almighty Ruler of the Universe, to defend the cause of the United American States, and finally to raise us up a powerful friend among the princes of the earth, to establish our liberty and independency upon a lasting foundation; it becomes us to set apart a day, for gratefully acknowledging the divine goodness, and celebrating the important event, which we owe to His divine interposition. The several brigades are to be assembled for this purpose, at nine o'clock to-morrow morning [May 7, 1778], when their chaplains will communicate the intelligence contained in the postscript of the *Pennsylvania Gazette* of the second instant, and offer up Thanksgiving, and deliver a discourse suitable to the occasion. At half-past ten o'clock, a cannon will be fired, which is to be the signal for the men to be under arms; the brigade inspectors will then inspect their dress and arms, and form the battalions according to the instructions given them, and announce to the commanding officers of the brigade, that the battalions are formed. The commanders of brigades will then appoint the field-officers to the battalions, after which each battalion will be ordered to load and ground their arms. At half-past eleven, a second cannon will be fired, as a signal for the march, upon which the several brigades will begin their march, by wheeling to the right by platoons, and proceed, by the nearest way, to the left of their ground by the new position; this will be pointed out, by the brigade inspectors. A third signal will be given, on which there will be a discharge of thirteen cannon; after which, a running fire of the infantry will begin on the right of Woodford's, and continue throughout the front line; it will then be taken upon the left of the second line, and continue to the right. Upon a signal given, the whole army will huzza, *long live the King of France*; the artillery then begins again, and fires thirteen rounds; this will be succeeded by a second general discharge of musketry, in a running fire, and huzza, *long live the friendly European powers.* The last discharge of thirteen pieces of artillery, will be given, followed by a general running fire, and huzza, *the American states.*

It will ever be the first wish of my heart, to inculcate a due sense of the dependence we ought to place in that All-Wise and Powerful Being, on whom alone our success depends.

It is not a little pleasing, nor less wonderful, to contemplate, that, after two years' manoeuvering, and undergoing the strangest vicissitudes that, perhaps, ever attended any one contest since the creation, both armies are brought back to the very point they set out from, and that the offending party at the beginning, is now reduced to the use of spade and pickaxe, for defence. The hand of Providence has been so conspicuous in this, that he must be worse than an infidel, that lacks faith, and more than wicked, that has not gratitude enough to acknowledge his obligations.

My friends may believe me sincere, in my professions of attachment to them, whilst Providence has a just claim to my humble and grateful thanks for its protection and direction of me, through the many difficult and intricate scenes which this contest has produced; and for its constant interposition in our behalf, when the clouds were heaviest, and seemed ready to burst upon us. To paint the distresses and perilous situation of the army, in the course of last winter, for want of clothes, provisions, and almost every other necessary essential to the well-being, I may say, existence, of an army, would require more time and an abler pen than mine; nor, since our prospects have so miraculously brightened, shall I attempt it, or even bear it in remembrance, further than as a memento of what is due to the Great Author of all the care and good that have been extended, in relieving us in difficulties and distress.

Ours is a kind of struggle, designed, I dare say, by Providence, to try the patience, fortitude, and virtue of men. None, therefore, who are engaged in it, will suffer himself, I trust, to sink under difficulties, or be discouraged by hardships. General McIntosh is only experiencing, upon a small scale, what I have had an ample share of, upon a large one; and must, as I have been obliged to do in a variety of instances, yield to necessity; that is, to use the vulgar phrase, "shape his coat according to his cloth"; or, in other words, if he cannot do what he wishes, he must do what he can.

1779

Our cause is noble. It is the cause of mankind; and the danger to it is to be apprehended from ourselves. Shall we slumber and sleep, then, while we should be punishing those miscreants who have brought these troubles upon us, and who are aiming to continue us in them; while we should be striving to fill our battalions, and devising ways and means to raise the value of the currency, on the credit of which every thing depends? I hope not.

I trust, the goodness of the cause, and the exertions of the people, and Divine protection, will give us that honorable peace for which we are contending.

Unanimity in our councils, disinterestedness in our pursuits, and steady perseverance in our national duty, are the only means to avoid misfortunes. If they come upon us after these, we shall have the consolation of knowing, that we have done our best. The rest is with God.

The hour is certainly come, when party disputes and dissensions should subside; when every man, especially those in office, should, with hand and heart, pull the same way, and with their whole strength.

Providence has done, and, I am persuaded, is disposed to do, a great deal for us; but we are not to forget the fable of Jupiter and the countryman.

The conduct of England in rejecting the mediation of Spain, is more strongly tinctured with insanity, than any thing she has done in the course of the contest, unless she be sure of very powerful aid from some of the northern powers.

The glorious success of [French Admiral] Count d'Estaing in the West Indies, at the same time that it adds dominion to France, and fresh lustre to her arms, is a source of new and unexpected misfortune to our tender and generous parent, and must serve to convince her of the folly of quitting the substance, in pursuit of the shadow; and, as there is no experience equal to that which is bought, I trust she will have the superabundance of this kind of knowledge, and be convinced, as I hope all the world and every tyrant in it will be, that the best and only safe road to honor, glory, and true dignity, is justice.

It is well worthy the ambition of a patriot statesman, at this juncture, to endeavor to pacify party differences, to give fresh vigor to the springs of government, to inspire the people with confidence, and, above all, to restore the credit of our currency.

Every other effort is in vain, unless something can be done to restore its credit. Congress, the States individually, and individuals of each State, should exert themselves to effect this great end. It is the only hope, the last resource, of the enemy. Nothing but our want of public virtue can induce a continuance of the war. Let them once see, that, as it is in our power, so it is our inclination and intention, to overcome this difficulty; and the idea of conquest, or hope of bringing us back to a state of dependence, will vanish like the morning dew. They can no more encounter this kind of opposition, than the hoar-frost can withstand the rays of the all-cheering sun. The liberty and safety of this country depend upon it.

The way is plain; the means are in our power. But it is virtue alone that can effect it.

Nothing, I am convinced, but the depreciation of our currency, has fed the hopes of the enemy, and kept the British arms in America to this day. They do not scruple to declare this themselves; and add, that we shall be our own conquerors. Cannot our common country, America, possess virtue enough to disappoint them? Is the paltry consideration of a little pelf to individuals, to be placed in competition with the essential rights and liberties of the present generation, and of millions yet unborn? Shall a few designing men, for their own aggrandizement, and to gratify their own avarice, overset the goodly fabric we have been rearing at the expense of so much time, blood, and treasure? Shall we at last become the victims of our own lust of gain? Forbid it, Heaven! Forbid it, all and every State of the Union, by enacting and enforcing efficacious laws for checking the growth of these monstrous evils, and restoring matters, in some degree, to the state they were in at the commencement of the war!

Let vigorous measures be adopted; not to limit the prices of articles, for this, I believe, is inconsistent with the very nature of things, and impracticable in itself; but to punish speculators, forestallers, and extortioners, and, above all, to sink the money by heavy taxes, to promote public and private economy, and encourage manufactures. Measures of this sort, gone heartily into by the several States, would strike at once at the root of all our evils, and give the coup de grace to the British hope of subjugating this continent, either by their arms or their arts. The former, they acknowledge, are unequal to the task; the latter, I am sure, will be so, if we are not lost to every thing that is good and virtuous.

Single men in the night will be more likely to ascertain facts, than the best glasses in the day.

A conduct of this kind [the breaking of parole] demands that every measure should he taken, to deprive them of the benefit of their delinquency, and to compel their return.

It is a fundamental maxim in our military trials, that the Judge-Advocate prosecutes, in the name and in behalf of the United States.

In order to preserve harmony and correspondence in the system of the army, there must be a controlling power, to which the several departments are to refer. If any department is suffered to act independently of the officer commanding, collisions of orders and confusion of affairs will be the inevitable consequences.

All that the common soldiery of any country can expect, is food and clothing. The pay given, in other armies, is little more than nominal; very low in the first instance, and subject to a variety of deductions, that reduce it to nothing. This is the case with the British troops; though, I believe, they receive more than those of any other State in Europe. The idea of maintaining the families of the soldiers, at the public expense, is peculiar to us, and is incompatible with the finances of the government. Our troops have been uniformly better fed than any others. They are, at this time, very well clad, and probably will continue to be so. While this is the case, they will have no just cause of complaint.

When men are employed, and have the incitements of military honor to encourage their ambition and pride, they will cheerfully submit to inconveniences, which, in a state of tranquillity, would appear insupportable.

The policy of our arming slaves is, in my opinion a moot point, unless the enemy set the example.

A disposition to peace, in these people [the Indians], can only be ascribed to the apprehension of danger, and would last no longer than till it was over, and an opportunity offered to resume their hostility, with safety and success. This makes it necessary, that we should endeavor to punish them severely, for what has passed, and by an example of rigor, intimidate them for the future.

My ideas of contending with the Indians, has been uniformly the same. I am clear in the opinion, that the cheapest (though this may also be attended with great expense), and most effectual mode of opposing them, where they can make incursions upon us, is to carry the war into their own country; for, supported on the one hand, by the British, and enriching themselves with the spoils of our people, they have every thing to gain, and nothing to lose, while we act on the defensive; whereas, the direct reverse would be the consequence of an offensive war on our part.

I suggest, as general rules that ought to govern our operations, to make, rather than receive, attacks, attended with as much impetuosity, shouting, and noise, as possible; and to make the troops act, in as loose and dispersed a way as is consistent with a proper degree of government, concert, and mutual support. It should be previously impressed upon the minds of the men, whenever they have an opportunity, to rush on, with the war-whoop and fixed bayonet. Nothing will disconcert and terrify the Indians, more than this.

Great caution is necessary, to guard against the snares which their [Indians'] treachery may hold out. Hostages are the only kind of security to be depended on.

I have uniformly made the departure of the enemy from these States, an essential condition to the invasion of Canada.

Your [the Marquis de Lafayette's] forward zeal in the cause of liberty; your singular attachment to this infant world; your ardent and persevering efforts, not only in America, but since your return to France, to serve the United States; your polite attentions to Americans, and your strict and uniform friendship for me, have ripened the first impressions of esteem and attachment which I imbibed for you, into such perfect love and gratitude, as neither time nor absence can impair.

A slender acquaintance with the world, must convince every man, that actions, not words, are the true criterion of the attachment of friends; and that the most liberal professions of good-will are very far from being the surest marks of it. I should be happy, if my own experience had afforded fewer examples of the little dependence to be placed upon them.

Conscious, that it is the aim of my actions to promote the public good, and that no part of my conduct is influenced by personal enmity to individuals, I cannot be insensible to the artifices, employed by some men, to prejudice me in the public esteem.

Our conflict is not likely to cease, so soon as every good man would wish. The measure of iniquity is not yet filled; and, unless we can return a little more to first principles, and act a little more upon patriotic grounds, I do not know when it will be, or what may be the issue of our contest.

Whatever services I have rendered to my country, in its general approbation I have received an ample reward.

Few men have virtue to withstand the highest bidder.

I hate deception, even where the imagination only is concerned.

I shall never attempt to palliate my own foibles by exposing the error of another.

To stand well in the estimation of one's country, is a happiness that no rational creature can be insensible of.

So far as they [slanders] are aimed at me personally, it is a misconception, if it be supposed I feel the venom of the darts. I have a consolation, which proves an antidote against their utmost malignity, rendering my mind, in the retirement I have long panted after, perfectly tranquil.

To persevere in one's duty and be silent, is the best answer to calumny.

Severe examples should, in my judgment, be made of those who were forgiven former offences, and are again in arms against us.

1780

The politics of princes are fluctuating; often, more guided by a particular prejudice, whim, or interest, than by extensive views of policy.

The change or caprice of a single minister, is capable of altering the whole system of Europe.

Commerce and industry are the best mines of a nation.

The favorable disposition of Spain, the promised succor from France, the combined force in the West Indies, the declaration of Russia (acceded to by other governments of Europe, and humiliating to the naval pride and power of Great Britain), the superiority of France and Spain, by sea in Europe, the Irish claims and English disturbances, formed in the aggregate an opinion in my breast, which is not very susceptible of peaceful dreams, that the hour of deliverance was not far distant; since, however unwilling Great Britain might be, to yield the point, it would not be in her power to continue the contest. But, alas! these prospects, flattering as they were, have proved delusory, and I see nothing before us but accumulating distress.

I see one head gradually changing into thirteen. I see one army branching into thirteen; and, instead of looking up to Congress, as the supreme controlling power of the United States, considering themselves as dependent on their respective States. In a word, I see the power of Congress declining too fast for the consequence and respect which are due to them, as the great representative body of America; and I am fearful of the consequences.

In general, I esteem it a good maxim, that the best way to preserve the confidence of the people durably, is to promote their true interest. There are particular exigencies, when this maxim has peculiar force. When any great object is in view, the popular mind is roused into expectation, and prepared to make sacrifices both of ease and property. If those to whom the people confide the management of their affairs do not call them to make these sacrifices, and the object is not attained, or they are involved in the reproach of not having contributed as much as they ought to have done towards it, they will be mortified at the disappointment; they will feel the censure; and their resentment will rise against those who, with sufficient authority, have omitted to do what their interest and their honor required.

The satisfaction I have, in any successes that attend us, even in the alleviation of misfortunes, is always allayed by a fear that it will lull us into security. Supineness, and a disposition to flatter ourselves, seem to make parts of our national character. When we receive a check, and are not quite undone, we are apt to fancy we have gained a victory; and, when we do gain any little advantage, we imagine it decisive, and expect the war immediately at an end. The history of the war is a history of false hopes, and temporary expedients. Would to God, they were to end here.

In modern wars, the longest purse must chiefly determine the event. I fear, that of the enemy will be found to be so. Though the Government is deeply in debt, the Nation is rich; and their riches afford a fund which will not be easily exhausted. Besides, their system of public credit is such, that it is capable of greater exertions than any other nation. Speculatists have been, a long time, foretelling Great Britain's downfall; but we see no symptoms of the catastrophe being very near. I am persuaded, it will at least last out the war; and then, in the opinion of many of the best politicians, it will be a national advantage. If the war should terminate successfully, the Crown will have acquired such influence and power, that it may attempt any thing; and a bankruptcy will probably be made the ladder to climb to absolute authority. The Administration may, perhaps, wish to drive matters to this issue. At any rate, they will not be restrained, by an apprehension of it, from forcing the resources of the State. It will promote their present purposes, on which their all is at stake; and it may pave the way to triumph more effectually over the Constitution. With this disposition, I have no doubt that ample means will be found, to prosecute the war with the greatest vigor.

The maritime resources of Great Britain are more substantial and real, than those of France and Spain united. Her commerce is more extensive than that of both her rivals; and it is an axiom, that the nation which has the most extensive commerce, will always have the most powerful marine.

There is nothing so likely to produce peace, as to be well prepared to meet the enemy.

The Court of France has made a glorious effort for our deliverance, and if we disappoint her intentions, by our supineness, we must become contemptible in the eyes of all mankind. Nor can we, after that, venture to confide, that our allies will persist in an attempt to establish what, it will appear, we want inclination or ability to assist them in.

The present instance of the friendship of the Court of France, is attended with every circumstance that can render it important and agreeable, that can interest our gratitude, or fix our emulation.

In the midst of a war, the nature and difficulties of which are peculiar and uncommon, I cannot flatter myself in any way to recompense the sacrifices they have made, but by giving them [French officers] such opportunities in the field of glory, as will enable them to display that gallantry, and those talents, which we shall always be happy to acknowledge with applause.

Regular troops alone are equal to the exigencies of modern war, as well for defence as offence; and, whenever a substitute [of militia troops] is attempted, it must prove illusory and ruinous.

No militia will ever acquire the habits necessary to resist a regular force. Even those nearest to the seat of war, are only valuable as light troops, to be scattered in the woods, and harass rather than do serious injury to the enemy.

The firmness requisite for the real business of fighting, is only to be attained, by a constant course of discipline and service. I have never yet been witness to a single instance, that can justify a different opinion; and it is most earnestly to be wished, that the liberties of America may no longer be trusted, in any material degree, to so precarious a dependence.

Extensive powers, not exercised as far as was necessary, have, I believe, scarcely ever failed to ruin the possessor.

There is no set of men in the United States, considered as a body, that have made the same sacrifices of their interest, in support of the common cause, as the officers of the American army. Nothing but a love of their country, of honor, and a desire of seeing their labors crowned with success, could possibly induce them to continue one moment in service. No officer can live upon his pay; and hundreds having spent their little all in addition to their scanty public allowance, have resigned, because they could no longer support themselves as officers. Numbers are, at this moment, rendered unfit for duty, for want of clothing, while the rest are wasting their property, and some of them verging fast to the gulf of poverty and distress.

Had we kept a permanent army on foot, the enemy could have had nothing to hope for, and would, in all probability, have listened to terms, long since.

I most firmly believe, the independence of the United States never will be established, till there is an army on foot for the war; and that, if we are to rely on occasional or annual levies, we must sink under the expense, and ruin must follow.

From long experience and the fullest conviction, I have been, and now am, decidedly in favor of a permanent force. But, knowing the jealousies which have been entertained on this head (Heaven knows how unjustly, and the cause of which could never be apprehended, were a due regard had to our local and other circumstances, even if ambitious views could be supposed to exist), and that our political helm was in another direction, I forbore to express my sentiments, for a time; but, at a moment when we are tottering on the brink of a precipice, silence would have been criminal.

To suppose, that this great Revolution can be accomplished by a temporary army, that this army will be subsisted by State supplies, and that taxation alone is adequate to our wants, is, in my opinion, absurd, and as unreasonable as to expect an inversion in the order of nature to accommodate itself to our views.

Nothing can be more obvious, than that a sound military establishment and the interests of economy are the same.

The opinion and advice of friends I receive, at all times, as a proof of their friendship, and am thankful when they are offered.

The circumstances under which he [Major Andre] was taken, justified it, and policy required a sacrifice. But, as he was more unfortunate than criminal, and, as there was much in his character to interest, while we yielded to the necessity of rigor, we could not but lament it.

If we do our duty, we may even hope to make the campaign decisive on this Continent. But we must do our duty in earnest, or disgrace and ruin will attend us.

To share the common lot, and participate the inconveniences which the army, from the peculiarity of our circumstances, are obliged to undergo, has, with me, been a fundamental principle.

I very much admire the patriotic spirit of the ladies of Philadelphia, and shall, with great pleasure, give them my advice, as to the application of their benevolent and generous donation to the soldiers of the army.

I cannot forbear taking the earliest moment, to express the high sense I entertain, of the patriotic exertions of the ladies of Maryland in favor of the army.

This [Benedict Arnold's treason] is an event, that occasions me equal regret and mortification; but, traitors are the growth of every country, and, in a Revolution of the present nature, it is more to be wondered at, that the catalogue is so small, than that there have been found a few.

In no instance, since the commencement of the war, has the interposition of Providence appeared more remarkably conspicuous, than in the rescue of the post and garrison of West Point from Arnold's villainous perfidy.

1781

We must not despair; the game is yet in our own hands; to play it well is all we have to do. And I trust, the experience of error will enable us to act better in future. A cloud may yet pass over us; individuals may be ruined, and the country at large, or particular States, undergo temporary distress; but certain I am, that it is in our power to bring the war to a happy conclusion.

I am very happy to be informed, by accounts from all parts of the continent, of the agreeable prospect of a very plentiful supply of almost all the productions of the earth. Blessed as we are with the bounties of Providence, necessary for our support and defence, the fault must surely be our own; and great indeed will it be, if we do not, by a proper use of them, obtain the noble prize for which we have so long been contending, the establishment of liberty, peace, and independence.

The fear of giving sufficient powers to Congress, is futile. Each Assembly, under its present constitution, will be annihilated, and we must once more return to the government of Great Britain, and be made to kiss the rod preparing for our correction. A nominal head, which, at present, is but another name for Congress, will no longer do. That honorable body, after hearing the interests and views of the several States fairly discussed and explained by their respective representatives, must dictate, and not merely recommend, and leave it to the States afterwards to do as they please, which is, in many cases, to do nothing at all.

Particular successes, obtained against all the chances of war, have had too much influence, to the prejudice of general and substantial principles.

No nation will have it more in its power, to repay what it borrows, than this. Our debts are, hitherto, small. The vast and valuable tracts of unlocated lands, the variety and fertility of climates and soils, the advantages of every kind which we possess, for commerce, insure to this country a rapid advancement in population and prosperity, and a certainty, its independence being established, of redeeming, in a short term of years, the comparatively inconsiderable debts it may have occasion to contract.

I conceive it to be a right, inherent in command, to appoint particular officers for special purposes.

It appears to me indispensable, that there should be an extension of the present corporal punishment, and that it would be useful, to authorize Courts-Martial, to sentence delinquents to labor on public works; perhaps, even for some crimes, particularly desertion, to transfer them from the land to the sea service, where they have less opportunity to indulge their inconstancy. . . . A variety in punishment is of utility, as well as a proportion. . . . The number of lashes may either be indefinite, left to the discretion of the Court, or limited to a larger number. In this case, I would recommend five hundred.

The arts and sciences essential to the prosperity of the State, and to the ornament and happiness of human life, have a primary claim to the encouragement of every lover of his country and of mankind.

I shall, with zeal, embrace every opportunity of seconding their [the American Academy of Arts and Sciences'] laudable views, and manifesting the exalted sense I have of the institution.

To be disgusted at the decision of questions, because not consonant to our own ideas, and to withdraw ourselves from public assemblies, or to neglect our attendance at them, upon suspicion that there is a party formed, who are inimical to our cause and to the true interests of the country, is wrong; because these things may originate in a difference of opinion. But supposing the fact otherwise, and that our suspicions are well founded, it is the indispensable duty of every patriot, to counteract them by the most steady and uniform opposition.

I know not what to say, on the subject of retaliation. Congress have it under consideration; and we must await their determination. . . . Of this I am convinced, that, of all laws, it is the most difficult to execute, where you have not the transgressor himself in your possession. Humanity will ever interfere, and plead strongly against the sacrifice of an innocent person for the guilt of another.

Amidst all the distress and sufferings of the army, from whatever sources they have arisen, it must be a consolation to our virtuous countrywomen, that they have never been accused of withholding their most zealous efforts, to support the cause we are engaged in, and encourage those who are defending them in the field. The army do not want gratitude, nor do they misplace it in this instance.

It embellishes the American character with a new trait, by proving, that the love of country is blended with those softer domestic virtues, which have always been allowed to be more peculiarly your own. You have not acquired admiration, in your own country only; it is paid to you abroad, and, you will learn with pleasure, by a part of your own sex, whose female accomplishments have attained their highest perfection, and who, from the commencement, have been the patronesses of American liberty.

The flattering distinction paid to the anniversary of my birth-day, is an honor for which I dare not attempt to express my gratitude. I confide in your Excellency's [Count de Rochambeau's] sensibility, to interpret my feelings for this, and for the obliging manner in which you are pleased to announce it.

Secrecy and despatch may prove the soul of success to an enterprise.

Nothing in human life can afford a liberal mind more rational and exquisite satisfaction, than the approbation of a wise, a great, and a virtuous man.

I have happily had but few differences, with those with whom I have the honor of being connected in the service. I bore much, for the sake of peace and the public good. My conscience tells me, that I acted right, in these transactions; and should they ever come to the knowledge of the world, I trust I shall stand acquitted.

It is much easier to avoid disagreements, than to remove discontents.

I never suffer reports, unsupported by proofs, to have weight in my mind.

The confidence and affection of fellow-citizens, are the most valuable and agreeable reward a citizen can receive. Next to the happiness of my country, this is the most powerful inducement I can have, to exert my self in its service.

We ought not to look back, unless it is to derive useful lessons from past errors, and for the purpose of profiting by dear-bought experience. To inveigh against things that are past and irremediable, is unpleasing; but to steer clear of the shelves and rocks we have struck upon, is the part of wisdom, equally as incumbent on political as other men, who have their own little bark, or that of others, to navigate through the intricate paths of life, or the trackless ocean, to the haven of security and rest.

The Great Director of events has carried us through a variety of scenes, during this long and bloody contest, in which we have been, for seven campaigns, most nobly struggling.

Our affairs are brought to a perilous crisis, that the hand of Providence, I trust, may be more conspicuous in our deliverance. The many remarkable interpositions of the Divine Government, in the hours of our deepest distress and darkness, have been too luminous, to suffer me to doubt the happy issue of the present contest.

The interposing hand of Heaven, in the various instances of our extensive preparations for this operation [the British surrender at Yorktown and Gloucester], has been most conspicuous and remarkable.

We have abundant reasons to thank Providence, for its many favorable interpositions in our behalf. It has, at times, been my only dependence; for, all other resources seemed to have failed us.

Divine service is to be performed tomorrow [October 21, 1781], in the several brigades and divisions. The Commander-in-chief earnestly recommends, that the troops not on duty should universally attend, with that seriousness of deportment and gratitude of heart, which the recognition of such reiterated and astonishing interpositions of Providence demands of us.

1782

Although we cannot, by the best concerted plans, absolutely command success, although the race is not always to the swift nor the battle to the strong, yet, without presumptuously waiting for miracles to be wrought, in our favor, it is our indispensable duty, with the deepest gratitude to Heaven for the past, and humble confidence in its smiles on our future operations, to make use of all means in our power for our defence and security.

There is nothing which will so soon produce a speedy and honorable peace, as a state of preparation for war; and we must either do this, or lay our account to patch up an inglorious peace, after all the toil, blood, and treasure we have spent. This has been my uniform opinion; a doctrine I have endeavored, amidst the universal expectation of an approaching peace, to inculcate, and which I am sure the event will justify.

If I may be allowed to speak figuratively, our Assemblies, in politics, are to be compared to the wheels of a clock, in mechanics. The whole, for the general purposes of war, should be set in motion by the great wheel, Congress; and, if all will do their parts, the machine will work easily; but a failure in one disorders the whole. Without the large one, which sets the whole in motion, nothing can be done. It is the united wisdom and exertions of the whole in Congress, that we are to depend upon. Without this, we are no better than a rope of sand, and as easily broken asunder.

I shall continue to exert all my influence and authority, to prevent the interruption of that harmony which is so essential, and which has so generally prevailed, between the Army and the inhabitants of the country. And I need scarcely add, that, in doing this, I shall give every species of countenance and support to the execution of the laws of the land.

The arts of dissimulation I despise; and my feelings will not permit me to make professions of friendship, to the man I deem my enemy, and whose system of conduct forbids it.

With a mixture of surprise and astonishment, I have read with attention the sentiments you [Colonel Lewis Nicola, suggesting the Army's wish to make Washington a King] have submitted to my perusal. Be assured, no occurrence, in the course of the war, has given me more painful sensations, than your information of there being such ideas existing in the army, as you have expressed, and I must view with abhorrence, and reprehend with severity. For the present, the communication of them will rest in my own bosom, unless some further agitation of the matter shall make a disclosure necessary. I am much at a loss, to conceive what part of my conduct could have given encouragement to an address, which to me seems big with the greatest mischiefs that can befall my country. If I am not deceived in the knowledge of myself, you could not have found a person, to whom your schemes are more disagreeable. At the same time, in justice to my own feelings, I must add, that no man possesses a more sincere wish to see ample justice done to the army, than I do, and, as far as my powers and influence, in a Constitutional way, extend, they shall be employed, to the utmost of my abilities, to effect it, should there be any occasion. . . . Let me conjure you, then, if you have any regard for your country, concern for yourself or posterity, or respect for me, to banish these thoughts from your mind, and never communicate, as from yourself or any one else, a sentiment of the like nature.

1783

Great Britain thought, she was only to hold up the rod, and all would be hushed.

A contemplation of the complete attainment (at a period earlier than could have been expected), of the object for which we contended against so formidable a power, cannot but inspire us with astonishment and gratitude.

The disadvantageous circumstances on our part, under which the war was undertaken, can never be forgotten. The singular interpositions of Providence in our feeble condition, were such as could scarcely escape the attention of the most unobserving; while the unparalleled perseverance of the armies of the United States, through almost every possible suffering and discouragement, for the space of eight long years, was little short of a standing miracle.

It is universally acknowledged, that the enlarged prospects of happiness, opened by the confirmation of our independence and sovereignty, almost exceed the power of description.

Unless the principles of the Federal Government are properly supported, and the powers of the Union increased, the honor, dignity, and justice of the nation will be lost for ever.

In such a country, so happily circumstanced, the pursuits of commerce and the cultivation of the soil will unfold to industry the certain road to competence. To those hardy soldiers who are actuated by the spirit of adventure, the fisheries will afford ample and profitable employment; and the extensive and fertile regions of the West will yield a most happy asylum to those, who, fond of domestic enjoyment, are seeking for personal independence.

We are now an independent people, and have yet to learn political tactics. We are placed among the nations of the earth, and have a character to establish; but how we shall acquit ourselves, time must discover. The probability is (at least, I fear it), that local or State politics will interfere too much with the more liberal and extensive plan of government, which wisdom and foresight, freed from the mist of prejudice, would dictate; and that we shall be guilty of many blunders, in treading this boundless theatre, before we shall have arrived at any perfection in this art; in a word that the experience which is purchased at the price of difficulties and distress, will alone convince us, that the honor, power, and true interest of this country, must be measured by a Continental scale, and that every departure therefrom weakens the Union, and may ultimately break the band which holds us together. To avert these evils, to form a new Constitution, that will give consistency, stability, and dignity to the Union, and sufficient powers to the Great Council of the nation for general purposes, is a duty incumbent upon every man who wishes well to his country, and will meet with my aid as far as it can be rendered in the private walks of life.

Happy, thrice happy shall they be pronounced, hereafter, who have contributed any thing, who have performed the meanest office, in erecting the stupendous *fabric of freedom and empire*, on the broad basis of independency; who have assisted in protecting the rights of human nature, and establishing an asylum for the poor and oppressed of all nations and religions.

I rejoice, most exceedingly, that there is an end of our warfare, and that such a field is opening to our view, as will, with wisdom to direct the cultivation of it, make us a great, a respectable, and happy people.

[France] is a country to which I shall ever feel a warm affection.

That no man can be more opposed to State feuds, or local prejudices, than myself, the whole tenor of my conduct has been continual evidence of. No man, perhaps, has had better opportunities, to see and feel the pernicious tendency of the latter than I have.

When we consider, that the Pennsylvania levies who have now mutinied, are recruits and soldiers of a day, who have not borne the heat and burden of the war, and who can have, in reality, very few hardships to complain of; and when we at the same time recollect, that those soldiers who have lately been furloughed from this army are the veterans, who have patiently endured hunger, nakedness, and cold, who have suffered and bled without a murmur, and who, with perfect good order, have retired to their homes without a settlement of their accounts, or a farthing of money in their pockets; we shall be as much astonished at the virtues of the latter, as we are struck with horror and detestation at the proceedings of the former; and every candid mind, without indulging ill-grounded prejudices, will undoubtedly make the proper discrimination.

The more its [the Army's] virtue and forbearance are tried, the more resplendent it appears. . . . My hope is, that the military exit of this valuable class of the community will exhibit such a proof of amor patriae [love of country], as will do them honor in the page of history.

The glorious task, for which we first flew to arms, being accomplished; the liberties of our country being fully acknowledged, and firmly secured by the smiles of Heaven, on the purity of our cause, and the honest exertions of a feeble people, determined to be free, against a powerful nation disposed to oppress them; and the character of those who have persevered through every extremity of hardship, suffering, and danger, being immortalized, by the illustrious appellation of the "Patriot Army"; nothing now remains, but for the actors of this mighty scene to preserve a perfect, unvarying consistency of character, through the very last act, to close the drama with applause, and to retire from the military theatre, with the same approbation of angels and men, which has crowned all their former virtuous actions.

I must beg the liberty, to suggest to Congress, an idea, which has been hinted to me, and which has affected my mind, very forcibly. That is, that, at the discharge of the men for the war, Congress should suffer those men, non-commissioned officers and soldiers, to take with them, as their own property, and as a gratuity, the arms and accoutrements they now hold. This act would raise pleasing sensations in the minds of those worthy and faithful men, who, from their early engaging in the war at moderate bounties, and from their patient continuance under innumerable distresses, have not only deserved nobly of their country, but have obtained an honorable distinction over those, who, with shorter times, have gained large pecuniary rewards. This, at a comparatively small expense, would be deemed an honorable testimonial from Congress, of the regard they bear to those distinguished worthies, and the sense they have had of their sufferings, virtues, and services, which have been so happily instrumental, towards the establishment and security of the rights, liberties, and independence of this rising empire. These constant companions of their toils, preserved with sacred attention, would be handed down from the present possessors to their children, as *honorary badges of bravery and military merit*; and would probably be brought forth, on some future occasion, with pride and exultation, to be improved with the same military ardor and emulation, in the hands of posterity, as they have been used by their forefathers, in the present establishment and foundation of our national independence.

There is nothing to be obtained but the soil they [the Indians] live on; and this can be had by purchase, at less expense, and without that bloodshed and those distresses, which helpless women and children are made partakers of, in all kinds of disputes with them.

True friendship is a plant of slow growth, and must undergo and withstand the shocks of adversity, before it is entitled to the appellation.

Be courteous to all, but intimate with few; and let those few be well tried, before you give them your confidence.

The company in which you will improve most, will be least expensive to you.

It is easy to make acquaintances, but difficult to shake them off, however irksome and unprofitable they are found, after we have once committed ourselves to them.

I was opposed to the policy of Great Britain, and became an enemy of her measures; but I always distinguished between a cause and individuals. And while the latter supported their opinions, upon liberal and generous grounds, personally I never could be an enemy to them.

Let your heart feel for the afflictions and distresses of every one. Let your hand give in proportion to your purse; remembering always, the estimation of the widow's mites, but, that it is not every one who asketh, that deserveth, charity. All, however, are worthy of inquiry; or the deserving may suffer.

The scheme which you [Lafayette] propose, as a precedent to encourage the emancipation of the black people in this country, from the state of bondage in which they are held, is a striking evidence of the benevolence of your heart. I shall be happy to join you, in so laudable a work.

The consciousness of having attempted faithfully to discharge my duty, and the approbation of my country, will be a sufficient recompense for my services.

Being now to conclude these his last public orders, to take his ultimate leave, in a short time, of the military character, and to bid a final adieu to the armies he has so long had the honor to command, he can only again offer, in their behalf, his recommendations to their grateful country, and his prayers to the God of Armies. May ample justice be done them here, and may the choicest of Heaven's favors, both here and hereafter, attend those who, under the Divine auspices, have secured innumerable blessings to others. With these wishes,

and his benediction, the Commander-in-chief is about to retire from service. The curtain of separation will soon be
drawn, and the military scene to him will be closed for ever.

Happy in the confirmation of our independence and sovereignty, and pleased with the opportunity afforded the United
States, of becoming a respectable nation, I resign with satisfaction the appointment I accepted with diffidence; a diffidence in my abilities to accomplish so arduous a task, which,
however, was superseded by a confidence in the rectitude of
our cause, the support of the supreme power of the Union,
and the patronage of Heaven. I consider it an indispensable
duty, to close this last solemn act of my official life, by com-
mending the interests of our dearest country to the protection of Almighty God, and those who have the
superintendence of them to His holy keeping.

If she wants advice upon it, a father and mother, who are at
hand, and competent to give it, are, at the same time, the
most proper to be consulted, on so interesting an event. For
my own part, I never did, nor do I believe I ever shall, give
advice, to a woman who is setting out on a matrimonial voyage; first, because I never could advise one to marry, without
her own consent; and secondly, because I know it is to no
purpose to advise her to refrain, when she has obtained it. A
woman very rarely asks an opinion, or requires advice, on
such an occasion, till her resolution is formed; and then it is,
with the hope and expectation of obtaining a sanction—not
that she means to be governed by your disapprobation—that
she applies. In a word, the plain English of the application
may be summed up in these words: "I wish you to think as
I do; but, if unhappily you differ from me in opinion, my
heart, I must confess, is fixed, and I have gone too far, now
to retract." . . . I will give my opinion of the *measure*, not of
the *man*, with candor, and to the following effect. I never
expected you would spend the residue of your days in widow-

hood. But, in a matter so important, and so interesting to yourself, children, and connections, I wish you would make a prudent choice. To do which, many considerations are necessary; such as, the family and connections of the man, his fortune (which is not the most essential in my eye), the line of conduct he has observed, and the disposition and frame of his mind. You should consider, what prospect there is of his proving kind and affectionate to you; just, generous, and attentive to your children; and how far his connections will be agreeable to you; for, when they are once formed, agreeable or not, the die being cast, your fate is fixed.

The hour of my resignation is fixed, at twelve today [December 23, 1783]; after which, I shall become a private citizen [at Mount Vernon] on the banks of the Potomac.

The scene is at last closed. I feel myself eased of a load of public care. I hope to spend the remainder of my days, in cultivating the affections of good men, and in the practice of the domestic virtues.

The private virtues of economy, prudence, and industry, are not less amiable, in civil life, than the more splendid qualities of valor, perseverance, and enterprise, in public life.

Do not conceive, that fine clothes make fine men, any more than fine feathers make fine birds. A plain, genteel dress is more admired, and obtains more credit, than lace and embroidery, in the eyes of the judicious and sensible.

I appeal to the Archives of Congress, and call on those sacred deposits to witness for me.

Avoid gaming. This is a vice which is productive of every possible evil; equally injurious to the morals and health of its votaries. . . . It is the child of avarice, the brother of iniquity, and the father of mischief. . . . It has been the ruin of many worthy families, the loss of many a man's honor, and the cause of suicide. . . . To all those who enter the lists, it is equally fascinating. The successful gamester pushes his good fortune, till it is overtaken by a reverse. The losing gamester, in hopes of retrieving past misfortunes, goes on, from bad to worse, till, grown desperate, he pushes at every thing, and loses his all. . . . Few gain, by this abominable practice; while thousands are injured.

I have made a tour through the Lakes George and Champlain, as far as Crown Point. Thence returning to Schenectady, I proceeded up the Mohawk River to Fort Schuyler (formerly Fort Stanwix), and crossed over to Wood Creek, which empties into the Oneida Lake, and affords the water communication with Ontario. I then traversed the country, to the head of the eastern branch of the Susquehanna, and viewed Lake Otsego, and the portage between that lake and the Mohawk River at Canajoharie. Prompted by these actual observations, I could not help taking a more extensive view of the vast inland navigation of these United States, from maps, and the information of others; and could not but be struck with the immense extent and importance of it, and with the goodness of that Providence, which has dealt its favors to us with so profuse a hand. Would to God, we may have wisdom enough to improve them.

I commend my friends, and, with them, the interests and happiness of our dear country, to the keeping and protection of Almighty God.

1784

It appears to be incompatible with the principles of our national Constitution, to admit the introduction of any kind of nobility, knighthood, or distinctions of a similar nature, amongst the citizens of our republic.

The disinclination of the individual States, to yield powers to Congress, for the Federal Government, their unreasonable jealousy of that body and of one another, and the disposition which seems to pervade each, of being all-wise and all-powerful within itself, will, if there be not a change in the system, be our downfall as a nation. This is as clear to me as A, B, C; and I think we have opposed Great Britain, and have arrived at the present state of peace and independency, to very little purpose, if we cannot conquer our own prejudices. The powers of Europe begin to see this; and our newly acquired friends, the British, are already and professedly acting upon this ground; and wisely too, if we are determined to persevere in our folly. They know, that individual opposition to their measures is futile; and boast, that we are not sufficiently united as a nation, to give a general one! Is not the indignity alone of this declaration, while we are in the very act of peace-making and conciliation, sufficient to stimulate us to vest more extensive and adequate powers in the Sovereign of these United States?

Men, chosen as the delegates in Congress are, cannot officially be dangerous. They depend upon the breath, nay, they are so much the creatures of the people, under the present Constitution, that they can have no views, which could possibly be carried into execution, nor any interests distinct from those of their constituents.

My political creed is, to be wise in the choice of delegates, support them like gentlemen while they are our representatives, give them competent powers for all Federal purposes, support them in the due exercise thereof, and, lastly, compel them to close attendance in Congress, during their delegation. These things, under the present mode and termination of elections, aided by annual instead of constant sessions, would, or I am exceedingly mistaken, make us one of the most wealthy, happy, respectable, and powerful nations that ever inhabited the terrestrial globe. Without them, we shall, in my opinion, soon be everything which is the direct reverse.

Annual sessions would always produce a full representation, and alertness in business. The delegates, after a separation of eight or ten months, would meet each other with glad countenances. They would be complaisant; they would yield to each other all that duty to their constituents would allow; and they would have better opportunities of becoming acquainted with their sentiments, and removing improper prejudices, when they are imbibed, by mixing with them during the recess. Men who are always together, get tired of each other's company. They throw off that restraint which is necessary to keep things in proper tune. They say and do things which are personally disgusting. This begets opposition; opposition begets faction; and so it goes on, till business is impeded, and often at a stand. I am sure (having the business prepared by proper boards, or a committee), an annual session of two months would despatch more business than is done in twelve, and this by a full representation of the Union.

That the prospect before us is fair, none can deny; what use we shall make of it, is exceedingly problematical. Not but that I believe all things will come right at last; but, like a young heir, come a little prematurely to a large inheritance, we shall wanton and run riot, until we have brought our reputation to the brink of ruin, and then, like him, shall have to labor with the current of opinion, when compelled perhaps to do what prudence and common policy pointed out, as plain as any problem of Euclid, in the first instance.

From trade our citizens will not be restrained; and, therefore, it behooves us to place it in the most convenient channels, under proper regulations, freed, as much as possible, from those vices which luxury, the consequence of wealth and power, naturally introduces.

I shall be mistaken, if [the New Yorkers] do not build vessels for the navigation of the lakes, which will supersede the necessity of coasting on either side.

In the moment of our separation, upon the road as I travelled, and every hour since, I have felt all that love, respect, and attachment for you [the Marquis de Lafayette], with which length of years, close connection, and your merits have inspired me. I often asked myself, as our carriages separated, whether that was the last sight I should ever have of you. And though I wished to say no, my fears answered yes. I called to mind the days of my youth, and found they had long since fled, to return no more; that I was now descending the hill I had been fifty-two years climbing; and that, though I was blessed with a good constitution, I was of a short-lived family, and might soon expect to be entombed in the mansion of my fathers. These thoughts darkened the shades, and gave a gloom to the picture, and consequently to my prospect of seeing you again. But I will not repine; I have had my day.

It is my wish, that the mutual friendship and esteem, which have been planted and fostered in the tumult of public life, may not wither and die in the serenity of retirement. . . . We should amuse our evening hours of life, in cultivating the tender plants [of friendship], and bringing them to perfection, before they are transplanted to a happier clime.

I repeat to you [the Chevalier de Chastellux] the assurances of my friendship, and of the pleasure I should feel in seeing you in the shade of those trees which my hands have planted; and which, by their rapid growth, at once indicate a knowledge of my declining years, and their disposition to spread their mantles over me before I go hence to return no more. For this, their gratitude, I will nurture them while I stay.

The friendship I have conceived, will not be impaired by absence; but it may be no unpleasing circumstance to brighten the chain, by a renewal of the covenant.

On the eve of Christmas, I entered these [Mount Vernon's] doors, an older man by nine years than when I left them. . . . I am just beginning to experience that ease and freedom from public cares, which, however desirable, takes some time to realize. It was not till lately, I could get the better of my usual custom of ruminating, as soon as I waked in the morning, on the business of the ensuing day; and of my surprise at finding, after revolving many things in my mind, that I was no longer a public man, nor had any thing to do with public transactions.

Freed from the clangor of arms, and the bustle of a camp, from the cares of public employment, and the responsibility of office, I am now enjoying domestic ease, under the shadow of my own vine and my own fig-tree. And in a small villa, with the implements of husbandry and lambkins around me, I expect to glide gently down the stream of life, till I am entombed in the mansion of my fathers.

Under the shadow of my own vine and my own fig-tree, free from the bustle of a camp, and the busy scenes of public life, I am solacing myself with those tranquil enjoyments, of which the soldier, who is ever in pursuit of fame, the statesman, whose watchful days and sleepless nights are spent in devising schemes to promote the welfare of his own, perhaps the ruin of other countries, as if the globe was insufficient for us all, and the courtier, who is always watching the countenance of his prince, in hopes of catching a gracious smile, can have very little conception. I have not only retired from all public employments, but I am retiring within myself, and shall be able to view the solitary walk, and tread the paths of private life, with a heartfelt satisfaction. Envious of none, I am determined to be pleased with all; and this being the order of my march, I will move gently down the stream of life, until I sleep with my fathers.

I do not think vanity is a trait of my character. Any memoirs of my life, distinct and unconnected with the general history of the war, would rather hurt my feelings, than tickle my pride, while I live. I had rather glide gently down the stream of life, leaving it to posterity, to think and say what they please of me, than, by any act of mine, to have vanity or ostentation imputed to me.

Where acts of Providence interfere to disable a tenant, I would be lenient, in the exaction of rent. But, when the cases are otherwise, I will not be put off; because it is on these my own expectations depend, and because an accumulation of undischarged rents is a real injury to the tenant.

I feel now, as I conceive a wearied traveller must do, who, after treading many a painful step, with a heavy burden on his shoulders, is eased of the latter, having reached the haven to which all the former were directed; and from his house-top is looking back, and tracing, with an eager eye, the me-anders, by which he escaped the quicksands and mires which lay in his way; and into which none but the All-powerful Guide and Dispenser of human events could have prevented his falling.

It is, indeed, a pleasure, from the walks of private life to view, in retrospect, all the meanderings of our past labors, the difficulties through which we have waded, and the happy haven to which the ship has been brought. Is it possible, after this, that it should founder? Will not the All-wise and All-powerful Director of human events preserve it? I think He will. He may, however, for some wise purpose of his own, suffer our indiscretions and folly to place our national character low in the political scale; and this, unless more wisdom and less prejudice take the lead in our government, will most certainly happen.

1785

It is really my wish, to have my mind and my actions which are the result of reflection, as free and independent as the air.

America may think herself happy, in having the Atlantic for a barrier.

If historiographers should be hardy enough, to fill the page of history with the advantages that have been gained, with unequal numbers, on the part of America in the course of this contest, and attempt to relate the distressing circumstances under which they have been obtained, it is more than probable, that posterity will bestow on their labors the epithet and marks of fiction; for it will not be believed, that such a force as Great Britain has employed, for eight years, in this country, could be baffled in their plan of subjugating it, by numbers infinitely less, composed of men oftentimes half starved, always in rags, without pay, and experiencing, at times, every species of distress which human nature is capable of undergoing.

To me it is a solecism in politics, indeed it is one of the most extraordinary things in nature, that we should confederate as a nation, and yet be afraid to give the rulers of that nation (who are the creatures of our own making, appointed for a limited and short duration, and who are amenable for every action, and may be recalled at any moment, and are subject to all the evils which they may be instrumental in producing), sufficient powers to order and direct the affairs of the same. By such policy as this, the wheels of government are clogged, and our brightest prospects, and that high expectation which was entertained of us by the wondering world, are turned into astonishment; and, from our high ground on which we stood, we are descending into the vale of confusion and darkness.

A coinage of gold, silver, and copper, is a measure which, in my opinion, has become indispensably necessary. Without a coinage, or lest some stop can be put to the cutting and clipping of money, our dollars, pistareens, etc., will be converted, as Teague says, into five quarters; and a man must travel with a pair of scales in his pocket, or run the risk of receiving gold, at one fourth less by weight than it counts.

The Agricultural Society lately established in Philadelphia, promises extensive usefulness, if its objects are prosecuted with spirit. I wish, most sincerely, that every State in the Union would institute similar ones; and that these societies would correspond fully and freely with each other, and communicate to the public all useful discoveries founded on practice, with a due attention to climate, soil, and seasons.

It has long been a speculative question among philosophers and wise men, whether foreign commerce is of real advantage to any country; that is, whether the luxury, effeminacy, and corruptions, which are introduced along with it, are counterbalanced by the convenience and wealth which it brings. The decision of this question is of very little importance to us. We have abundant reason to be convinced, that the spirit of trade, which pervades these States, is not to be restrained. It behooves us, then, to establish just principles; and this cannot, any more than other matters of national concern, be done by thirteen heads differently constructed and organized.

The necessity, therefore, of a controlling power, is obvious; and why it should be withheld, is beyond my comprehension.

We are either a united people, under one head and for federal purposes; or we are thirteen independent sovereignties, eternally counteracting each other. If the former, whatever such a majority of the States as the Constitution points out, conceives to be for the benefit of the whole, should, in my humble opinion, be submitted to by the minority. Let the Southern States always be represented; let them act more in union; let them declare, freely and boldly, what is for the interest of, and what is prejudicial to, their constituents; and there will, there must be, an accommodating spirit. In the establishment of a Navigation Act, this, in a particular manner, ought, and will doubtless be attended to. If the assent of nine States, or, as some propose, of eleven, is necessary to give validity to a commercial system, it insures this measure, or it cannot be obtained.

Our trade, in all points of view, is as essential to Great Britain, as hers is to us. And she will exchange it, upon reciprocal and liberal terms, if better cannot be had. Had we not better encourage seamen among ourselves, with less imports, than divide them with foreigners, and, by increasing the amount of them, ruin our merchants, and greatly injure the mass of our citizens?

My first wish is, to see this plague of mankind [war] banished from the earth, and the sons and daughters of this world employed in more pleasing and innocent amusements, than in preparing implements, and exercising them, for the destruction of mankind.

Rather than quarrel about territory, let the poor, the needy, and oppressed of the earth, and those who want land, resort to the fertile plains of our Western country, the second land of promise, and there dwell in peace, fulfilling the first and great commandment.

There is not, I conceive, an unbiassed mind, that would refuse the officers of the late army the right of associating, for the purpose of establishing a fund for the support of the poor and distressed of their fraternity, when many of them, it is well known, are reduced to their last shifts, by the ungenerous conduct of their country, in not adopting more vigorous measures to render their certificates productive.

It is not the letters of my friends, which give me trouble, or add aught to my perplexity.

To correspond with those I love, is among my highest gratifications.

Letters of friendship require no study; the communications they contain, flow with ease; and allowances are expected and made.

When I was first called to the station, with which I was honored during the late conflict for our liberties, to the diffidence which I had so many reasons to feel in accepting it, I thought it my duty, to join a firm resolution to shut my hand against every pecuniary recompense. To this resolution I have invariably adhered; and from it, if I had the inclination, I do not feel at liberty now to depart.

In for a penny, in for a pound, is an old adage. I am so hackneyed to the touches of the painter's pencil, that I am now altogether at their beck, and sit like Patience on a monument, whilst they are delineating the lines of my face. It is a proof, among many others, of what habit and custom can effect. At first, I was as impatient at the request, and as restive under the operation, as a colt is of the saddle. The next time, I submitted very reluctantly, but with less flouncing. Now, no dray moves more readily to the thill, than I do to the painter's chair.

My time is now occupied by rural amusements, in which I have great satisfaction. And my first wish is (although it is against the profession of arms, and would clip the wings of some of our young soldiers, who are soaring after glory), to see *the whole world in peace*, and the inhabitants of it, as *one band of brothers*, striving who should contribute most to the happiness of mankind.

With those who are disposed to cavil, or who have the itch of writing strongly upon them, nothing can be made to suit their palates. The best way, therefore, to disconcert and defeat them, is to take no notice of their publications. All else is but food for declamation.

Should any thing tending to give me anxiety, present itself, I shall never undertake the painful task of recrimination; nor do I know, that I should even enter upon my justification.

Although no man's sentiments are more opposed to any kind of restraint upon religious principles than mine are, yet I must confess, that I am not amongst the number of those, who are so much alarmed at the thought of making people pay, towards the support of that which they profess, if of the denomination of Christians, Jews, Mahometans, or otherwise, and thereby obtain proper relief.

I shall always strive, to prove faithful and impartial of genuine, vital religion.

I am clearly in sentiment with her Ladyship [the Countess of Huntington], that Christianity will never make any progress among the Indians, or work any considerable reformation in their principles, until they are brought to a state of greater civilization. And the mode by which she means to attempt this, as far as I have been able to give it consideration, is as likely to succeed, as any other that could have been devised, and may, in time, effect the great and benevolent objects of her Ladyship's wishes. But that love of ease, impatience under any sort of control, and disinclination to any sort of pursuit but those of hunting and of war, would discourage any person, possessed of less piety, zeal, and philanthropy, than are characteristic of Lady Huntington.

If it should please the [Virginia] General Assembly, to permit me to turn the destination of the fund vested in me, from my private emolument, to objects of a *public* nature, it will be my study, in selecting these, to prove the sincerity of my gratitude for the honor conferred on me, by preferring such as may appear most subservient to the enlightened and patriotic views of the legislature.

1786

Here [on European battlefields] have fallen thousands of gallant spirits, to satisfy the ambition of their Sovereigns, or to support them, perhaps, in acts of oppression and injustice! Melancholy reflection! For what wise purpose does Providence permit this? Is it as a scourge to mankind, or is it to prevent them from becoming too populous? If the latter, would not the fertile plains of the Western World receive the redundancy of the Old?

Influence is not government.

Let us have a government by which our lives, liberties, and properties will be secured.

The foundation of a great empire is laid; and I please myself with the persuasion, that Providence will not leave its work imperfect.

It is one of the evils of democratical governments, that the people, not always seeing, and frequently misled, must often feel before they can act right; but then evils of this nature seldom fail to work their own cure.

We have probably had too good an opinion of human nature, in forming our Confederation. Experience has taught us, that men will not adopt and carry into execution measures the best calculated for their own good, without the intervention of a coercive power.

I am told, that even respectable characters speak of a monarchial form of government, without horror. From thinking proceeds speaking; thence to acting is often but a single step. But, how irrevocable and tremendous! What a triumph for our enemies to verify their predictions! What a triumph for the advocates of despotism, to find, that we are incapable of governing ourselves, and that systems founded on the basis of equal liberty, are merely ideal and fallacious!

Let the reins of government be braced, and held with a steady hand, and every violation of the Constitution be reprehended. If defective, let it be amended, but not suffered to be trampled upon, whilst it has an existence.

Nations are not influenced, as individuals may be, by disinterested friendships; but, when it is their interest to live in amity, we have little reason to apprehend any rupture.

Nothing, in my opinion, would contribute more to the welfare of these States, than the proper management of lands. Nothing, in Virginia particularly, seems to be less understood. The present mode of cropping, practised among us, is destructive to landed property, and must, if persisted in much longer, ultimately ruin the holders of it.

There are many articles of manufacture, which we stand absolutely in need of, and shall continue to have occasion for, so long as we remain an agricultural people, which will be, while lands are so cheap and plenty, that is to say, for ages to come.

However unimportant America may be considered at present, and however Britain may affect to despise her trade, there will assuredly come a day, when this country will have some weight in the scale of empires.

It gives me great pleasure, to find a spirit for inland navigation prevailing so generally. No country is more capable of improvements in this way, than our own; none will be more benefited; and to begin well is all in all.

When the [Cincinnati] Society was formed, I am persuaded not a member of it conceived, that it would give birth to those jealousies, or be charged with those dangers, real or imaginary, with which the minds of many, and of some respectable characters in these States, seem to be agitated.

If the assurances of the sincerest esteem and affection, if the varieties of uncultivated nature, the novelty of exchanging the gay and delightful scenes of Paris, with which you [the Marchioness de Lafayette] are surrounded, for the rural amusements of a country in its infancy, if the warbling notes of the feathered songsters of our lawns and meads, can, for a moment, make you forget the melody of the opera, and the pleasures of the court, these all invite you to give us this honor, and the opportunity of expressing to you, personally, those sentiments of attachment and love, with which you have inspired us.

There is not a man living, who wishes more sincerely than I do, to see a plan adopted, for the abolition of [slavery]. But there is only one proper and effectual mode by which it can be accomplished, and that is, by legislative authority. This, as far as my suffrage will go, shall never be wanting. But when slaves, who are happy and contented with their present masters, are tampered with and seduced to leave them; when masters are taken unawares by these practices; when a conduct of this kind begets discontent on one side, and resentment on the other; and when it happens to fall on a man whose purse will not measure with that of the society, and he loses his property for want of means to defend it; it is oppression in such a case, and not humanity in any, because it introduces more evils than it can cure.

Your [Lafayette's] purchase of an estate in the colony of Cayenne, with a view of emancipating the slaves on it, is a generous and noble proof of your humanity. Would to God, a like spirit might diffuse itself generally, into the minds of the people of this country. But I despair of seeing it. . . . Some petitions were presented to the Assembly, at its last session, for the abolition of slavery, but they could scarcely obtain a reading. . . . To set the slaves afloat, at once, would, I believe, be productive of much inconvenience and mischief; but, by degrees, it certainly might, and assuredly ought to be effected; and that, too, by legislative authority.

I never mean, unless some particular circumstances should compel me to it, to possess another slave by purchase, it being among my first wishes, to see some plan adopted, by which slavery, in this country, may be abolished by law.

In my estimation, more permanent and genuine happiness is to be found, in the sequestered walks of connubial life, than in the giddy rounds of promiscuous pleasure, or the more tumultuous and imposing scenes of successful ambition.

There is more of wickedness than ignorance mixed in our Councils. Ignorance and design are difficult to combat. Out of these proceed illiberal sentiments, improper jealousies, and a train of evils, which oftentimes, in republican governments, must be sorely felt, before they can be removed. Ignorance being a fit soil for design to work in, tools are employed, which a generous mind would disdain to use; and which nothing but time, and their own puerile or wicked productions, can show the inefficacy and dangerous tendency of. I often think of our situation, and view it with concern.

It is to be lamented, that great characters are seldom without a blot. If the enlightened and virtuous part of the community will make allowances for my involuntary errors, I will promise, that they shall have no cause to accuse me of wilful ones.

In all matters of great national moment, the only true line of conduct is, dispassionately to compare the advantages and disadvantages of the measure proposed, and decide from the balance.

As the member of an infant empire, as a philanthropist by character, and, if I may be allowed the expression, as a citizen of the Great Republic of Humanity at large, I cannot help turning my attention, sometimes, to this subject. I would be understood to mean, I cannot avoid reflecting, with pleasure, on the probable influence that commerce may hereafter have on human manners, and society in general. On these occasions I consider, how mankind may be connected, like *one great family*, in fraternal ties. I indulge a fond, perhaps an enthusiastic idea, that, as the world is evidently much less barbarous than it has been, its melioration must still be progressive; that nations are becoming more humanized in their policy; that the subjects of ambition and causes for hostility are daily diminishing; and, in fine, that the period is not very remote, when the benefits of a liberal and free commerce will pretty generally succeed to the devastations and horrors of war.

Thus, some of the pillars of the Revolution fall. Others are mouldering, by insensible degrees. May our country never want props, to support the glorious fabric.

Life and the concerns of this world, one would think, are so uncertain, and so full of disappointments, that nothing is to be counted upon from human actions.

1787

Honesty in States, as well as in individuals, will ever be found the soundest policy.

It is among the evils, and perhaps not the smallest, of democratical governments, that the people must feel, before they will see. When this happens, they are roused to action. Hence it is, that those kinds of government are so slow.

The power under the Constitution, will always be in the people. It is intrusted, for certain defined purposes, and for a certain limited period, to representatives of their own choosing; and, whenever it is exercised contrary to their interest, or not agreeably to their wishes, their servants can and undoubtedly will be recalled.

I am fully of opinion, that those who lean to a monarchial government have either not consulted the public mind, or that they live in a region, which (the levelling principles in which they were bred being entirely eradicated), is much more productive of monarchial ideas, than is the case in the

Southern States, where, from the habitual distinctions which have always existed among the people, one would have expected the first generation, and the most rapid growth, of them.

There must be reciprocity, or no Union. Which of the two is preferable, will not become a question in the mind of any true patriot.

The various and opposite interests which were to be conciliated, the local prejudices which were to be subdued, the diversity of opinions and sentiments which were to be reconciled, and, in fine, the sacrifices which were necessary to be made, on all sides, for the general welfare, combined to make it a work of so intricate and difficult a nature, that I think it is much to be wondered at, that any thing could have been produced with such unanimity, as the Constitution proposed.

Submit your sentiments with diffidence. A dictatorial style, though it may carry conviction, is always accompanied with disgust.

Being no bigot myself, to any mode of worship, I am disposed to indulge the professors of Christianity in the Church, with that road to heaven, which to them shall seem the most direct, plainest, easiest, and least liable to exception.

The ties of nature must have their yearnings, before calm resignation will preponderate.

1788

It is a little strange, that the men of large property in the South, should be more afraid that the Constitution will produce an aristocracy or a monarchy, than the genuine demo-cratical people of the East.

The rights of mankind, the privileges of the people, and the true principles of liberty, seem to have been more generally discussed, and better understood, throughout Europe, since the American Revolution, than they were at any former period.

It is far from my design to intimate an opinion, that her-aldry, coat-armor, etc., might not be rendered conductive to public and private uses with us; or that they can have any tendency unfriendly to the purest spirit of republicanism. On the contrary, a different conclusion is deducible from the practice of Congress, and the States; all of which have estab-lished some kind of armorial devices, to authenticate their official instruments.

Liberty, when it begins to take root, is a plant of rapid growth.

The political state of affairs in France, seems to be in a deli-cate situation. What will be the issue, is not easy to deter-mine; but the spirit which is diffusing itself, may produce changes in that government, which, a few years ago, could hardly have been dreamt of.

Treaties which are not built upon reciprocal benefits, are not likely to be of long duration.

We exhibit the novel and astonishing spectacle of a whole people, deliberating calmly on what form of government will be most conducive to their happiness; and deciding, with an unexpected degree of unanimity in favor of a system which they conceive calculated to answer the purpose.

I do most firmly believe, that, in the aggregate, it is the best Constitution that can be obtained at this epoch; and that this, or a dissolution of the Union awaits our choice, and is the only alternative before us.

The general Government is not invested with more powers, than are indispensably necessary to perform the functions of a good government. These powers are so distributed among the Legislative, Executive, and Judicial branches, into which the general Government is arranged, that it can never be in danger of degenerating into a monarchy, an oligarchy, an aristocracy, or any other despotic or oppressive form, so long as there shall remain any virtue in the body of the people.

It should be the policy of United America, to administer to the wants of other nations, without being engaged in their quarrels; and it is not in the ability of the proudest and most polite people on earth, to prevent us from becoming a great, a respectable, and a commercial nation, if we shall continue united and faithful to ourselves.

I look forward, with a kind of political faith, to scenes of national happiness, which have not heretofore been offered for the fruition of the most favored nations. The natural, political, and moral circumstances of our nascent empire justify the anticipation.

We have an almost unbounded territory, whose natural advantages for agriculture and commerce equal those of any on the globe. In a civil point of view, we have the unequalled privilege of choosing our own political institutions and of improving upon the experience of mankind, in the formation of a confederated government, where due energy will not be incompatible with the unalienable rights of freemen; and the information and morals of our citizens appear to be peculiarly favorable for the introduction of such a plan of government.

Under an energetic general Government, such regulations might be made, and such measures taken, as would render this country the asylum of pacific and industrious characters from all parts of Europe; encourage the cultivation of the earth, by the high price which its products would command; and draw the wealth and wealthy men of other nations into our bosom, by giving security to property, and liberty to its holders.

It is a flattering and consolatory reflection, that our rising Republics have the good wishes of all the philosophers, patriots, and virtuous men, in all nations; and that they look upon them, as a kind of asylum for mankind. God grant, that we may not disappoint their honest expectations by our folly or perverseness.

I hope, some day, we shall become a storehouse and granary for the world.

It is a point conceded, that America, under an efficient government, will be the most favorable country of any in the world, for persons of industry and frugality, possessed of a moderate capital. It is also believed, that it will not be less advantageous to the happiness of the lowest class of the people, on account of the equal distribution of property, the great plenty of unoccupied lands, and the facility of procuring the means of subsistence.

The scheme of purchasing a good tract of freehold estate, and bringing out a number of able-bodied men, indented for a certain time, appears to be indisputably a rational one.

Would to God, the harmony of nations were an object that lay nearest to the hearts of sovereigns; and that the incentives to peace, of which commerce, and facility of understanding each other, are not the most inconsiderable, might be daily increased.

Our situation is such as makes it not only unnecessary, but extremely imprudent, for us to take a part in their [foreign] quarrels; and, whenever a contest happens among them, if we wisely and properly improve the advantage which nature has given us, we may be benefited by their folly, provided we conduct ourselves with circumspection and under proper restrictions.

Separated as we are, by a world of water, from other nations, if we are wise, we shall surely avoid being drawn into the labyrinth of their politics, and involved in their destructive wars.

I have always believed, that some apparent cause, powerful in its nature, and progressive in its operation, must be employed, to produce a change in national sentiments.

The life of the husbandman, of all others, is the most delightful. It is honorable, it is amusing, and, with judicious management, it is profitable.

An extensive speculation, a spirit of gambling, or the introduction of any thing which will divert our attention from agriculture, must be extremely prejudicial, if not ruinous, to us.

For the sake of humanity, it is devoutly to be wished, that the manly employment of agriculture, and the humanizing benefit of commerce, would supersede the waste of war, and the rage of conquest that the swords might be turned into ploughshares, the spears into pruning-hooks, and, as the Scriptures express it, "the nations learn war" no more.

It has been understood, by wise politicians and enlightened patriots, that giving a facility to the means of travelling [public roads], for strangers, and of intercourse, for citizens, was an object of legislative concern, and a circumstance highly beneficial to the country.

The maritime genius of this country is now steering our vessels in every ocean; to the East Indies, the North West coasts of America, and the extremities of the globe.

There are three circumstances, which are thought to give the British merchants an advantage over all others. First: their extensive credit, which, I confess, I wish to see abolished. Secondly: their having in one place magazines, containing all kinds of articles than can be required. Thirdly: their knowledge of the precise kinds of merchandise and fabrics which are wanted.

Men may speculate as they will; they may talk of patriotism; they may draw a few examples, from ancient story, of great achievements performed by its influence; but whoever builds upon them, as a sufficient basis for conducting a long and bloody war, will find himself deceived, in the end.

I rely fully in your [the Trustees of William and Mary College's] strenuous endeavors for placing the system on such a basis, as will render it most beneficial to the State, and the republic of letters, as well as to the more extensive interests of humanity and religion.

I entertain a high idea of the utility of periodical publications, insomuch that I could heartily desire copies of the

["American Museum,"] and magazines, as well as common gazettes, might be spread through every city, town, and village in America. I consider such easy vehicles of knowledge more happily calculated than any other, to preserve the liberty, stimulate the industry, and meliorate the morals of an enlightened and free people.

It is a wonder to me, that there should be found a single monarch, who does not realize, that his own glory and felicity must depend on the prosperity and happiness of his people. How easy is it for a sovereign, to do that, which shall not only immortalize his name, but attract the blessings of millions!

The great Searcher of human hearts is my witness, that I have no wish which aspires beyond the humble and happy lot, of living and dying a private citizen, on my own farm.

I hope I shall always possess firmness and virtue enough, to maintain, what I consider the most enviable of all titles, the character of an "Honest Man."

The various passions and motives, by which men are influenced, are concomitants of fallibility, and ingrafted into our nature.

The good opinion of honest men, friends to freedom, and well-wishers to mankind, wherever they may be born or happen to reside, is the only kind of reputation a wise man would ever desire.

Though I prize as I ought the good opinion of my fellow-citizens, yet, if I know myself, I would not seek or retain popularity, at the expense of one social duty or moral virtue.

While doing what my conscience informed me was right, as it respected my God, my country, and myself, I could despise all the party clamor, and unjust censure, which might be expected from some, whose personal enmity might be occasioned by their hostility to the Government.

My chief reason for supposing the West India trade detrimental to us, was, that rum, the principal article received from thence, is the bane of morals, and the parent of idleness. . . . I could wish to see the direct commerce with France encouraged, to the greatest degree; and that almost all the foreign spirits which we consume, should consist of the wines and brandies made in that country. The use of these liquors would, at least, be more innocent to the health and morals of the people, than the thousands of hogsheads of poisonous rum, which are annually consumed in the United States.

We may, with a kind of pious and grateful exultation, trace the finger of Providence through these dark and mysterious events, which first induced the States to appoint a General Convention, and then led them, one after another, by such steps as were best calculated to effect the object, into the adoption of a system recommended by that General Convention; thereby, in all human probability, laying a lasting foundation for tranquillity and happiness, when we had but too much reason to fear, that confusion and misery were coming rapidly upon us. That the same good Providence may still continue to protect us, and prevent us from dashing the cup of national felicity, just as it has been lifted to our lips, is my earnest prayer.

I earnestly pray, that the Omnipotent Being, who has not deserted the cause of America in the hour of its extreme hazard, may never yield so fair a heritage to anarchy or despotism.

If I should, unluckily for me, be reduced to the necessity of giving an answer to the question [of whether he would accept the office of President of the United States], I would fain do what is, in all respects, best. But how can I know what is best, or on what I shall determine? May Heaven assist me, in forming a judgment; for, at present, I see nothing but clouds and darkness before me.

I trust in that Providence, which has saved us in six troubles, yea, in seven, to rescue us again from any imminent, though unseen dangers. Nothing, however, on our part, ought to be left undone.

If an event so long and so earnestly desired, as that of converting the Indians to Christianity, and consequently to civilization, can be effected, the Society of Bethlehem bids fair to bear a very considerable part in it.

Should any efforts of mine, to procure information respecting the different dialects of the aborigines of America, serve to reflect a ray of light on the obscure subject of language in general, I shall be highly gratified. I love to indulge the contemplation of human nature, in a progressive state of improvement and amelioration; and, if the idea would not be considered visionary and chimerical, I could fondly hope, that the present plan of the great potentate of the North [Catherine the Great, Empress of Russia] might, in some measure, lay the foundation for that assimilation of manners and interests, which should, one day, remove many of the causes of hostility from among mankind.

To know the affinity of tongues, seems to me to be one step towards promoting the affinity of nations.

I observe with singular satisfaction, the cases in which your [the Massachusetts Humane Society's] benevolent institution has been instrumental, in recalling some of our fellow-creatures, as it were, from beyond the gates of eternity, and has given occasion for the hearts of parents and friends to leap for joy. . . . The provision made for the preservation of ship-wrecked mariners, is also highly estimable, in the view of every philanthropic mind, and greatly consolatory to that suffering part of the community. These things will draw upon you the blessings of those who were nigh to perish. . . . These works of charity and good will towards men reflect, in my estimation, great lustre upon the authors, and presage an era of still further improvements. . . . How pitiful, in the eye of reason and religion, is that false ambition, which desolates the world with fire and sword, for the purposes of conquest and fame, when compared to the milder virtues of making our neighbors and our fellow-men as happy as their frail condition and perishable nature will permit them to be!

Time alone can blunt the keen edge of afflictions. Philosophy and our religion hold out to us such hopes as will, upon proper reflection, enable us to bear, with fortitude, the most calamitous incidents of life; and this is all that can be expected from the feelings of humanity.

1789

My politics are plain and simple. I think every nation has a right to establish that form of government under which it conceives it may live most happy; provided it infracts no right, or is not dangerous to others; and that no governments ought to interfere with the internal concerns of another, except for the security of what is due to themselves.

The American Revolution, or the peculiar light of the age, seems to have opened the eyes of almost every nation in Europe.

A spirit of equal liberty appears fast to be gaining ground everywhere; which must afford satisfaction to every friend of mankind.

Did it not savor too much of partiality for my countrymen, I might say, that I cannot help flattering myself, that the new Congress, on account of the self-created respectability and various talents of its members, will not be inferior to any Assembly in the world.

It should be the highest ambition of every American, to extend his views beyond himself, and to bear in mind, that his conduct will not only affect himself, his country, and his immediate posterity, but that its influence may be co-extensive with the world, and stamp political happiness or misery on ages yet unborn. To establish this desirable end, and to establish the government of laws, the Union of these States is absolutely necessary. Therefore, in every proceeding, this great, this important object should ever be kept in view; and, so long as our measures tend to this, and are marked with the wisdom of a well-informed and enlightened people, we may reasonably hope, under the smiles of Heaven, to convince the world, that the happiness of nations can be accomplished by pacific revolutions in their political systems, without the destructive intervention of the sword.

In every nomination to office, I have endeavored, as far as my own knowledge extended, or information could be obtained, to make fitness of character my primary object.

As a public man, acting only with reference to the public good, I must be allowed to decide upon all points of my duty, without consulting my private inclinations and wishes. I must be permitted, with the best lights I can obtain, and upon a general view of characters and circumstances, to nominate such persons alone to offices as, in my judgment, shall be the best qualified to discharge the functions of the departments to which they shall be appointed.

The virtue, moderation and patriotism, which marked the steps of the American people, in framing, adopting, and thus far carrying into effect our present system of government, have excited the admiration of nations. It only now remains for us, to act up to those principles, which should characterize a free and enlightened people, that we may gain respect abroad, and insure happiness to ourselves and our posterity.

It doubtless is important, that all treaties and compacts formed by the United States with other nations, whether civilized or not, should be made with caution, and executed with fidelity.

It is said to be the general understanding and practice of nations, as a check on the mistakes and indiscretions of ministers and commissioners, not to consider any treaty, negotiated and signed by such officers, as final and conclusive, until ratified by the sovereign or government from whom they derive their powers.

The concurrence of virtuous individuals, and the combination of economical societies, to rely, as much as possible, on the resources of our own country, may be productive of great national advantages, by establishing the habits of industry and economy.

Within our territories there are no mines either of gold or silver; and this young nation, just recovering from the waste and desolation of a long war, has not as yet had time to acquire riches by agriculture and commerce. But our soil is bountiful, and our people industrious; and we have reason to flatter ourselves, that we shall gradually become useful to our friends.

Though I would not force the introduction of manufactures, by extravagant encouragements, and to the prejudice of agriculture, yet, I conceive, much might be done in that way, by women, children, and others, without taking one really necessary hand from tilling the earth.

I have been writing to General Knox, to procure me homespun broadcloth of the Hartford fabric, to make a suit of clothes for myself. I hope it will not be a great while, before it will be unfashionable for a gentleman to appear in any other dress. Indeed we have already been too long subject to British prejudices. I use no porter or cheese in my family, but such as is made in America. Both those articles may now be purchased, of an excellent quality.

The promotion of domestic manufactures will, in my conception, be among the first consequences which may naturally be expected to flow from an energetic government. For myself, having an equal regard for the prosperity of the farming, trading, and manufacturing interests, I will only observe, that I cannot conceive the extension of the latter (so far as it may afford employment to a great number of hands, which would be otherwise, in a manner, idle), can be detrimental to the former.

While the measures of government ought to be calculated to protect its citizens from all injury and violence, a due regard should be extended to those Indian tribes, whose happiness, in the course of events, so materially depends on the national justice and humanity of the United States.

I am not a little flattered, by being considered, by the patrons of literature, as one of their number. Fully apprised of the influence which sound learning has on religion and manners, on government, liberty, and laws, I shall only lament my want of abilities to make it still more extensive.

Men's minds are as variant as their faces. Where the motives of their actions are pure, the operation of the former is no more to be imputed to them as a crime, than the appearance of the latter; for both, being the work of nature, are alike unavoidable.

A difference of opinion on political points, is not to be imputed to freemen, as a fault. It is to be presumed, that they are all actuated by an equally laudable and sacred regard for the liberties of their country. If the mind is so formed, in different persons, as to consider the same object to be somewhat different in its nature and consequences, as it happens to be placed in different points of view; and if the oldest, the ablest, and the most virtuous statesmen, have often differed in judgment, as to the best forms of government, we ought, indeed, rather to rejoice, that so much has been effected, than to regret, that more could not all at once be accomplished.

I have obeyed a summons, to which I can never be insensible.

When my country demands the sacrifice, personal ease must always be a secondary consideration.

The love of my country will be the ruling influence of my conduct.

It is but justice, to assign great merit to the temper of those citizens whose estates were more immediately the scene of warfare. Their personal services were rendered, without constraint; and the derangement of their affairs submitted to, without dissatisfaction. It was the triumph of patriotism over personal considerations. And our present enjoyments of peace and freedom reward the sacrifice.

I am sensible, that I am embarking, with the voice of the people, and a good name of my own, on this voyage. What returns may be made for them, Heaven alone can foretell. Integrity and firmness are all I can promise. These, be the voyage long or short, shall never forsake me, though I may be deserted by all men; for, of the consolation to be derived from these the world cannot deprive me.

It appears to me, that little more than common sense and common honesty, in the transactions of the community at large, would be necessary to make us a great and happy nation; for, if the general government lately adopted shall be arranged and administered in such a manner, as to acquire the full confidence of the American people, I sincerely believe they will have greater advantages, from their natural, moral, and political circumstances, for public felicity, than any other people ever possessed.

The eyes of Argus are upon me; and no slip will pass unnoticed.

Every one who has any knowledge of my manner of acting in public life, will be persuaded, that I am not accustomed to impede the despatch, or frustrate the success, of business, by a ceremonious attention to idle forms.

That great and glorious Being is the Beneficent Author of all the good that was, that is, or that will be.

When I contemplate the interposition of Providence, as it was manifested in guiding us through the Revolution, in preparing us for the reception of a general government, and in conciliating the good will of the people of America towards one another, after its adoption, I feel myself oppressed, and almost overwhelmed, with a sense of the Divine Munificence.

May we unite, in most humbly offering our prayers and supplications to the Great Lord and Ruler of Nations, and beseech him to pardon our national and other transgressions; to enable us all, whether in public or private stations, to perform our several and relative duties, properly and punctually; to render our national government a blessing to all the people, by constantly being a government of wise, just, and constitutional laws, discreetly and faithfully executed and obeyed; to protect and guide all sovereigns and nations (especially such as have shown kindness to us), and to bless them with good governments, peace and concord; to promote the knowledge and practice of true religion and virtue, and the increase of science, among them and us; and, generally, to grant unto all mankind such a degree of temporal prosperity, as He alone knows to be best.

Whilst just government protects all, in their religious rites, true religion affords government its surest support.

I believe, its mild yet efficient operations will tend to remove every remaining apprehension of those with whose opinions it may not entirely coincide, as well as to confirm the hopes of its numerous friends; and the moderation, patriotism, and wisdom of the present Federal Legislature seem to promise the restoration of order and our ancient virtues, the extension of genuine religion, and the consequent advancement of our respectability abroad, and of our substantial happiness at home.

It is the duty of all nations, to acknowledge the Providence of Almighty God, to obey His will, to be grateful for His benefits, and humbly to implore His protection and favor.

It always affords me satisfaction, when I find a concurrence in sentiment and practice between all conscientious men, in acknowledgments of homage to the great Governor of the Universe, and in professions of support to just civil government.

I know the delicate nature of the duties, incident to the part I am called upon to perform; and I feel my incompetence, without the singular assistance of Providence, to discharge them in a satisfactory manner.

If such talents as I possess have been called into action by great events, and those events have terminated happily for our country, the glory should be ascribed to the manifest interposition of an overruling Providence.

I was but the humble agent of favoring Heaven, whose benign influence was so often manifested in our behalf, and to whom alone the praise of victory is due.

The success which has hitherto attended our united efforts, we owe to the gracious interposition of Heaven; and to that interposition let us gratefully ascribe the praise of victory, and the blessings of peace.

I flatter myself, that opportunities will not be wanting, for me to show my disposition to encourage the domestic and public virtues of industry, economy, patriotism, philanthropy, and that righteousness which exalteth a nation.

While I reiterate the professions of my dependence upon Heaven, as the source of all public and private blessings, I will observe, that the general prevalence of piety, philanthropy, honesty, industry, and economy, seems, in the ordinary course of human affairs, particularly necessary for advancing and confirming the happiness of our country. While all men within our territories are protected, in worshipping the Deity according to the dictates of their consciences, it is rationally to be expected from them, in return, that they will all be emulous of evincing the sanctity of their professions, by the innocence of their lives, and the beneficence of their actions; for no man who is profligate in his morals, or a bad member of the civil community, can possibly be a *true Christian*, or a credit to his own religious society.

Your love of liberty, your respect for the laws, your habits of industry, and your practice of the moral and religious obligations, are the strongest claims to national and individual happiness.

Government being, among other purposes, instituted to protect the persons and *consciences* of men from oppression, it certainly is the duty of rulers, not only to abstain from it themselves, but, according to their stations, to prevent it in others.

If I could have entertained the slightest apprehension, that the Constitution, framed in the convention where I had the honor to preside, might possibly endanger the religious rights of any ecclesiastical society, certainly I would never have placed my signature to it. If I could conceive, that the general Government might ever be so administered, as to render the liberty of conscience insecure, no one would be more zealous than myself, to establish effectual barriers against the horrors of spiritual tyranny, and every species of religious persecution.

I trust, the people of every denomination, who demean themselves as good citizens, will have occasion to be convinced, that I shall always strive to be a faithful and impartial patron of genuine, vital religion.

It shall be my endeavor to manifest, by overt acts, the purity of my inclinations for promoting the happiness of mankind, as well as the sincerity of my desires to contribute whatever may be in my power, towards the preservation of the civil and religious liberties of the American people.

The liberty enjoyed by the people of these States, of worshipping Almighty God agreeably to their consciences, is not only among the choicest of their blessings, but also of their rights.

While men perform their social duties faithfully, they do all that society or the State can, with propriety, demand or expect; and remain responsible only to their Maker, for the religion, or modes of faith, which they may prefer or profess.

In my opinion, the conscientious scruples of all men should be treated with great delicacy and tenderness; and it is my wish and desire, that the laws may always be as extensively accommodated to them, as a due regard to the protection of the essential interests of the nation may justify or permit.

I have often expressed my sentiments, that every man, conducting himself as a good citizen, and being accountable to God alone for his religious opinions, ought to be protected, in worshipping the Deity according to the dictates of his own conscience.

In proportion as the general government of the United States shall acquire strength by duration, it is probable they may have it in their power, to extend a salutary influence to the Aborigines in the extremities of their territory. In the mean time, it will be a desirable thing, for the protection of the Union, to co-operate, as far as circumstances may conveniently admit, with the disinterested efforts of your Society [the Society of the United Brethren for Propagating the Gospel among the Heathen], to civilize and Christianize the savages of the wilderness.

Awful and affecting as the death of a parent is, there is consolation in knowing, that Heaven has spared ours [his mother, Mary Washington], to an age beyond which few attain, and favored her with the full enjoyment of her mental faculties, and as much bodily strength as usually falls to the lot of fourscore. Under these circumstances, and the hope that she is translated to a happier place, it is the duty of her relations, to yield due submission to the decrees of the Creator.

Do not flatter me with vain hopes. I am not afraid to die, and therefore can hear the worst. Whether to-night, or twenty years hence, makes no difference. I know, that I am in the hands of a good Providence.

The want of regular exercise, and the cares of office, will, I have no doubt, hasten my departure for that country from which no traveller returns. But a faithful discharge of whatever trust I accept, as it ever has been, so it always will be, the primary consideration, in every transaction of my life, be the consequences what they may.

1790

Common danger brought the States into confederacy; and on their Union our safety and importance depend.

A spirit of accommodation was the basis of the present Constitution.

The aggregate happiness of society, which is best promoted by the practice of a virtuous policy, is, or ought to be, the end of all government.

My greatest fear has been, that the [French] nation would not be sufficiently cool and moderate, in making arrangements for the security of that liberty of which it seems to be possessed.

That the government, though not actually perfect, is one of the best in the world, I have little doubt.

If we mean to support the liberty and independence, which it has cost us so much blood and treasure to establish, we must drive far away the demon of party spirit and local reproach.

Should the conduct of the Americans, whilst promoting their own happiness, influence the feelings of other nations, and thereby render a service to mankind, they will receive a double pleasure.

The establishment of our new government, seemed to be the last great experiment, for promoting human happiness by a reasonable compact in civil society. It was to be, in the first instance, in a considerable degree, a government of accommodation, as well as a government of laws.

A spirit for political improvement, seems to be rapidly and extensively spreading through the European countries. I shall rejoice in seeing the condition of the human race happier than ever it has hitherto been. But I shall be sorry to see, that those who are for prematurely accelerating those improvements, were making more haste than good speed, in their innovations.

It remains with the people themselves, to preserve and promote the great advantages of their political and natural situation. Nor ought a doubt to be entertained, that men, who so well understand the value of social happiness, will ever cease to appreciate the blessings of a free, equal, and efficient government.

The value of liberty was enhanced in our estimation, by the difficulty of its attainment, and the worth of character appreciated by the trial of adversity. The tempest of war having at length been succeeded by the sunshine of peace, our citizen-soldiers impressed a useful lesson of patriotism on mankind, by nobly returning, with impaired constitutions and unsatisfied claims, after such long sufferings and severe disappointments, to their former occupations. Posterity, as well as the present age, will doubtless regard, with admiration and gratitude, the patience, perseverance and valor, which achieved our Revolution. They will cherish the remembrance of virtues which had but few parallels in former times, and which will add new lustre to the most splendid page of history.

I always believed, that an unequivocally free and equal representation of the people in the legislature, together with an efficient and responsible Executive, was the great pillar on which the preservation of American freedom must depend.

As, under the smiles of Heaven, America is indebted for freedom and independence, rather to the joint exertions of the citizens of the several States than to the conduct of the Commander-in-chief, so is she indebted, for their support, rather to a continuation of those exertions, than to the prudence and ability manifested in the exercise of the powers delegated to the President of the United States.

A change in the national Constitution, conformed to experience and the circumstances of our country, has been most happily effected by the influence of reason alone. In this change, the liberty of the citizen continues unimpaired, while the energy of government is so increased, as to promise full protection to all the pursuits of science and industry, together with the firm establishment of public credit, and the vindication of our national character.

All see, and most admire, the glare which hovers round the external happiness of elevated office. To me, there is nothing in it beyond the lustre, which may be reflected from its connection with the power of promoting human felicity.

The prospect of national prosperity now before us is truly animating, and ought to excite the exertions of all good men, to establish and secure the happiness of their country, in the permanent duration of its freedom and independence. America, under the smiles of Divine Providence, the protection of a good government, the cultivation of manners, morals, and piety, can hardly fail of attaining an uncommon degree of eminence in literature, commerce, agriculture, improvements at home, and respectability abroad.

An adequate provision for the support of the public credit, is a matter of high importance to the national honor and prosperity.

I have always been persuaded, that the stability and success of the National Government, and consequently the happiness of the people of the United States, would depend, in a considerable degree, on the interpretation and execution of its laws.

In my opinion, it is important, that the Judiciary System should not only be independent in its operations, but as perfect as possible in its formation.

Seconded by such a body of yeomanry, as repaired to the standard of liberty, fighting in their own native land, fighting for all that freemen hold dear, and whose docility soon supplied the place of discipline, it was scarcely in human nature, under its worst character, to abandon them in their misfortunes; nor is it for me to claim any singular merit for having shared in a common danger, and triumphed with them, after a series of the severest toil and most accumulated distress, over a formidable foe.

The basis of our proceedings with the Indian Nations has been, and shall be, *justice*, during the period in which I have any thing to do with the administration of this government.

The welfare of the country, is the great object to which our cares and efforts ought to be directed. . . . I shall derive great satisfaction from a cooperation in the pleasing, though arduous task, of insuring to our fellow-citizens the blessings which they have a right to expect from a free, efficient, and equal government.

I can truly say, I had rather be at Mount Vernon, with a friend or two about me, than to be attended, at the seat of government, by the officers of state, and the representatives of every power in Europe.

Mrs. Washington's wishes coincide with my own, as to simplicity of dress, and every thing which can tend to support propriety of character, without partaking of the follies of luxury and ostentation.

A good moral character is the first essential in a man. It is therefore highly important, to endeavor not only to be learned, but virtuous.

As mankind become more liberal, they will be more apt to allow, that all those who conduct themselves as worthy members of the community, are equally entitled to the protection of civil government. . . . I hope ever to see America among the foremost nations, in examples of justice and liberality.

May the same Wonder-working Deity, who long since delivered the Hebrews from their Egyptian oppressors, and
planted them in the Promised Land; whose providential
agency has lately been conspicuous, in establishing these
United States as an independent nation, still continue to
water them with the dews of heaven, and to make the inhabitants, of every denomination, participate in the temporal
and spiritual blessings of that people whose God is Jehovah.

It gives me the most sensible pleasure to find, that, in our
nation, however different are the sentiments of citizens, on
religious doctrines, they generally concur in one thing; for
their political professions and practice are almost universally
friendly to the order and happiness of our civil institutions.

Our citizen-soldiers have impressed a useful lesson of patriotism on mankind.

In looking forward to that awful moment when I must b
adieu to sublunary things, I anticipate the consolation,
leaving our country in a prosperous condition. And while t
curtain of separation shall be drawing, my last breath wil
trust, expire in a prayer for the temporal and eternal feli
of those, who have not only endeavored to gild the even
of my days with unclouded serenity, but extended their
sires to my happiness hereafter, in a brighter world.

1791

The tumultuous populace of large cities, are ever
dreaded. Their indiscriminate violence prostrates, fc
time, all public authority; and its consequences are
times extensive and terrible.

It is among nations, as with individuals; the party
advantage [in treaty negotiations] of the distresses

other, will lose infinitely more, in the opinion of manki, and in consequent events, than it will gain by the stroke the moment.

From the gallantry and fortitude of her citizens, under the auspices of Heaven, America has derived her independence. To their industry, and the natural advantages of the country, she is indebted for her prosperous situation. From their virtue she may expect long to share the protection of a free and equal government, which their wisdom has established, and which experience justifies, as admirably adapted to our social wants and individual felicity.

The impressions naturally produced by similarity of political sentiment, are justly to be regarded as causes of national sympathy, calculated to confirm the amicable ties which may otherwise subsist between nations. This reflection, independent of its more particular reference, must dispose every benevolent mind to unite in the wish, that a general diffusion of the true principles of liberty, assimilating as well as ameliorating the condition of mankind, and fostering the maxims of an ingenuous and virtuous policy, may tend to strengthen the fraternity of the human race, to assuage the jealousies and animosities of its various subdivisions, and to convince them, more and more, that their true interest and felicity will best be promoted, by mutual good-will and universal harmony.

Unless treaties are mutually beneficial to the parties, it is in vain to hope for a continuance of them, beyond the moment when the one which conceives itself overreached, is in a situation to break off the connection.

In this age of free inquiry and enlightened reason, it is to be hoped, that the condition of the people in every country will be bettered, and the happiness of mankind promoted. Spain

appears to be so much behind the other nations of Europe in liberal policy, that a long time will undoubtedly elapse, before the people of that kingdom can taste the sweets of liberty, and enjoy the natural advantages of their country.

In two hours after the books [of the Bank of the United States] were opened by the Commissioners, the whole number of shares was taken up, and four thousand more applied for, than were allowed by the institution; besides a number of subscriptions which were coming on. This circumstance was not only pleasing, as it related to the confidence in the Government, but as it exhibited an unexpected proof of the resources of our citizens.

The disorders in the existing currency, and especially the scarcity of small change (a scarcity, so peculiarly distressing to the poorer classes), strongly recommend the carrying into immediate effect the resolution already entered into, concerning the establishment of a Mint.

The importance of the Post-Office and Post-Roads, on a plan sufficiently liberal and comprehensive, as they respect the expedition, safety, and facility of communication, is increased, by their instrumentality in diffusing a knowledge of the laws and proceedings of the Government, which, while it contributes to the security of the people, serves also to guard them against the effects of misrepresentation and misconception.

This [the militia of the United States] is certainly an object of primary importance, whether viewed in reference to the national security, to the satisfaction of the community, or to the preservation of order.

The safety of the United States, under Divine protection, ought to rest on the basis of systematic and solid arrange-

ment, exposed, as little as possible, to the hazards of fortuitous circumstances.

The Great Ruler of Events will not permit the happiness of
so many millions to be destroyed.

1792

The just medium cannot be expected to be found in a moment. The first vibrations always go to the extremes; and
cool reason, which can alone establish a permanent and equal
government, is as little to be expected in the tumults of popular commotion, as an attention to the liberties of the people
is to be found in the dark divan of a despotic tyrant.

I entertain a strong hope, that the state of the national finances is now sufficiently matured, to enable you [the House
of Representatives] to enter upon a systematic and effectual
arrangement, for the regular redemption and discharge of the
public debt, according to the right which has been reserved
to the Government. No measure can be more desirable,
whether viewed with an eye to its intrinsic importance, or to
the general sentiment and wish of the nation.

As the All-wise Disposer of events has hitherto watched over
my steps, I trust, that, in the important one I may soon be
called upon to take, He will mark the course so plainly, that
I cannot mistake the way.

Of all the animosities which have existed among mankind,
those which are caused by a difference of sentiments in religion, appear to be the most inveterate and distressing, and
ought most to be deprecated. I was in hopes, that the enlightened and liberal policy which has marked the present
age, would at least have reconciled Christians of every denomination, so far, that we should never again see their religious disputes carried to such a pitch, as to endanger the
peace of society.

Impressed as I am with the opinion, that the most effectual means of securing the permanent attachment of our savage neighbors, is to convince them that we are just, and to show them, that a proper and friendly intercourse with us would be for our mutual advantage, I cannot conclude, without giving you [Roman Catholic Archbishop Carroll] my thanks, for your pious and benevolent wishes to effect this desirable end, upon the mild principles of religion and philanthropy. And when a proper occasion shall offer, I have no doubt that such measures will be pursued, as may seem best calculated to communicate liberal instruction, and the blessings of society, to their untutored minds.

1793

The rapidity of national revolutions appears no less astonishing than their magnitude. In what they will terminate, is known only to the Great Ruler of events; and, confiding in His wisdom and goodness, we may safely trust the issue to Him, without perplexing ourselves to seek for that which is beyond our ken; only taking care to perform the parts assigned to us, in a way that reason and our own consciences approve.

To complete the American character, it remains for the citizens of the United States to show to the world that the reproach heretofore cast on republican governments, for their want of stability, is without foundation, when that government is the deliberate choice of an enlightened people. And I am fully persuaded, that every well-wisher to the happiness and prosperity of this country will evince, by his conduct, that we live under a government of laws, and that, while we preserve inviolate our national faith, we are desirous to live in amity with all mankind.

True to our duties and interests as Americans, firm to our purpose as lovers of peace, let us unite our fervent prayers to the great Ruler of the Universe, that the justice and moderation of all concerned may permit us to continue in the uninterrupted enjoyment of a blessing, which we so greatly prize, and of which we ardently wish them a speedy and permanent participation.

No pecuniary consideration is more urgent, than the regular redemption and discharge of the public debt. On none can delay be more injurious, or an economy of time more valuable.

The friends of humanity will deprecate war, wheresoever it may appear; and we have experience enough of its evils, in this country, to know, that it should not be wantonly or unnecessarily entered upon. I trust, that the good citizens of the United States will show to the world, that they have as much wisdom in preserving peace at this critical juncture, as they have hitherto displayed valor in defending their just rights.

Time may unfold more, than prudence ought to disclose.

We have abundant reason to rejoice, that, in this land, the light of truth and reason have triumphed over the power of bigotry and superstition, and that every person may here worship God, according to the dictates of his own heart. In this enlightened age, and in this land of equal liberty, it is our boast, that a man's religious tenets will not forfeit the protection of the laws, nor deprive him of the right of attaining and holding the highest offices that are known in the United States.

I am at a loss, for whose benefit to apply the little I can give, and in whose hands to place it; whether for the use of the fatherless children and widows, made so by the late calamity [a fever epidemic in Philadelphia], who may find it difficult, whilst provisions, wood, and other necessaries are so dear, to support themselves; or to other and better purposes, if any, I know not, and therefore have taken the liberty of asking your [Right Reverend Dr. William White's] advice.

1794

My opinion with respect to emigration is, that, except of useful mechanics, and some particular descriptions of men or professions, there is no need of encouragement; whilst the policy or advantage of its taking place in a body (I mean the settling of them in a body), may be much questioned; for, by so doing, they retain the language, habits, and principles, good or bad, which they bring with them. Whereas, by an intermixture with our people, they or their descendants get assimilated to our customs, measures, and laws; in a word, soon become our people.

The affairs of this country cannot go amiss. There are so many watchful guardians of them! and such infallible guides! that no one is at a loss for a director at every turn.

My policy, in our foreign transactions, has been, to cultivate peace with all the world; to observe the treaties with pure and absolute faith; to check every deviation from the line of impartiality; to explain what may have been misapprehended, and correct what may have been injurious to any nation; and having thus acquired the right, to lose no time in acquiring the ability, to insist upon justice being done to ourselves.

Having determined, as far as lay within the power of the Executive, to keep this country in a state of neutrality, I have made my public conduct accord with the system; and, whilst so acting as a public character, consistency and propriety as a private man forbid those intemperate expressions in favor of one nation, or to the prejudice of another which many have indulged themselves in, and, I will venture to add, to the embarrassment of government, without producing any good to the country.

The Mint of the United States has entered upon the coinage of the precious metals, and considerable sums of defective coins and bullion have been lodged with the director, by individuals. There is a pleasing prospect, that the institution will, at no remote day, realize the expectation which was originally formed of its utility.

The dispensation of justice belongs to the civil magistrate; and let it ever be our pride and our glory, to leave the sacred deposit there inviolate.

I exhort all individuals, officers, and bodies of men, to contemplate with abhorrence the measures leading, directly or indirectly, to those crimes which produce this resort to military coercion [the Whiskey Rebellion]; to check, in their respective spheres, the efforts of misguided or designing men to substitute their misrepresentations in the place of truth, and their discontents in the place of stable government; and to call to mind, that, as the people of the United States have been permitted, under the Divine favor, in perfect freedom, after solemn deliberation, in an enlightened age, to elect their own government, so will their gratitude for this inestimable blessing be best distinguished, by firm exertions to maintain the Constitution and the laws.

The spirit which blazed out on this occasion, as soon as the object was fully understood, and the lenient measures of the government were made known to the people, deserves to be communicated. There are instances of general officers going at the head of a single troop, and of light companies; of field officers, when they came to the places of rendezvous, and found no command for them in that grade, turning into the ranks, and proceeding as private soldiers, under their own captains; and of numbers, possessing the first fortunes in the country, standing in the ranks as private men, and marching, day by day, with their knapsacks and haversacks at their backs, sleeping on straw, with a single blanket, in a soldier's tent, during the frosty nights which we have had, by way of example to others. Nay, more; many young Quakers, of the first families, character, and property, not discouraged by the elders, have turned into the ranks, and are marching with the troops.

That a National University, in this country, is a thing to be desired, has always been my decided opinion; and the appropriation of grounds and funds for it, in the Federal City, has long been contemplated.

I have no scruple in disclosing to you [Tobias Lear, his private secretary] that my motives to these sales are to reduce my income, be it more or less, to specialities—that the remainder of my days may thereby be more tranquil, and free from care; and that I may be enabled, knowing what my dependence is, to do as much good as my resources will admit. Although, in the estimation of the world, I possess a good and clear estate, yet so unproductive is it, that I am oftentimes ashamed to refuse aid which I cannot afford, unless I sell part of it to answer this purpose. Besides these, I have another motive, which makes me earnestly wish for these things. It is, indeed, more powerful than all the rest; namely, to liberate a certain species of property, which I possess very reluctantly to my own feelings, but which imperious necessity compels, until I can substitute some other expedient, by which expenses not in my power to avoid (however well disposed I may be to do it), can be defrayed.

Against the malignity of the discontented, the turbulent, and the vicious, no abilities, no exertions, nor the most unshaken integrity, are any safeguard.

Let us unite, in imploring the Supreme Ruler of Nations, to spread his holy protection over these United States; to turn the machinations of the wicked, to the confirming of our Constitution; to enable us, at all times, to root out internal sedition, and put invasion to flight; to perpetuate to our country that prosperity, which His goodness has already conferred, and to verify the anticipations of this government being a safeguard of human rights.

I will direct my manager to pay my annual donation, for the education of orphan children, or the children of indigent parents, who are unable to be at the expense themselves. I had pleasure in appropriating this money to such uses, as I always shall have in paying it.

1795
The Constitution is the guide which I never can abandon.

Such, for wise purposes it is presumed, is the turbulence of human passions in party disputes, when victory, more than truth, is the palm contended for, that "the post of honor is a private station."

In every act of my administration, I have sought the happiness of my fellow-citizens. My system for the attainment of this object, has uniformly been, to overlook all personal, local, and partial considerations; to contemplate the United States as one great whole; to confide, that sudden impressions, when erroneous, would yield to candid reflection; and to consult only the substantial and permanent interests of the country.

If any power on earth could, or the Great Power above would, erect a standard of infallibility, in political opinions, there is no being that inhabits the terrestrial globe, that would resort to it with more eagerness than myself, so long as I remain a servant of the public. But as I have found no better guide hitherto, than upright intentions and close investigation, I shall adhere to those maxims, while I keep the watch; leaving it to those who will come after me, to explore new ways, if they like or think them better.

Republicanism is not the phantom of a deluded imagination. On the contrary, laws, under no form of government, are better supported, liberty and property better secured, or happiness more effectually dispensed to mankind.

In a government as free as ours, where the people are at liberty, and will express their sentiments (oftentimes imprudently, and, for want of information, sometimes unjustly), allowances must be made for occasional effervescences; but, after the declaration which I have made of my political creed, you can run no hazard in asserting, that the Executive branch of this government never has suffered, nor will suffer while I preside, any improper conduct of its officers to escape with impunity, nor give its sanction to any disorderly proceedings of its citizens.

Of two men equally well affected to the true interests of their country, of equal abilities, and equally disposed to lend their support, it is the part of prudence, to give preference to him against whom the least clamor can be excited.

In the appointments to the great offices of Government, my aim has been, to combine geographical situation, and sometimes other considerations, with abilities, and fitness of known character.

I shall not, whilst I have the honor to administer the Government, bring a man into any office of consequence, knowingly, whose political tenets are adverse to the measures which the general Government are pursuing; for this, in my opinion, would be a sort of political suicide.

I can most religiously aver, I have no wish that is incompatible with the dignity, happiness, and true interest of the people of this country. My ardent desire is, and my aim has been, so far as depended on the Executive department, to comply strictly with all our engagements, foreign and domestic; but to keep the United States free from political connections with every other country, to see them independent of all, and under the influence of none. In a word, I want an American character, that the powers of Europe may be convinced we act for ourselves, and not for others. This, in my judgment, is the only way to be respected abroad, and happy at home; and not, by becoming the partisans of Great Britain or France, create dissensions, disturb the public tranquillity, and destroy, perhaps for ever, the cement which binds the Union.

My policy has been, and will continue to be, while I have the honor to remain in the administration, to maintain friendly terms with, but to be independent of, all the nations of the earth; to share in the broils of none; to fulfil our own engagements; to supply the wants, and be carriers for them all; being thoroughly convinced, that it is our policy and interest to do so.

Nothing short of self-respect, and that justice which is essential to a national character, ought to involve us in [a foreign] war; for sure I am, if this country is preserved in tranquillity twenty years longer, it may bid defiance, in a just cause, to any power whatever; such, in that time, will be its population, wealth, and resources.

The affairs of the country are in a violent paroxysm; and it is the duty of its old and uniform friends, to assist in piloting the vessel in which we are all embarked, between the rocks of Scylla and Charybdis; for more pains never were taken, I believe, than at this moment, to throw it upon one or the other, and to embroil us in the disputes of Europe.

The Constitution has assigned to the President the power of making treaties, with the advice and consent of the Senate. It was doubtless supposed, that these two branches of Government would combine, without passion, and with the best means of information, those facts and principles, upon which the success of our foreign relations will always depend; that they ought not to substitute, for their own conviction, the opinions of others, or to seek truth through any channel but that of a temperate and well-informed investigation.

The madness of the European powers, and the calamitous situation into which all of them are thrown by the present ruinous war, ought to be a serious warning to us, to avoid a similar catastrophe, so long as we can with honor and justice to our national character.

The army are the mere agents of civil power. Out of camp, they have no other authority than other citizens; and their offences against the laws are to be examined, not by a military officer, but by a magistrate. They are not exempt from arrests and indictments for violations of the laws.

The plan of annual presents [to the Indians], in an abstract view, unaccompanied with other measures, is not the best mode of treating ignorant savages, from whose hostile conduct we experience much distress; but, it is not to be forgotten, that they in turn are not without serious causes of complaint, from the encroachments which are made on their lands by our people, who are not to be restrained by any law now in being, or likely to be enacted. They, poor wretches, have no press, through which their grievances are related. And it is well known, that, when one side only of a story is heard and often repeated, the human mind becomes impressed with it, insensibly. The annual presents, however, are not given so much with a view to purchase peace, as by way of contribution for injuries not otherwise to be redressed.

We ought to deprecate the hazard attending ardent and susceptible minds, from being too strongly, and too easily, prepossessed [by foreign education], in favor of other political systems, before they are capable of appreciating their own.

It is with indescribable regret, that I have seen the youth of the United States, migrating to foreign countries, in order to acquire the higher branches of erudition, and to obtain a knowledge of the sciences.

My friendship, so far from being diminished, has increased in the ratio of his [Lafayette's] misfortunes.

A month from this day [January 22, 1795], if I should live to see the completion of it, will place me on the wrong (perhaps it would be better to say the advanced) side of my grand climacteric; and although I have no cause to complain of the want of health, I can religiously aver, that no man was ever more tired of public life, or more devoutly wished for retirement, than I do.

Whilst I am in office, I shall never suffer private convenience to interfere with what I conceive to be my official duty.

Next to the approbation of my own mind, arising from a consciousness of having uniformly, diligently, and sincerely timed, by doing my duty, to promote the true interests of my country, the approbation of my fellow-citizens is dear to my heart. In a free country, such approbation should be a citizen's best reward; and so it would be, if truth and candor were always to estimate the conduct of public men. But the reverse is so often the case, that he who wishes to serve his country, if not influenced by higher motives, runs the risk of being miserably disappointed. Under such discouragements, the good citizen will look beyond the applauses and reproaches of men, and, persevering in his *duty*, stand firm in conscious rectitude, and in the hope of approving Heaven.

While I feel the most lively gratitude for the many instances of approbation from my country, I can not otherwise deserve it, than by obeying the dictates of my conscience.

I am resolved, that no misrepresentations, falsehoods, or calumny, shall make me swerve from what I conceive to be the strict line of duty.

The sentiments we have mutually expressed, of profound gratitude to the source of those numerous blessings, the Author of all good, are pledges of our obligations, to unite our sincere and zealous endeavors, as the instruments of Divine Providence, to preserve and perpetuate them.

Mrs. H. [an indigent woman] should endeavor to do what she can for herself. This is the duty of every one. But you must not let her suffer, as she has thrown herself upon me. Your advances, on this account, will be allowed always at settlement. I agree readily to furnish her with provisions; and, from the good character you give of her daughter, make the latter a present, in my name, of a handsome but not costly gown, and other things which she may stand mostly in need of. You may charge me also with the worth of your tenement on which she is placed; and where, perhaps, it is better she should be, than at a greater distance from your attentions to her.

1796

Born in a land of liberty; having early learned its value; having engaged in the perilous conflict to defend it; having, in a word, devoted the best years of my life to secure its permanent establishment in my own country; my anxious recollections, my sympathetic feelings, and my best wishes are irresistibly attracted, whensoever in any country I see an oppressed nation unfurl the banners of freedom.

I concur with the legislature in repeating, with pride and joy, what will be an everlasting honor to our country, that our Revolution was so distinguished for moderation, virtue, and humanity, as to merit the eulogium they have pronounced, of its being unsullied with a crime.

Whatever my own opinion may be, on any subject interesting to the community at large, it always has been and will continue to be my earnest desire, to learn, and, as far as it is consistent, to comply with, the public sentiment; but it is on great occasions only, and after time has been given for cool and deliberate reflection, that the real voice of the people can be known.

I am sure, the mass of citizens in these United States mean well; and I firmly believe they will always act well, whenever they can obtain a right understanding of matters. But, in some parts of the Union, where the sentiments of their delegates and leaders are adverse to the government, and great pains are taken to inculcate a belief, that their rights are assailed and their liberties endangered, it is not easy to accomplish this; especially, as is the case invariably, when the inventors and abettors of pernicious measures use infinitely more industry, in disseminating poison, than the well-disposed part of the community, in furnishing the antidote. To this source all our discontents may be traced and from it all our embarrassments proceed. Hence serious misfortunes, originating in misrepresentation, frequently flow, and spread, before they can be dissipated by truth.

Let me impress the following maxims upon the executive officers. In all important matters, deliberate maturely, but execute promptly and vigorously; and do not put things off until to-morrow which can be done, and require to be done, to-day. Without an adherence to these rules, business never will be well done, or done in an easy manner, but will always be in arrear, with one thing treading upon the heels of another.

Men in responsible situations cannot, like those in private life, be governed solely by the dictates of their own inclinations, or by such motives as can only affect themselves.

Good measures should always be executed, as soon as they are conceived, and circumstances will admit.

I have always given it as my decided opinion, that no nation had a right to intermeddle in the internal concerns of another; that every one had a right to form and adopt whatever government they liked best to live under, themselves; and that if this country could, consistently with its engagements, maintain a strict neutrality and thereby preserve peace, it was bound to do so, by motives of policy, interest, and every other consideration that ought to actuate a people situated as we are, already deeply in debt, and in a convalescent state from the struggles we have been engaged in, ourselves.

The nature of foreign negotiations requires caution; and their success must often depend on secrecy. Even when brought to a conclusion, a full disclosure of all the measures, demands, or eventual concessions, which have been proposed or contemplated, would be extremely impolitic; for this might have a pernicious influence on future negotiations, or produce immediate inconveniences, perhaps danger or mischief, in relation to other powers.

Having been a member of the General Convention, and knowing the principles on which the Constitution was formed, I have ever entertained but one opinion on this subject; and, from the first establishment of the Government to this moment, my conduct has exemplified that opinion, that the power of making treaties is exclusively vested in the President, by and with the advice and consent of the Senate, provided two-thirds of the Senators present concur; and that every treaty, so made and promulgated, thenceforward became the law of the land. It is thus that the treaty-making power has been understood by foreign nations; and, in all the treaties made with them, we have declared, and they have believed, that, when ratified by the President, with the advice and consent of the Senate, they became obligatory.

To call your nation [France] brave, were to pronounce but common praise. Wonderful people! Ages to come will read with astonishment the history of your brilliant exploits.

Posterity may have cause to regret, if, from any motive, intervals of tranquillity are left unimproved for accelerating this valuable end [repayment of the national debt].

It is a maxim with me, not to ask what, under similar circumstances, I would not grant.

It is a fact declared by the General Convention, and universally understood, that the Constitution of the United States was the result of a spirit of amity and mutual concession. And it is well known, that, under this influence, the smaller States were admitted to an equal representation in the Senate, with the larger States, and that this branch of the Government was invested with great powers; for, on the equal participation of those powers the sovereignty and political safety of the smaller States were deemed essentially to depend.

The situation in which I now stand, for the last time, in the midst of the representatives of the people of the United States, naturally recalls the period, when the administration of the present form of government commenced. And I cannot omit the occasion, to congratulate you [Congress], and my country, on the success of the experiment, nor to repeat my fervent supplications to the Supreme Ruler of the Universe and Sovereign Arbiter of Nations, that his providential care may still be extended to the United States, that the virtue and happiness of the people may be preserved, and that the government which they have instituted for the protection of their liberties, may be perpetual.

I am sorry to hear of the death of Mrs. H. [an indigent woman]; and will very cheerfully receive her daughter, the moment I get settled at this place; sooner, it would not be possible, because this house will be, as it has been, empty, from the time we shall quit it in October, until my final establishment in the spring. Such necessaries as she needs in the mean time, may, however, be furnished her at my expense; and if it is inconvenient for you to retain her in your own house, let her be boarded in some respectable family, where her morals and good behavior will be attended to; at my expense also. Let her want for nothing that is decent or proper; and if she remains in your family, I wish, for the girl's sake, as well as for the use she may be of to your aunt, when she comes here, that [she be] industriously employed always, and instructed in the care and economy of housekeeping.

1797

Candor is not a more conspicuous trait, in the character of governments, than it is of individuals.

In all free governments, contentions in elections will take place; and, whilst it is confined to our own citizens, it is not to be regretted; but severely indeed ought it to be repro- bated, when occasioned by foreign machinations. I trust that the good sense of our countrymen will guard the public weal against this and every other innovation, and that, although we may be a little wrong now and then, we shall return to the right path with more avidity. I can never believe, that Providence, which has guided us so long, and through such a labyrinth, will withdraw its protection at this crisis.

With respect to the nations of Europe, their situation appears so awful, that nothing short of omnipotence can predict the issue; although every human mind must feel the miseries it endures. Our course is plain; they who run may read it. Theirs is so bewildered and dark, so entangled and embar- rassed, and so obviously under the influence of intrigue, that one would suppose, if any thing could open the eyes of our misled citizens, that the deplorable situation of those people could not fail to effect it.

I pray devoutly, that we [England and America] may both witness, and that shortly, the return of peace; for a more bloody, expensive, and eventful war is not recorded in modern, if to be found in ancient, history.

Our own experience, if it has not already had this effect, will soon convince us, that the idea of disinterested favors or friendship from any nation whatever, is too novel to be calculated on; and there will always be found a wide difference between the words and actions of any of them.

No policy, in my opinion, can be more clearly demonstrated, than that we should do justice to all, and have no political connection with any of the European powers, beyond those which result from, and serve to regulate, our commerce with them.

Unfortunately, the nature of man is such, that the experience of others is not attended to as it ought to be. We must feel, ourselves, before we can think, or perceive the danger that threatens us.

For having performed duties, which I conceive every country has a right to require of its citizens, I claim no merit; but no man can feel, more sensibly, the reward of approbation for such services than I do.

Although guided by our excellent Constitution in the discharge of official duties, and actuated, through the whole course of my public life, solely by a wish to promote the best interests of our country; yet, without the beneficial interposition of the Supreme Ruler of the Universe, we could not have reached the distinguished situation which we have attained with such unprecedented rapidity. To Him, therefore, should we bow with gratitude and reverence, and endeavor to merit a continuance of his special favors.

Believing, as I do, that religion and morality are essential pillars of civil society, I view, with unspeakable pleasure, that harmony and brotherly love, which characterize the clergy of different denominations, as well in this [Philadelphia], as in other parts of the United States; exhibiting to the world a new and interesting spectacle, at once the pride of our country, and the surest basis of universal harmony.

For me to express my sentiments, with respect to the administration of the concerns of another government, might incur a charge of stepping beyond the line of prudence. But the principles of humanity will justify an avowal of my regret, and I do regret exceedingly, that any causes whatever should have produced and continued until this time a war, more bloody, more expensive, more calamitous, and more pregnant with events, than modern or perhaps any other times can furnish an example of. And I most sincerely and devoutly wish, that the exertions of those having this object in view, may effect what *human nature* cries aloud for—a *general peace*.

It is not for man, to scan the wisdom of Providence. The best we can do is, to submit to the decrees of Providence. . . . Reason, religion, and philosophy teach us to submit; but it is time alone, that can ameliorate the pangs of humanity, and soften its woes.

1798

Peace with all the world, is my sincere wish. I am sure it is our true policy, and am persuaded it is the ardent desire of the government.

Standing as it were in the midst of falling empires, it should be our aim to assume a station and attitude, which will preserve us from being overwhelmed in their ruins.

It was not difficult for me to perceive, that, if we entered into a serious contest with France, the character of the war would differ materially from the last we were engaged in. In the latter, time, caution, and worrying the enemy, until we could be better provided with arms and other means, and had better disciplined troops to carry it on, was the plan for us. But if we should be engaged with the former, they ought to be attacked at every step.

My first wish would be, that my military family and the whole army should consider themselves as a band of brothers, willing and ready to die for each other.

It has been, very properly, the policy of our government to cultivate peace. But, in contemplating the possibility of our being driven to unqualified war, it will be wise to anticipate, that, frequently, the most effectual way to defend is to attack.

The principles by which my conduct has been actuated through life, would not suffer me, in any great emergency, to withhold any services I could render, required by my country; especially in a case, where its dearest rights are assailed by lawless ambition and intoxicated power, contrary to every principle of justice, and in violation of solemn compacts and laws, which govern all civilized nations; and this, too, with the obvious intent to sow thick the seeds of disunion, for the purpose of subjugating the government, and destroying our independence and happiness.

All officers, non-commissioned officers, and soldiers, are positively forbid playing at cards, or other games of chance. At this time of public distress, men may find enough to do, in the service of their God and their country, without abandoning themselves to vice and immorality.

Satisfied, that we have sincerely wished and endeavored to avert war, and exhausted, to the last drop, the cup of reconciliation, we can, with pure hearts, appeal to Heaven for the justice of our cause, and may confidently trust the final result to that kind Providence, which has hitherto, and so often, signally favored the people of the United States.

The vicissitudes of war are in the hands of the Supreme Director, where is no control.

It is in vain, I perceive, to look for ease and happiness in a world of troubles.

1799

It is not uncommon, in prosperous gales, to forget, that adverse winds may blow. Such was the case with France. Such may be the case with the coalesced powers against her. A bystander sees more of the game, generally, than those who are playing it. So neutral nations may be better able to draw a line between the contending parties, than those who are actors in the war. My own wish is, to see every thing settled upon the best and surest foundation, for the peace and happiness of mankind, without regard to this, that, or the other nation. A more destructive sword never was drawn, at least in modern times, than this war has produced. It is time to sheathe it, and give peace to mankind.

Offensive operations, oftentimes, are the surest, if not in some cases the only, means of defence.

The establishment of an institution of this kind [a military academy], upon a respectable and extensive basis, has ever been considered by me, as an object of primary importance to this country; and, while I was in the chair of Government, I omitted no proper opportunity of recommending it, in my public speeches and otherwise, to the attention of the legislature.

It is a maxim with me, that, in times of imminent danger to the country, every true patriot should occupy the post in which he can render his services most effectually.

When, in the decline of life, I gratify the fond wish of my heart in retiring from public labors, and find the language of approbation and fervent prayers for future happiness following that event, my heart expands with gratitude, and my feelings become unutterable.

No wish of my retirement can exceed that of seeing our country happy; and I can entertain no doubt of its being so, if all of us act the part of *good citizens*, contributing our best endeavors to maintain the Constitution, support the laws, and guard our independence against all assaults from whatsoever quarter they may come. Clouds may, and doubtless often will, in the vicissitudes of events, hover over our political concerns; but a steady adherence to these principles will not only dispel them, but render our prospect the brighter by such temporary obscurities.

The affection and attachment of my fellow-citizens, through the whole period of my public employments, will be the subject of my most agreeable recollections. The belief, which the affecting sentiments of the people of Massachusetts, expressed by their Senate and House of Representatives, with those of my fellow-citizens in general, have inspired, that I have been the happy instrument of much good to my country and to mankind, will be a source of unceasing gratitude to Heaven.

Rural employments, while I am spared, which, in the natural course of things, cannot be long, will now take the place of toil, responsibility, and the solicitude attending the walks of public life. And with a desire for the peace, happiness, and prosperity of a country in whose service the prime of my life has been spent, and with the best wishes for the tranquillity of all nations and all men, the scene to me will close; grateful to that Providence, which has directed my steps and shielded me, in the various changes and chances through which I have passed, from my youth to the present moment.

To have finished my public career to the satisfaction of my fellow-citizens, will, to my latest moments, be a matter of pleasing reflection. And to find an evidence of this approbation among my neighbors and friends (some of whom have been the companions of my juvenile years), will contribute not a little to heighten this enjoyment.

Without virtue, and without integrity, the finest talents and the most brilliant accomplishments can never gain the respect, and conciliate the esteem, of the truly valuable part of mankind.

In times of turbulence, when the passions are afloat, calm reason is swallowed up, in the extremes to which measures are attempted to be carried; but, when those subside, and its empire is resumed, the man who acts from principle, who pursues the path of truth, moderation, and justice, will regain his influence.

Conscious integrity has been my unceasing support; and, while it gave me confidence in the measures I pursued, the belief of it, by acquiring to me the confidence of my fellow-citizens, insured the success which they have had. This consciousness will accompany me in my retirement. Without it, public applause could be viewed only as a proof of public error, and felt as the upbraiding of personal demerit.

The ways of Providence are inscrutable, and mortals must submit.

December 14, 1799

I find I am going. My breath cannot last long. I believed from the first, that the disorder would prove fatal.

Do you [his secretary, Tobias Lear] arrange and record all my late military letters and papers. Arrange my accounts, and settle my books, as you know more about them than any one else; and let Mr. Rawlins finish recording my other letters, which he has begun.

I am afraid I fatigue you too much.

Well, it is a debt we must pay to each other; and I hope, when you want aid of this kind, you will find it.

Doctor [James Craik, the family physician], I die hard, but I am not afraid to go. I believed, from my first attack, that I should not survive it. My breath cannot last long.

I feel myself going. I thank you for your attention. But I pray you to take no more trouble about me. Let me go off quietly. I cannot last long.

I am just going. Have me decently buried. And do not let my body be put into the vault, in less than three days after I am dead. Do you understand me? . . . 'Tis Well.

Father of Mercies, take me to thyself.

THE LAST WILL AND TESTAMENT
OF GEORGE WASHINGTON

George Washington died at his home at Mount Vernon, Virginia, on December 14, 1799, in his sixty-seventh year. In his *Last Will And Testament*, dated July 9, 1799, Washington described and disposed of his real and personal property and provided for the future of his immediate family, including Martha Washington, his wife of forty years, and his extended family of brothers, sisters, nieces, and nephews, and his friends.

THE LAST WILL AND TESTAMENT
OF GEORGE WASHINGTON
JULY 9, 1799

In the name of God, amen!

I, George Washington of Mount Vernon, a citizen of the United States and lately President of the same, do make, ordain and declare this instrument, which is written with my own hand and every page thereof subscribed with my name, to be my last Will and Testament, revoking all others.

Imprimus. All my debts, of which there are but few, and none of magnitude, are to be punctually and speedily paid, and the legacies hereinafter bequeathed are to be discharged as soon as circumstances will permit, and in the manner directed.

Item. To my dearly beloved wife, Martha Washington, I give and bequeath the use, profit and benefit of my whole estate, real and personal, for the term of her natural life, except such parts thereof as are specially disposed of hereafter—my improved lot in the town of Alexandria, situated on Pitt and Cameron Streets, I give to her and her heirs forever, as I also do my household and kitchen furniture of every sort and kind with the liquors and groceries which may be on hand at the time of my decease, to be used and disposed of as she may think proper.

Item. Upon the decease of my wife, it is my will and desire, that all the slaves which I hold in my own right shall receive their freedom. To emancipate them during her life, would tho earnestly wished by me, be attended with such insuperable difficulties, on account of their intermixture by marriages with the dower negroes as to excite the most painful sensations—if not disagreeable consequences from the latter while both descriptions are in the occupancy of the same proprietor, it not being in my power under the tenure by which the dower Negroes are held to manumit them. And whereas among those who will receive freedom according to this devise there may be some who from old age, or bodily infirmities and others who on account of their infancy, that will be unable to support themselves, it is my will and desire that all who come under the first and second description shall be comfortably clothed and fed by my heirs while they live and that such of the latter description as have no parents living, or if living are unable, or unwilling to provide for them, shall be bound by the Court until they shall arrive at the age of twenty-five years, and in cases where no record can be produced whereby their ages can be ascertained, the judgment of the Court upon its own view of the subject shall be adequate and final. The negroes thus bound are (by their masters and mistresses) to be taught to read and write and to be brought up to some useful occupation, agreeably to the laws of the Commonwealth of Virginia, providing for the support of orphans and other poor children—and I do hereby expressly forbid the sale or transportation out of the said Commonwealth of any slave I may die possessed of, under any pretense, whatsoever—and I do moreover most positively, and most solemnly enjoin it upon my executors hereafter named, or the survivors of them to see that this clause respecting slaves and every part thereof be religiously fulfilled at the epoch at which it is directed to take place without evasion, neglect or delay after the crops which may then be on the ground are harvested, particularly as it respects the aged and infirm, seeing that a regular and permanent fund be established for their support so long as there are subjects requiring it, not trusting to the uncertain provisions to be made by individuals. And to my mulatto man, William (calling himself William Lee) I give immediate freedom or if he should prefer it (on account of the accidents which have befallen him and which have rendered him incapable of walking or of any active employment) to remain in the situation he now is, it shall be optional in him to do so. In either case, however, I allow him an annuity of thirty dollars during his natural life which shall be independent of the victuals and clothes he has been accustomed to receive; if he chooses the last alternative, but in full with his freedom, if he prefers the first, and this I give him as a testimony of my sense of his attachment to me and for his faithful services during the Revolutionary War.

Item. To the Trustees (Governors or by whatsoever other name they may be designated) of the academy in the town of Alexandria, I give and bequeath, in trust, four thousand dollars, or in other words twenty of the shares which I hold in the Bank of Alexandria towards the support of a free school, established at, and annexed to the said academy for the purpose of educating such orphan children, or the children of such other poor and indigent persons as are unable to accomplish it with their own means, and who in the judgment of the trustees of the said seminary, are best entitled to the benefits of this donation. The aforesaid twenty shares I give and bequeath in perpetuity—the dividends only of which are to be drawn for and applied by the said Trustees for the time being, for the uses above mentioned, the stock to remain entire and untouched unless indications of a failure of the said bank should be so apparent or discontinuance thereof should render a removal of this fund necessary, in either of these cases the amount of the stock here devised is to be vested in some other bank or public institution whereby the interest may with regularity and certainty be drawn and applied as above. And to prevent misconception, my meaning is, and is hereby declared to be that, these twenty shares are in lieu of and not in addition to the thousand pounds given by a missive letter some years ago in consequence whereof an annuity of fifty pounds has since been paid towards the support of this institution.

Item. Whereas by a law of the Commonwealth of Virginia, enacted in the year 1785, the Legislature thereof was pleased (as an evidence of its approbation of the services I had rendered the public, during the Revolution—and partly, I believe in consideration of my having suggested the vast advantages which the community would derive from the extension of its inland navigation, under legislative patronage) to present me with one hundred shares, of one hundred dollars each, in the incorporated company established for the purpose of extending the navigation of James River from tide water to the mountains; and also with fifty shares of one hundred pounds sterling each in the corporation of another company likewise established for the similar purpose of opening the navigation of the River Potomac from tide water to Fort Cumberland; the acceptance of which, although the offer was highly honorable and grateful to my feelings, was refused, as inconsistent with a principle which I had adopted, and had never departed from, namely not to receive pecuniary compensation for any services I could render my country in its arduous struggle with Great Britain for its rights; and because I had evaded similar propositions from other States in the Union—adding to this refusal, however, an intimation, that, if it should be the pleasure of the Legislature to permit me to appropriate the said shares to public uses, I would receive them on those terms with due sensibility—and this it having consented to in flattering terms, as will appear by a subsequent law and sundry resolutions, in the most ample and honorable manner, I proceed after this recital for the more correct understanding of the case to declare—

That as it has always been a source of serious regret with me to see the youth of these United States sent to foreign countries for the purpose of education, often before their minds were formed or they had imbibed any adequate ideas of the happiness of their own, contracting too frequently not only habits of dissipation and extravagance, but principles unfriendly to republican government and to the true and genuine liberties of mankind, which thereafter are rarely overcome. For these reasons it has been my ardent wish to see a plan devised on a liberal scale which would have a tendency to spread systematic ideas through all parts of this rising Empire, thereby to do away local attachments and state prejudices as far as the nature of things would, or indeed ought to admit, from our national councils. Looking anxiously forward to the accomplishment of so desirable an object as this is (in my estimation), my mind has not been able to contemplate any plan more likely to effect the measure than the establishment of a university in a central part of the United States to which the youth of fortune and talents from all parts thereof might be sent for the completion of their education in all the branches of polite literature in arts and sciences—in acquiring knowledge in the principles of politics and good government and (as a matter of infinite importance in my judgment) by associating with each other and forming friendships in juvenile years, be enabled to free themselves in a proper degree from those local prejudices and habitual jealousies which have just been mentioned and which when carried to excess are never failing sources of disquietude to the public mind and pregnant of mischievous consequences to this country—under these impressions so fully dilated—

Item. I give and bequeath in perpetuity the fifty shares which I hold in the Potomac Company (under the aforesaid Acts of the Legislature of Virginia) towards the endowment of a university to be established within the limits of the District of Columbia, under the auspices of the general Government, if that Government should incline to extend a fostering hand towards it, and until such seminary is established, and the funds arising on these shares shall be required for its support, my further will and desire is that the profit accruing therefrom shall whenever the dividends are made be laid out in purchasing stock in the Bank of Columbia or some other bank at the discretion of my executors, or by the Treasurer of the United States for the time being under the direction of Congress, provided that honorable body should patronize the measure. And the dividends proceeding from the purchase of such stock is to be vested in more stock and so on until a sum adequate to the accomplishment of the object is obtained, of which I have not the smallest doubt before many years pass away, even if no aid or encouraged is given by legislative authority or from any other source.

Item. The hundred shares which I held in the James River Company I have given and now confirm in perpetuity to and for the use and benefit of Liberty Hall Academy in the County of Rockbridge, in the Commonwealth of Virginia.

Item. I release, exonerate and discharge the estate of my deceased brother, Samuel Washington, from the payment of the money which is due to me for the land I sold to Philip Pendleton (lying in the County of Berkley) who assigned the same to him the said Samuel, who by agreement was to pay me therefor. And whereas by some contract (the purport of which was never communicated to me) between the said Samuel and his son, Thornton Washington, the latter became possessed of the aforesaid land without any conveyance having passed from me either to the said Pendleton, the said Samuel or the said Thornton, and without any consideration having been made, by which neglect neither the legal or equitable title has been alienated; it rests therefore with me to declare my intentions concerning the premises—and these are to give and bequeath the said land to whomsoever the said Thornton Washington (who is also dead) devised the same or to his heirs forever, if he died intestate. Exonerating the estate of the said Thornton, equally with that of the said Samuel from payment of the purchase money, which with interest agreeably to the original contact with the said Pendleton would amount to more than a thousand pounds—and whereas two other sons of my said deceased brother Samuel—namely, George Steptoe Washington and Lawrence Augustine Washington—were by the decease of those to whose care they were committed, brought under my protection, and in consequence have occasioned advances on my part for their education at college and other schools, for their board, clothing, and other incidental expenses to the amount of near five thousand dollars over and above the sums furnished by their estate, which sum may be inconvenient for them or their father's estate to refund—I do for these reasons acquit them and the said estate from the payment thereof—my intention being that all accounts between them and me and their father's estate and me shall stand balanced.

Item. The balance due to me from the estate of Bartholomew Dandridge, deceased (my wife's brother), and which amounted on the first day of October, 1795, to four hundred and twenty-five pounds (as will appear by an account rendered by his deceased son, John Dandridge, who was the executor of his father's will) I release and acquit from the payment thereof. And the negroes (then thirty-three in number) formerly belonging to the said estate who were taken in execution—sold—and purchased in, on my account . . . and ever since have remained in the possession and to the use of Mary, widow of the said Bartholomew Dandridge with their increase, it is my will and desire shall continue and be in her possession, without paying hire or making compensation for the same for the time past or to come during her natural life, at the expiration of which, I direct that all of them who are forty years old and upwards shall receive their freedom, all under that age and above sixteen shall serve seven years and no longer, and all under sixteen years shall serve until they are twenty-five years of age and then be free. And to avoid disputes respecting the ages of any of these negroes they are to be taken to the Court of the county in which they reside and the judgment thereof in this relation shall be final and a record thereof made, which may be adduced as evidence at any time thereafter if disputes should arise concerning the same. And I further direct that the heirs of the said Bartholomew Dandridge shall equally share the benefits arising from the services of the said negroes according to the tenor of this devise upon the decease of their mother.

Item. If Charles Carter who intermarried with my niece, Betty Lewis, is not sufficiently secured in the title to the lots he had of me in the town of Fredericksburg, it is my will and desire that my executors shall make such conveyances of them as the law requires to render it perfect.

Item. To my nephew, William Augustine Washington, and his heirs (if he should conceive them to be objects worth prosecuting) . . . a lot in the town of Manchester (opposite to Richmond) No. 265—drawn on my sole account and also the tenth of one or two hundred acre lots and two or three half-acre lots in the city and vicinity of Richmond, drawn in partnership with nine others, all in the lottery of the deceased William Byrd are given—as is also a lot which I purchased of John Hood conveyed by William Willie and Samuel Gordon, trustees of the said John Hood, numbered 139 in the town of Edenburgh in the county of Prince George, State of Virginia.

Item. To my nephew, Bushrod Washington, I give and bequeath all the papers in my possession which relate to my civil and military administration of the affairs of this Country—I leave to him also such of my private papers as are worth preserving; and at the decease of my wife and before, if she is not inclined to retain them, I give and bequeath my library of books and pamphlets of every kind.

Item. Having sold lands which I possessed in the State of Pennsylvania and part of a tract held in equal right, with George Clinton, late Governor of New York, in the State of New York—my share of land and interest in the Great Dismal Swamp and a tract of land which I owned in the County of Gloucester; withholding the legal titles thereto until the consideration money should be paid—and having moreover leased and conditionally sold (as will appear by the tenor of the said leases), all my lands upon the Great Kanawha and the tract upon Difficult Run in the County of Loudon, it is my will and direction that whensoever the contracts are fully and respectively complied with according to the spirit, true intent, and meaning thereof on the part of the purchaser, their heirs, or assigns, that then and in that case conveyances are to be made agreeably to the terms of the said contracts and the money arising therefrom when paid to be vested in bank stock, the dividends whereof, as of that also which is already vested therein, is to inure to my said wife during her life but the stock itself is to remain and be subject to the general distribution hereafter directed.

Item. To the Earl of Buchan I recommit, "The Box made of the oak that sheltered the Great Sir William Wallace after the battle of Falkirk"—presented to me by his Lordship in terms too flattering for me to repeat—with a request "To pass it, on the event of my decease to the man in my country who should appear to merit it best, upon the same conditions that have induced him to send it to me"—whether easy or not to select the man who might comport with his Lordship's opinion in this respect, is not for me to say, but conceiving that no disposition of this valuable curiosity, can be more eligible than the recommitment of it to his own cabinet agreeably to the original design of the Goldsmith's Company of Edinburgh, who presented it to him, and at his request, consented that it should be transferred to me; I do give and bequeath the same to his Lordship, and in case of his decease, to his heir with my grateful thanks for the distinguished honor of presenting it to me, and more especially for the favorable sentiments with which he accompanied it.

Item. To my brother, Charles Washington, I give and bequeath the gold-headed cane left me by Doctor Franklin in his will—I add nothing to it because of the ample provision I have made for his issue. To the acquaintances and friends of my juvenile years, Lawrence Washington and Robert Washington of Chotanck, I give my other two gold-headed canes, having my arms engraved on them, and to each (as they will be useful where they live), I leave one the spy glasses which constituted part of my equipage during the late war. To my compatriot in arms and old and intimate friend Doctor Craik, I give my bureau (or as the cabinet makers called it tambour secretary) and the circular chair, an appendage of my study. To Doctor David Stuart I give my large shaving and dressing table, and my telescope. To the Reverend, now Bryan Lord Fairfax I give a Bible in three large folio volumes with notes, presented to me by the Right Reverend Thomas Wilson, Bishop of Sodor and Man. To General de la Fayette I give a pair of finely wrought steel pistols taken from the enemy in the Revolutionary War. To my sisters in law, Hannah Washington and Mildred Washington; to my friends Eleanor Stuart; Hannah Washington of Fairfield and Elizabeth Washington of Hayfield, I give each a mourning ring of the value of one hundred dollars. These bequests are not made for the intrinsic value of them, but as mementos of my esteem and regard. To Tobias Lear I give the use of the farm which he now holds in virtue of a lease from me to him and his deceased wife (for and during their natural lives) free from rent during his life, at the expiration of which it is to be disposed as is hereafter directed. To Sally B. Hanyie (a distant relation of mine) I give and bequeath three hundred dollars. To Sarah Green, daughter of the deceased Thomas Bishop, and to Ann Walker, daughter of John Alton, also deceased, I give each one hundred dollars in consideration of the attachment of their fathers to me, each of whom having lived nearly forty years in my family. To each of my nephews, William Augustine Washington, George Lewis, George Steptoe Washington, Bushrod Washington, and Samuel Washington, I give one of the swords or cutteaux of which I may die possessed, and they are to choose in the order they are named. These swords are accompanied with an injunction not to unsheath them for the purpose of shedding blood except it be for self-defense, or in defense of their Country and its rights, and in the latter case to keep them unsheathed, and prefer falling with them in their hands to the relinquishment thereof.

And now, having gone through these specific devises, with explanations for the more correct understanding of the meaning and design of them, I proceed to the distribution of the more important parts of my estate, in manner following.

First. To my nephew, Bushrod Washington, and his heirs (partly in consideration of an intimation to his deceased father, while we were bachelors and he had kindly undertaken to superintend my estate, during my military services in the former war between Great Britain and France, that if I shall fall therein, Mt. Vernon (then less extensive in dominion than at present, should become his property) I give and bequeath all that part thereof which is comprehended within the following limits—viz.—beginning at the ford of Dogue Run near my mill and extending along the road and bounded thereby as it now goes, and ever has gone since my recollection of it, to the ford of little hunting Creek, at the gum spring until it comes to a knowl opposite to an old road which formerly passed through the lower field of Muddy-Hole Farm; at which, on the north side of the said road are three red or Spanish oaks marked as a corner, and a stone placed—thence by a line of trees to be marked rectangular to the black line, or outer boundary of the tract between Thomson Mason and myself, thence with that line easterly (now double ditching with a post and rail fence thereon) to the run of little hunting Creek, thence with that run, which is the boundary of the lands of the late Humphrey Peake and me, to the tide water of the said Creek thence by that water to Potomac River, thence with the River to the mouth of Dogue Creek, and thence with the said Dogue Creek to the place of beginning, at the aforesaid ford, containing upwards of four thousand acres, be the same more or less together with the mansion house, and all other buildings and improvements, thereon.

Secondly. In consideration of the consanguinity between them and my wife, being as nearly related to her as to myself, as on account of the affection I had for, and the obligation I was under to their father when living, who from his youth had attached himself to my person and followed my fortunes through the vicissitudes of the late Revolution, afterwards devoting his time to the superintendence of my private concerns for many years whilst my public employments rendered it impracticable for me to do it myself, thereby affording me essential services, and always performing them in a manner the most filial and respectful; for these reasons I say, I give and bequeath to George Fayette Washington and Lawrence Augustine Washington and their heirs my estate east of little hunting creek lying on the River Potomac, including the farm of 360 acres, leased to Tobias Lear as noticed before and containing in the whole, by deeds, two thousand and twenty-seven acres be it more or less which said estate, it is my will and desire should be equitably and advantageously divided between them, according to quantity, quality and other circumstances when the youngest shall have arrived at the age of twenty-one years, by three judicious and disinterested men, one to be chosen by each of the brothers and the third by these two. In the mean time if the termination of my wife's interest therein should have ceased the profits, arising therefrom are to be applied for their joint uses and benefit.

Third. And whereas it has always been my intention, since my expectation of having issue has ceased, to consider the grand children of my wife in the same light as I do my own relations and to act a friendly part by them, more especially by the two whom we have reared from their earliest infancy, namely, Eleanor Parke Custis and George Washington Parke Custis; and whereas the former of these hath lately intermarried with Lawrence Lewis, a son of my deceased sister Betty Lewis, by which union the inducement to provide for them both has been increased—wherefore I give and bequeath to the said Lawrence Lewis and Eleanor Parke Lewis, his wife, and their heirs, the residue of my Mount Vernon estate, not already devised to my nephew Bushrod Washington comprehended within the following description—viz.—all the land north of the road leading from the ford of Dogue Run to the Gum Spring as described in the devise of the other part of the tract to Bushrod Washington until it comes to the stone and three red or Spanish oaks on the knowl—thence with the rectangular line to the back line (between Mr. Mason and me)—thence with that line westerly, along the new double

ditch to Dogue Run, by the tumbling dam of my mill—
thence with the said Run to the ford aforementioned—to
which I add all the land I possess west of the said Dogue Run
and Dogue Creek bounded, easterly and southerly thereby—
together with the mill, distillery, and all other houses and
improvements on the premises making together about two
thousand acres be it more or less.

Fourth. Actuated by the principle already mentioned, I give
and bequeath to George Washington Parke Custis, the grand
son of my wife and my ward, and to his heirs, the tract I
hold on four mile Run in the vicinity of Alexandria containing one thousand, two hundred acres, more or less—and
my entire square, numbering twenty-one, in the city of
Washington.

Fifth. All the rest and residue of my estate, real and personal,
not disposed of in manner aforesaid—in whatsoever consisting—wheresoever lying, and wheresoever found—a
schedule of which as far as is recollected, with a reasonable
estimate of its value is hereunto annexed—I desire may be
sold by my executors at such times, in such manner, and in
such credits (if an equal valid and satisfactory distribution of
the specific property cannot be made without) as, in their
judgment shall be most conducive to the interests of the parties concerned, and the monies arising therefrom to be divided into twenty-three equal parts and applied as
follows—viz.:

To William Augustine Washington, Elizabeth Spotswood,
Jane Thornton, and the heirs of Ann Ashton; son and daughters of my deceased brother Augustine Washington, I give
and bequeath four parts—that is—one part to each of them.

To Fielding Lewis, George Lewis, Robert Lewis, Howell
Lewis, and Betty Carter, sons and daughter of my deceased

sister, Betty Lewis, I give and bequeath five other parts—one to each of them.

To George Steptoe Washington, Lawrence Augustine Washington, Harriot Parke, and the heirs of Thornton Washington, sons and daughter of my deceased brother Samuel Washington, I give and bequeath other four parts, one part to each of them.

To Corbin Washington, and the heirs of Jane Washington, I give and bequeath two parts—one part to each of them.

To Samuel Washington, Frances Ball, and Mildred Hammond, son and daughters of my brother Charles Washington I give and bequeath three parts—one part to each of them. And to George Fayette Washington, Charles Augustine Washington and Maria Washington, sons and daughter of my deceased nephew, George Augustine Washington, I give one other part—that is—to each a third of that part.

To Elizabeth Parke Law, Martha Parke Peter, and Eleanor Parke Lewis, I give and bequeath three other parts—that is, a part to each of them.

And to my nephew, Bushrod Washington, and Lawrence Lewis, and to my ward, the grandson of my wife, I give and bequeath one other part—that is a third part to each of them. And if it should so happen, that any of the persons whose names are here enumerated (unknown to me) should now be deceased, or should die before me, that in either of these cases, the heirs of such deceased persons shall, notwithstanding derive all the benefit of the bequest, in the same manner as if he, or she was actually living at the time.

And by way of advice, I recommended it to my executors not to be precipitate in disposing of the landed property (herein directed to be sold) if from temporary causes the sale thereof should be dull, experience having fully evinced, that the price of land (especially above the Falls of the Rivers and on the Western Waters) have been progressively rising, and cannot be long checked in its increasing value—and I particularly recommend it to such of the legatees (under this clause of my will) as can make it convenient, to take each a share of my stock in the Potomac Company in preference to the amount of what it might sell for; being thoroughly convinced myself, that no uses to which the money can be applied will be so productive as the tolls arising from this navigation when in full operation (and this from the nature of things it must be 'ere long) and more especially if that of the Shenandoah is added thereto.

The family vault at Mount Vernon requiring repairs, and being improperly situated besides, I desire that a new one of brick, and upon a larger scale, may be built at the foot of what is commonly called the vineyard inclosure—on the ground which is marked out—in which my remains, with those of my deceased relatives (now in the old vault) and such others of my family as may choose to be entombed there, may be deposited. And it is my express desire that my corpse may be interred in a private manner, without parade or funeral oration.

Lastly. I constitute and appoint my dearly beloved wife, Martha Washington, my nephews, William Augustine Washington, Bushrod Washington, George Steptoe Washington, Samuel Washington, and Lawrence Lewis, and my ward, George Washington Parke Custis (when he shall have arrived at the age of twenty years), executrix and executors of this Will and Testament. In the construction of which it will readily be perceived that no professional character has been consulted or has had any agency in the draught—and that, although it has occupied many of my leisure hours to digest and to through it into its present form, it may notwithstanding, appear crude and incorrect. But having endeavored to be plain and explicit in all the devises—even at the expense of prolixity, perhaps of tautology, I hope, and trust, that no disputes will arise concerning them; but if contrary to expectation the case should be otherwise from the want of legal expression, or the usual technical terms, or because too much or too little, has been said on any of the devises to be consonant with law, my will and direction expressly is, that all disputes (if unhappily any should arise) shall be decided by three impartial and intelligent men, known for their probity and good understanding; two to be chosen by the disputants, each having the choice of one, and the third by those two—which three men thus chosen, shall unfettered by law, or legal constructions declare their sense of the testator's intention; and such decision is, to all intents and purposes to be as binding on the parties as if it had been given in the Supreme Court of the United States.

In witness of all and of each of the things herein contained I have set my hand and seal this ninth day of July, in the year one thousand, seven hundred and ninety-nine, and of the independence of the United States, the twenty-fourth.

BIBLIOGRAPHY

Adler, David A. *George Washington: Father of Our Country.*
New York, NY: Holiday House, 1988.

Alden, John R. *George Washington: A Biography.*
Baton Rouge, LA: Louisiana State University Press, 1984.

Ambler, Charles H. *George Washington and the West.*
New York, NY: Russell & Russell, 1971.

Bancroft, Aaron. *The Life of George Washington.*
Philadelphia, PA: Porter & Coates, 1808.

Bellamy, Francis R. *The Private Life of George Washington.*
New York, NY: Crowell, 1951.

Billias, George A. *George Washington's Generals.*
New York, NY: William Morrow, 1964.

Bloom, Sol. *Our Heritage: George Washington and the
Establishment of the American Union.*
New York, NY: G.P. Putnam's Sons, 1944.

Boller, Paul F. *George Washington and Religion.*
Dallas, TX: Southern Methodist University Press, 1963.

Bordon, Morton. *George Washington.*
Englewood Cliffs, NJ: Prentice-Hall, 1969.

Bourne, Miriam Anne. *First Family: George Washington and
His Intimate Relations.*
New York, NY: Norton, 1982.

Bremer, Howard F. *George Washington.*
Dobbs Ferry, NY: Oceana Publications, 1967.

Brookhiser, Richard. *Founding Father: Rediscovering George Washington.*
New York, NY: Free Press, 1996.

Busch, Noel F. *Winter Quarters: George Washington and the Continental Army at Valley Forge.*
New York, NY: Liveright, 1974.

Callahan, North. *George Washington, Soldier and Man.*
New York, NY: Morrow, 1972.

Carrington, Henry B. *Washington: The Soldier.*
New York, NY: Charles Scribner's Sons, 1899.

Clark, E. Harrison. *All Cloudless Glory: The Life of George Washington.*
Washington, DC: Regency Pub., 1995.

Cleland, Hugh. *George Washington in the Ohio Valley.*
Pittsburgh, PA: University of Pittsburgh Press, 1955.

Corbin, John. *The Unknown Washington.*
New York, NY: Charles Scribner's Sons, 1930.

Cunliffe, Marcus. *George Washington, Man and Monument.*
Boston, MA: Little, Brown, 1958.

Custis, George Washington Parke. *Recollections and Private Memoirs of Washington.*
New York, NY: Derby & Jackson, 1860.

D'Aulaire, Ingri. *George Washington.*
New York, NY: Doubleday, 1936.

Davidson, Thomas W. *Wisdom of George Washington.*
San Antonio, TX: Naylor Co., 1964.

Davis, Burke. *George Washington and the American Revolution.*
New York, NY: Random House, 1975.

Decatur, Stephen. *Private Affairs of George Washington, From the Records and Accounts of Tobias Lear, Esq., His Secretary.*
New York, NY: Da Capo Press, 1969.

Easton, Jeanette. *Leader by Destiny: George Washington, Man and Patriot.*
New York, NY: Harcourt, Brace, 1938.

Emery, Noemi. *Washington: A Biography.*
New York, NY: Putnam, 1976.

Everett, Edward. *The Life of George Washington.*
New York, NY: Sheldon & Co., 1860.

Faey, Bernard. *George Washington, Republican Aristocrat.*
Boston: Houghton Mifflin Co., 1931.

Ferling, John E. *The First of Men: A Life of George Washington.*
Knoxville, TN: University of Tennessee Press, 1988.

Fitzpatrick, John C. *George Washington, Colonial Traveller, 1732–1775.*
Indianapolis, IN: Bobbs-Merrill, 1927.

Fitzpatrick, John C. *George Washington Himself.*
Indianapolis, IN: Bobbs-Merrill Co., 1933.

Fleming, Thomas J. *First in Their Hearts: A Biography of George Washington.*
New York, NY: W.W. Norton, 1968.

Flexner, James T. *George Washington: The Forge of Experience, 1732–1775.*
Boston, MA: Little, Brown, 1965.

Flexner, James T. *George Washington in the American Revolution, 1775–1783.*
Boston, MA: Little, Brown, 1968.

Flexner, James T. *George Washington and the New Nation, 1783–1793.*
Boston, MA: Little, Brown, 1970.

Flexner, James T. *George Washington: Anguish and Farewell.*
Boston, MA: Little, Brown, 1972.

Flexner, James T. *George Washington: The Indispensable Man.*
Boston, MA: Little, Brown, 1974.

Ford, Paul L. *The True George Washington.*
Philadelphia, PA: J. B. Lippincott Co., 1896.

Freeman, Douglas Southall. *George Washington: A Biography.*
New York, NY: Scribner, 1948.

Frothingham, Thomas. *George Washington, Commander-in-Chief.*
Boston, MA: Houghton Mifflin Co., 1930.

Hapgood, Norman. *George Washington.*
New York, NY: The Macmillan Co., 1901.

Headley, Joel T. *Washington and His Generals.*
New York, NY: Baker & Scribner, 1848.

Hodges, George. *The Apprenticeship of Washington.*
New York, NY: Moffat, Yard & Co., 1909.

Hughes, Rupert. *George Washington.*
New York, NY: William Morrow & Co., 1926.

Irving, Washington. *Life of George Washington.*
Boston, MA: Twayne Publishers, 1982.

Jackson, Donald, Editor. *The Diaries of George Washington.*
Charlottesville, VA: University of Virginia Press, 1976.

Jones, Robert F. *George Washington.*
Boston, MA: Twayne Publishers, 1979.

Ketchum, Richard M. *The World of George Washington.*
New York, NY: Harmony Books, 1984.

Kingston, John. *The Life of General George Washington.*
Baltimore, MD: J. Kingston, 1813.

Kinnaird, Clark. *George Washington, The Pictorial Biography.*
New York, NY: Hastings House, 1967.

Knipe, Alden A. *Everybody's Washington.*
New York, NY: Dodd, 1931.

Knollenberg, Bernhard. *George Washington, the Virginia
Period, 1732–1775.*
Durham, NC: Duke University Press, 1964.

Koral, Bella. *George Washington: The Father of Our Country.*
New York, NY: Random House, 1954.

Little, Shelby. *George Washington.*
New York, NY: Minton, Balch & Co., 1929.

Lodge, Henry Cabot. *George Washington.*
Boston, MA: Houghton, Mifflin & Co., 1889.

Madison, Lucy F. *Washington.*
Philadelphia, PA: Pennsylvania Publishing, 1927.

Marshall, John. *The Life of George Washington.*
Philadelphia, PA: C. P. Wayne, 1804.

McDonald, Forrest. *The Presidency of George Washington.*
Lawrence, KS: University of Kansas Press, 1974.

Moore, Charles. *The Family Life of George Washington.*
Boston, MA: Houghton Mifflin Co., 1926.

Morgan, Edmund S. *The Genius of George Washington.*
New York, NY: Norton, 1980.

Nettels, Curtis P. *George Washington and American Independence.*
Boston, MA: Little, Brown & Co., 1951.

Niles, Blair. *Martha's Husband.*
New York, NY: McGraw-Hill, 1951.

Nordham, George Washington. *The Age of Washington: George Washington's Presidency, 1789–1797.*
Chicago, IL: Adams Press, 1989.

Penniman, James H. *George Washington as Commander-in-Chief.*
Philadelphia, PA: J. Wanamaker, 1917.

Rivoire, Mario. *The Life and Times of Washington.*
Philadelphia, PA: Curtis Books, 1967.

Schroeder, John F. *Life and Times of Washington.*
New York, NY: M. Belcher Publishing, 1903.

Schwartz, Barry. *George Washington: The Making of an American Symbol.*
New York, NY: Free Press, 1987.

Scudder, Horace E. *George Washington: An Historical Biography.*
Boston, MA: Houghton, Mifflin & Co., 1889.

Sears, Louis M. *George Washington.*
New York, NY: Thomas Y. Crowell Co., 1932.

Sears, Louis M. *George Washington and the French Revolution.*
Detroit, MI: Wayne State University Press, 1960.

Smith, James M. *George Washington: A Profile.*
New York, NY: Hill & Wang, 1969.

Smith, Richard N. *Patriarch: George Washington and the New American Nation.*
Boston, MA: Houghton, Mifflin, 1993.

Sparks, Jared. *The Life of George Washington.*
Boston, MA: Tappan & Dennet, 1842.

Stephenson, Nathaniel W., and Waldo Hilary Dunn. *George Washington.*
New York, NY: Oxford University Press, 1940.

Tebbel, John W. *George Washington's America.*
New York, NY: Dutton, 1954.

Thane, Elswyth. *Potomac Squire.*
New York, NY: Duell, Sloan & Pearce, 1963.

Thayer, William R. *George Washington.*
Boston, MA: Houghton Mifflin Co., 1922.

Vestal, Samuel Curtis. *Washington, The Military Man.*
Washington, DC: George Washington Bicentennial
Commission, 1931.

Weems, Mason L. *The Life of George Washington the Great.*
Augusta, GA: George P. Randolph, 1806.

Wills, Garry. *Cincinnatus: George Washington and the
Enlightment.*
Garden City, NY: Doubleday, 1984.

Wilson, Woodrow. *George Washington.*
New York, NY: Harper & Brothers, 1897.

Wister, Owen. *The Seven Ages of Washington: A Biography.*
New York, NY: Macmillan Co., 1909.

Woodward, William E. *George Washington, The Image and the
Man.*
New York, NY: Boni and Liveright, 1926.

Wright, Esmond. *Washington and the American Revolution.*
New York, NY: Collier Books, 1962.

Wrong, George M. *Washington and His Comrades in Arms.*
New York, NY: United States Publishers, 1921.

INDEX